INCREASING STUDENT ENGAGEMENT AND RETENTION USING MULTIMEDIA TECHNOLOGIES: VIDEO ANNOTATION, MULTIMEDIA APPLICATIONS, VIDEOCONFERENCING AND TRANSMEDIA STORYTELLING

CUTTING-EDGE TECHNOLOGIES IN HIGHER EDUCATION

Series Editor: Charles Wankel

Recent Volumes:

CUTTING-EDGE TECHNOLOGIES IN HIGHER
EDUCATION   VOLUME 6F

INCREASING STUDENT ENGAGEMENT AND RETENTION USING MULTIMEDIA TECHNOLOGIES: VIDEO ANNOTATION, MULTIMEDIA APPLICATIONS, VIDEOCONFERENCING AND TRANSMEDIA STORYTELLING

EDITED BY

LAURA A. WANKEL
Northeastern University, Massachusetts, USA

PATRICK BLESSINGER
St. John's University, New York, USA

IN COLLABORATION WITH

JURATE STANAITYTE
NEIL WASHINGTON

Created in partnership with the Higher Education
Teaching and Learning Association

http://hetl.org/

United Kingdom – North America – Japan
India – Malaysia – China

Emerald Group Publishing Limited
Howard House, Wagon Lane, Bingley BD16 1WA, UK

First edition 2013

Copyright © 2013 Emerald Group Publishing Limited

Reprints and permission service
Contact: permissions@emeraldinsight.com

British Library Cataloguing in Publication Data
A catalogue record for this book is available from the British Library

ISBN: 978-1-78190-513-5
ISSN: 2044-9968 (Series)

ISOQAR certified
Management System,
awarded to Emerald
for adherence to
Environmental
standard
ISO 14001:2004.

Certificate Number 1985
ISO 14001

INVESTOR IN PEOPLE

CONTENTS

LIST OF CONTRIBUTORS

Peter Adds	Victoria University of Wellington, New Zealand
Sheila M. Aird	SUNY-Empire State College, USA
Maria Bargh	Victoria University of Wellington, New Zealand
Patrick Blessinger	St. John's University, Queens, NY, USA
Meg Colasante	RMIT University, Australia
Karen Corneille	RMIT University, Australia
Kathy Douglas	RMIT University, Australia
Sarsha-Leigh Douglas	Victoria University of Wellington, New Zealand
Meegan Hall	Victoria University of Wellington, New Zealand
Wayne Jacoby	Global Education Motivators, USA
Felix A. Kronenberg	Rhodes College, USA
Narelle Lemon	RMIT University, Australia
Audeliz Matias	SUNY-Empire State College, USA
Bruce McFadgen	Victoria University of Wellington, New Zealand
O. Ripeka Mercier	Victoria University of Wellington, New Zealand
Leila A. Mills	University of North Texas, USA
Stephanie E. Raible	Global Education Motivators, USA
Kyle F. Reinson	St. John Fisher College, USA

Sean Robinson	Morgan State University, USA
Jenny S. Wakefield	University of North Texas, USA
Laura A. Wankel	Northeastern University, Boston, USA
Scott J. Warren	University of North Texas, USA
Tahu Wilson	Victoria University of Wellington, New Zealand
David F. Wolf II	SUNY-Empire State College, USA
Müberra Yüksel	Kadir Has University, Turkey

PART I
ADOPTION OF MULTIMEDIA TECHNOLOGIES

INVENTIVE APPROACHES IN HIGHER EDUCATION: AN INTRODUCTION TO USING MULTIMEDIA TECHNOLOGIES

Laura A. Wankel and Patrick Blessinger

INTRODUCTION

The chapters in this book focus on using different types of multimodal, multimedia, and transmedia technologies to create technology-rich learning environments that have the potential to enable higher levels of academic motivation, participation, and engagement. Developments in relatively low cost and abundant digital technologies, coupled with the improvements in contemporary learning theories and pedagogical practices, are quickly enhancing and transforming the way we teach and learn in the 21st century and changing our understanding of what it means to teach and learn in a highly web-based multimedia world. At the individual, group, and institutional levels, these technologies are being used in a variety of ways for a variety of purposes. In teaching and learning, they offer promising and innovative ways to create more interesting and enjoyable academic environments and offer more meaningful and authentic ways to better engage the senses of learners. Mayer (1997) states that multimedia-based

Increasing Student Engagement and Retention using Multimedia Technologies:
Video Annotation, Multimedia Applications, Videoconferencing and Transmedia Storytelling
Cutting-edge Technologies in Higher Education, Volume 6F, 3–16
ISSN: 2044-9968/doi:10.1108/S2044-9968(2013)000006F003

teaching and learning offers many benefits to educators (e.g., a variety of instructional options, more effective learning, and more efficient use of instructor time especially for very large classes). This is based on the core multimedia principle posited by Mayer (2005): people tend to learn more deeply with both words and images than from words alone.

Technology alone cannot guarantee student engagement and retention. Technology should be used in a purposeful manner and grounded in relevant learning theory and in line with clearly defined learning goals and course objectives. The reality of the postindustrial digital age is that technology is pervasive and we cannot and should not try to escape it or consider it a passing fad. Communication in the modern era has become ubiquitous and global and increasingly based on integrated multimedia. Shirky (2008) reminds us that the Internet and social networks are increasingly breaking down boundaries (e.g., political, economic, and social) and breaking down formal hierarchies, and that these ubiquitous, low-cost, open-access tools and networks have, in many ways, become more effective in connecting and organizing people than traditional institutions and networks. We now live in a world saturated with a diverse set of multimodal, multimedia technologies that are empowering people to not only be knowledge consumers on a large scale but also knowledge creators and disseminators.

The ultimate goal of using these technologies is to increase motivation and, ultimately, academic achievement. For instance, in the learning environment (e.g., physical space or electronic space or blended), students (and faculty) can use these tools to extend the dialogue beyond the formal class setting. Rather than assuming that these tools are inherently a distraction from learning, one could design the course and the classroom interactions in such a way that they become tools to enhance the learning experience by, for instance, allowing students to engage in such ways that is more interesting and meaningful and authentic to them. Imposing a one-size-fits-all teaching and learning paradigm on students will likely lead to frustration and discontent. Most learning tools today should, regardless of the mode of delivery, focus more on collaboration and engagement across all learning domains (cognitive, affective, social). E-portfolios, for instance, can create a tangible learning outcome that embodies multimedia representations and can serve several educational functions (e.g., course assessment, evidence of institutional learning outcome, evidence of skill and knowledge competence).

As stated before, these tools are unlikely to yield more effective learning if these tools, as with any tool, are not used in a purposeful manner and in a way that is meaningful to the learners (Sadik, 2008). Also, it is important to note that learners' identities are formed to a large degree via their social interactions (Berger & Luckmann, 1967). So, the social aspects of using these technologies (e.g., group video conferencing, collaborative storytelling using VoiceThread) should also be taken into account. In other words, academic success depends, in large part, on how appropriately instructors utilize these technologies to match the objectives of the course and how they are specifically used to mediate meaningful learning activities for students.

There is no one right way to use these technologies for all courses. Each instructor must figure out for him/herself what is appropriate and what is not appropriate depending on the context of his/her course. Nonetheless, these technologies provide educators with new possibilities and greater opportunities to enhance or transform how they interact with their students and how students interact with each other and the instructional content and how they participate in the learning activities. These tools provide instructors with another opportunity to expand their notions of teaching and learning while at the same time allowing them to sustain the central principles of the academy (e.g., academic freedom, academic rigor, pedagogical pluralism).

Mayer (2005) gives a straightforward definition of multimedia technologies: learning from words (e.g., verbal and printed text) and images (graphs, charts, maps, animation, video, photos, and illustrations). So, multimedia in and of itself does not guarantee that learning will be enhanced, but when it is constructed in an integrated, purposeful, and meaningful way within the context of a particular course, it can be a powerful catalyst to increase learner engagement. Mayer's broad definition can serve as a viable starting point for drilling down into the specifics of who, what, where, when, why, and how of these technologies in an educational context. Irrespective of whether multimedia technologies are used at the undergraduate level or post graduate level, or whether they are used in a humanities course or a mathematics course, the notion of multimedia integration to enable more comprehensive and coherent sense-making is important. This broad definition connotes the idea that better learning (i.e., more integrated, more meaningful, more purposeful, more authentic) is one of the main outcomes of their use (Kegan, 1994; Magolda, 1999). To that end, these technologies can create new possibilities to enhance or even transform existing pedagogical practices.

For instance, multimedia projects can be used as part of inquiry-based and problem-based learning activities to create more active learning scenarios (Herrington, Reeves, Oliver, & Woo, 2004). Multimedia discourse tools can also be used with a broad set of other teaching and learning tools and approaches to (1) increase student participation through more authentic and effective ways to hold their attention and interest, (2) create a learning environment that is more consistent with modern learning theory and how the human mind learns best, and (3) improve learner sense-making by creating instructional methods, course materials, and learning activities that are appropriately integrated and coherently constructed using multimedia that more completely engages the human senses. Hence, the power of using multimedia resides in its ability to increase cognitive and emotional interest and attention by creating more coherent and authentic representations of knowledge. Using multimedia technologies in conjunction with allied teaching and learning approaches (e.g., digital storytelling, digital mapping, video conferencing) expands the boundaries for teaching and learning and makes for a more flexible and interesting class experience. For instance, digital storytelling (i.e., telling stories using digital technologies – Alexander, 2011) helps to empower learners at all levels to construct narratives that are meaningful to them and allows them to cultivate their own voice and self-identity.

Technology is neither inherently good nor inherently bad but rather depends on how it is used. For instance, an instructor could decide to use digital storytelling as a means to give students a greater voice in the classroom and turn the universal desire for self-expression into personally meaningful learning activities. In contrast, the more traditional, authoritarian approach would be to suppress this natural desire for self-expression and participation by requiring students to sit in silence while the instructor delivers a unidirectional, unimodal monologue for the entire class period. Learning, either in the classroom or outside the classroom, should be as much a social and emotional experience as it is a cognitive experience.

However, doing this may require an attitudinal shift in the mind of the instructor (and the institution) wherein they see technological tools as opportunities for better learning through engagement rather than viewing them as distractions. Novelty or technical sophistication alone of these technologies is not sufficient to engage and interest learners. As with any technologies, these tools must be used in a purposeful and meaningful way and integrated in a way suitable to the course. So, using valid and reliable pedagogical methods and learning principles and theories is critical. In addition to relevant and established theory, it is also important to be cognizant of the epistemological, ontological, and phenomenological bases that are germane to utilizing such technologies.

ADOPTION PRINCIPLES

Two key principles emerge from the findings of the chapters in the adoption section of the book that help to frame the content of the book and this specific set of technologies:

1. Multimedia technology can be used as a viable way to create more engaging and interesting learning environments by *integrating instructional messages and integrating learning activities using multiple forms and modes of media*; by appropriately integrating text-based content with image-based content, content and pedagogy becomes more coherent, more rich, more dynamic, and more meaningful by appealing to multiple human senses which is an important factor in catalyzing student interest and their motivation to participate.

2. Multimedia technology has the potential to increase cognitive attention and emotional interest in the subject matter and the learning activity by *creating a learning environment that reflects coherent and authentic representations of knowledge* and is consistent with modern learning theories that explain how the human mind learns best and how human emotions and social actions are related to cognition.

These principles are also reflective of a growing emphasis on student-centeredness, meaning-centeredness, active learning, contextual learning, situated learning, integrative learning, authentic learning, and developing learning environments and activities that are interesting and enjoyable. Authentic learning entails aligning course objectives with meaningful learning activities. Situated learning entails learning that is rooted within a specific personal and social context. Contextual learning occurs by the complex interplay of situated interactions (i.e., connecting subject specific content to one's real-life context). Integrative learning involves the ability to connect knowledge and meanings across varied courses and life experiences. The growing importance of these types of learning is reflective of life in an increasingly globalized and digital world where interconnectedness and interdependence play such a vital role in our lives. All else being equal, it follows that students will be more interested in learning activities that are more meaningful to their personal life-worlds.

The great flexibility of multimedia allows it to be customized to work in any course in any discipline and at any level. Also, all these approaches can be used within a single course or to create a theme or key concept that is threaded across multiple courses. Instructor and student participation with these multimodal and multimedia technologies should therefore endeavor to create a more cognitively coherent and emotionally interesting way to engage both instructors and students in the course content and learning activities. For instance, multimedia technologies can be used with digital storytelling or mapping activities in humanities course as an interpretive medium to evoke emotional responses within the social and personal context of each student's own values and aspirations and thus encourage group dialogue and personal reflection. They can also be used with animation or video models in engineering or science courses to explain difficult concepts or complex theories visually. Again, used appropriately and in a purposeful manner, these technologies can produce several positive effects in the classroom.

APPLICATION BENEFITS

As illustrated in the chapters in the application section, these types of meaning-centered, multimedia-based learning environments have the potential to:

1. improve sense-making by providing a more coherent and accurate integration of knowledge representations,
2. improve sense-making by creating more diverse and comprehensive ways to learn from words, images, and sounds,
3. create more personally meaningful learning environments by appealing more directly to the emotional and social needs of students,
4. create more personally meaningful learning environments by fostering more collaborative and participatory learning activities, and
5. provide instructors with a wide array of tools to choose from regardless of the type or level of course they are teaching.

If integrated into the course in a purposeful manner using sound design principles and learning theories, multimedia technologies have the potential to create a more engaging and interesting learning environment for both instructors and students. Technologies such as digital storytelling, digital mapping, interactive videos, and the like can help create a more coherent and integrated learning experience. In turn, these technologies can help foster deeper critical thinking, deeper personal reflection, and more deeply engaged sense-making. In short, the question becomes: how can we use these promising technologies to not only improve academic achievement but also to better enable students to more holistically explore the questions of who, what, where, when, why, and how of their own continually unfolding personal story.

THEORETICAL FRAMING

Through various approaches, the authors in this volume explain how they operationalize the use of multimodal, multimedia, and transmedia technologies in the spirit of cognitive learning theory and social constructivism which are supported by the learning theories of Piaget, Vygotsky, Bandura, Bruner, Mayer, et al. Cognitive theory of multimedia learning (Mayer, 1997, 2005) is especially useful in understanding the effectiveness of using multimedia. This theory states that learning occurs best when instructional content consists of both words (e.g., verbal and written text) and images (e.g., graphs, charts, maps) that are delivered simultaneously in a coherent and integrated fashion. The social and emotional aspect of learning is addressed with social constructivism which can be broadly defined as cognitive and social learning wherein the learner constructs new knowledge and meaning based on his/her contextualized and situated experiences. Thus, cognitive theory and social constructivism provides a plausible framework for designing multimedia learning contexts.

So, it is critical that these technologies be used in such a way that is germane to the context of the learning environment (e.g., the type and nature of the course, the grade level, the learning objectives of the course, learning needs of the students) and the pedagogical approach of the instructor. For instance, Mayer (2005) states that multimedia-based classes will be most effective in enhancing learning when the instructional messages are grounded in sound design principles based on how the mind actually works (cognitive theory) and, as such, is much more likely to lead to meaningful learning. Mayer also noted that not all multimedia representations are the same; merely adding images and other non-textual representations will not automatically enhance learning. Mayer concludes that the most important element in multimedia learning is making *meaningful* connections and relationships between text and images (i.e., an integrated and coherent representation) where integration entails creating meaningful connections between text (verbal models) and images (pictorial models) relative to the student's prior knowledge. Also, through the lens of cognitive load theory, Sweller (2005) notes that instructional messages that are meaningfully integrated (i.e., integrated instructions created from multiple sources of information) produce a relatively lower cognitive load on the brain, as compared to split-attention instruction.

If used with sound design principles relevant to the context of the course, multimodal, multimedia, and transmedia learning have the potential to increase student participation and engagement. As such, these technologies have the potential to be used across a wide range of inquiry (from basic to advanced), across a wide range of courses (from foundational courses to advanced), and a wide range of pedagogical practices. Lambert and McCombs (1998) define learning as the ability to synthesize and apply complex information in *meaningful* ways. Thus, more effective learning can be achieved by using multimedia to stimulate multiple senses in an integrated and coherent way, and thereby increase the ability to get and hold attention and concentration for longer periods of time.

TECHNOLOGY

The technology described in this volume is especially useful to support instructors who wish to create more dynamic and interesting learning environments and activities. One of the benefits of these tools is that they are so diverse and so flexible that they do not necessarily require instructors to make radical changes in their teaching methods but, rather, they can provide a flexible way to enrich existing learning environments. In this way, multi-media technology supports meaningful learning and pedagogical pluralism. As such, these tools are just one of several ways in which instructors can enhance their own teaching methods and improve student learning by creating more dynamic and coherent instructional messages.

For instance, transmedia (i.e., a distinct learning experience or episode that is connected by and threaded across several types of media) can be used to create learning threads where the focus is on the streams of learning that are important to the learners rather than merely on the technology itself. In fact, in well-constructed multimedia learning, the technology almost becomes transparent to the users. Transmedia often involves using a narrative storyline to create meaningful and purposeful stories. Human storytelling (in one form or another) is presumably as old as human history. Stories not only enable self-authorship, self-agency, and self-expression but stories also provide students with an opportunity to engage emotionally and socially, in addition to cognitively. So, digital storytelling using transmedia tools can also help to expand the traditional boundaries related to using word (text and verbal) only classrooms. Thus, when used in a coherent way that is properly aligned with learner needs and course objectives, these multimedia technologies can expand the capacity for greater meaning-making as well as more personally meaningful learning experiences.

CHAPTER OVERVIEWS

In "Higher Education: A Medium in Search of a Message," by Kyle F. Reinson, the author explores how the age of information has ostensibly shifted content delivery to the cloud, which over time has itself become an increasingly reliable aggregator of useful content. Content, however, serves as an effective shield for instructors that can fit every size learner. In a content-driven classroom, students are forced into an unnatural mode of one-way communication where they are accountable for what is conveyed in class rather than what they *may have learned* in class about either the content or themselves. Handheld student technology is capable of assisting student learning if instructors keep an open mind toward its use. At the same time, new technological leaps are presenting perfect timing for higher education to speed adoption of cutting-edge technology because the learning curve is ongoing, not too steep and, in fact, not really more difficult than creating a Facebook account. The conversational classroom is on the near horizon and it will liberate both instructors and students to find new ways of seeking, sharing, and creating knowledge. The message of higher education as an adaptive medium itself is explored.

In "Using Technology and Digital Narratives to Engage Doctoral Students in Self-Authorship and Learning Partnerships," by Sean Robinson, the author explores how using digital narratives and storytelling with the doctoral educational milieu is one particular activity that can serve to help doctoral students become critical and reflective thinkers, to develop or refine a professional identity, and to transform their assumptions about their knowledge and about themselves. Such an approach can lead to innovative practices in the classroom, deeper, more reflective learning for students, and greater overall success for our institutions. By combining multimedia tools, technology, and activities with an adult learning-centered pedagogy built around self-authoring practices of student development, faculty can more effectively organize doctoral education to engage and involve students in the process and to truly cultivate a new generation of scholars, researchers, and practitioners. Stories and narratives can help validate students' experiences and connect individuals together, but they can also encourage dialogue and reflection, and offer a change to take a risk, while providing both a means of challenge and support for others. Digital narratives and storytelling offer a way to break down traditional barriers of text-only technologies prevalent in most technology-mediated classrooms. The use of digital narratives in a technology-mediated classroom invites and creates a new type of social ecology and interconnectedness in such a virtual world. Digital stories and narratives can allow students to see, hear, and experience their peers not as external objects, but as true subjects with different experiences worthy of time, energy, and attention. Finally, digital narratives allow for possibilities for both self-directed learning, since students can be free to tell a particular story from a particular vantage point, and critical reflective practice as they analyze their own narratives and respond to feedback and ideas from their peers.

In "Learning and Teaching as Communicative Actions: Transmedia Storytelling," by Scott J. Warren, Jenny S. Wakefield, and Leila A. Mills, the authors explain how transmedia — a single experience that spans across multiple forms of media — is still a *new* media in the educational landscape and therefore may pose a challenge to educators wanting to create opportunities for interactive media communications in their classrooms. In this chapter, we share an instance in which a university professor introduced transmedia to support graduate student learning to encourage inquiry, critical thinking, problem solving, creativity, contemplation, and critical discourses. Further, we examine how two of the graduate students took their learning a step further by designing and creating a model transmedia lesson tailored for the 6th grade Social Studies classroom. This chapter provides a theoretical framework within which transmedia may be used: Learning and teaching as communicative actions theory — LTCA.

In "Technology and the Changing Nature of Narratives in Language Learning and Teaching," by Felix A. Kronenberg, the author examines two different newer forms of narratives and their use for language learning and teaching. The first is that of digital storytelling, a form of communication that enables anyone, even those with limited communicative skills and experience, to create a compelling, authentic narrative that can be shared through various distribution channels. The second type of narrative discussed is that of stories found in video games. Rooted in contemporary popular culture, these interactive narratives are increasingly used for language learning and teaching purposes not only for their motivational factors but also their immersive and multimodal advantages.

In "Promoting Engagement Through a Student-Built Digital Atlas of Maori Studies," by O. Ripeka Mercier, Sarsha-Leigh Douglas, Meegan Hall, Bruce McFadgen, Peter Adds, Maria Bargh, and Tahu Wilson, the authors explain how, in 2010, they began implementing map-based assignments in their undergraduate courses at Te Kawa a Māui (the School of Māori Studies) at Victoria University of Wellington, New Zealand, diversifying the learning and assessment spectrum from traditional research essays. The work students have produced in individual and group efforts, using primary and secondary research, covers a diverse range of topics of relevance to students, engages students in cutting-edge digital technologies, and enables students and staff to visualize Māori studies differently. The best work of the 250 students from 10 different courses has contributed to the Te Kawa a Māui Atlas (TeKaMA), an online database of student projects. This chapter presents and describes some of those projects. We used quantitative and qualitative surveys of students to discuss how student engagement in this project was facilitated by digital technology. In line with other findings in the literature, digital aspects of our project had to be carefully managed and balanced, so that they did not disengage students from learning. However, our TeKaMA exercises provided multiple ways by which students could engage, with cultural mapping and place-based education in general engaging all students, not just Māori.

In "Learner Engagement in an Intercultural Virtual Experience," by Müberra Yüksel, the author explains how Kadir Has University in Istanbul undertook a challenging project with the initiative of College of Staten Island (CSI) and became the international partner of a distant learning course through video conference. The conceptual model is called the Global Experience Through Technology Project with the goal of using Internet technology to make university students of different cultures get engaged in a virtual classroom context to enhance their intercultural competencies.

In "Video Annotation for Collaborative Connections to Learning: Case Studies from an Australian Higher Education Context," by Narelle Lemon, Meg Colasante, Karen Corneille, and Kathy Douglas, the authors present a case of implementing a new media annotation tool (MAT) into an Australian university, from idea inception in 2005, to design and development, to trial followed by pilot implementation in 2009, and multiple disciplinary use in 2011. At each of these stages − from design through to cross-discipline implementation − data from student and teacher feedback has been integral to guide the next steps. MAT requires teachers in higher education learning contexts to adapt new modes of technology-supported collaboration with and for students in a higher education environment. Perspectives shared are the wide range of issues and perspectives associated for MAT as a technology selection, technology deployment, and assessment (up-take in a variety of learning environments across one Australian university). This chapter shares the learning design, pedagogy, and voice of both the teachers and students, all seen as active learners, in how MAT is being used for alternative and appropriate models of learning and assessment. Strong connections are made to work-relevant learning, supported by industry partnerships via input into the learning process.

In "Innovative Teaching Methods for Using Multimedia Maps to Engage Students at a Distance," by Audeliz Matias, Sheila M. Aird, and David F. Wolf II, the authors explain how knowledge of space is critical to attitudes and decision making as global citizens. This chapter demonstrates the use of current technology to create multimedia maps that offer new educational affordances for students at a distance with the potential to link geographic and cultural understanding within the context of a variety of disciplines. The authors present the development of a mapping and blogging interactive learning environment, MapBlog, as a visual platform for representing information spatially. In the blog view students can add and edit their own blog posts as well as add to and view comments by other students; whereas the map view displays an interactive map. Posts can include text, links, images, and video. The advantage of this format is that it offers a familiar interface for students to interact with the MapBlog. Through this tool, students get introduced to the geography of a particular region, develop research and communication skills, and a stronger grasp of the topic. This approach shifts emphasis away from a memorizing facts and information to an inquiry-based learning. The four MapBlog categories explored are: external content, student-created content, static content, and thematic.

In "Developing Global Perspectives, Responsibility, and Partnerships Through Videoconferencing," Stephanie E. Raible and Wayne Jacoby, the authors present a qualitative case study of Philadelphia-based Global Education Motivators, an NGO housed within a college campus that has served both the college community and schools in the local and regional area by connecting them with other students and educators from across the globe using videoconferencing technology. The case study features reports from five educators, one of whom is a former student of the college, who have built a long-standing relationship with the NGO in order to internationalize the curriculum of their respective classrooms and schools. In the reports, the educators discuss the impact of international video-conferencing on their practice and their professional perspectives as educators. Rather than investigate engagement in its behavioral and cognitively oriented forms, the reports focus on how continuous engage-ment has yielded a meaningful, lifelong learning orientation toward their commitment to internationalizing their curriculum through the participation in and facilitation of international videoconferencing events. This orientation was adopted in order to better understand the cognitive, affective, and conative domains of their learning, as manifested through each of the five reports − perspectives, responsibility, and partnerships respectively, and the chapter concludes how the participant responses relate to the three themes.

CONCLUSION

In this collection of chapters, we have presented different perspectives on how to use multimodal, multimedia, and transmedia technologies in order to create more coherent and integrated instructional messages and thus more fully engage learners. Current research suggests that these enabling technologies have the potential to increase engagement and retention but the technology is just one piece of the teaching and learning puzzle. These technologies should be used in conjunction with both sound pedagogical principles and content knowledge as well as grounded in appropriate learning theories (e.g., authentic learning, meaning-centered learning, cognitive theory). Compared with passive methods of learning (e.g., pure lecture, textbooks), these technologies have the potential to foster a more interesting and engaging learning environment.

Education should be a place where self-regulated learning is fostered and where other forms of learning are encouraged (e.g., collateral learning, informal learning, tacit knowledge). These other forms of learning are also important for students in becoming self-regulated lifelong learners. In this way, the classroom environment in microcosm, and the college environment more broadly, serves as an incubator to help nurture the attitudes and values important in sustaining learning throughout life. Please join us in exploring the inventive application of these technologies as we search for more imaginative and effective ways to better engage students.

REFERENCES

Alexander, B. (2011). *The new digital storytelling: Creating narratives with new media*. Santa Barbara, CA: Praeger.

Berger, P. L., & Luckmann, T. (1967). *The social construction of reality: A treatise in the sociology of knowledge*. New York, NY: Anchor Books.

Herrington, J., Reeves, T. C., Oliver, R., & Woo, Y. (2004). Designing authentic activities in web-based courses. *Journal of Computing and Higher Education, 16*(1), 3–29.

Kegan, R. (1994). *In over our heads: The mental demands of modern life.* Cambridge: Harvard University Press.

Lambert, N., & McCombs, B. L. (Eds.). (1998). *How students learn: Reforming schools through learner-centered education.* Washington, DC: APA Books.

Magolda, M. B. (1999). *Creating contexts for learning and self authorship.* Nashville, TN: Vanderbilt University Press.

Mayer, R. E. (1997). Multimedia learning: Are we asking the right questions? *Educational Psychologist, 32*, 1–19.

Mayer, R. E. (2005). Cognitive theory of multimedia learning. In R. E. Mayer (Ed.), *The Cambridge handbook of multimedia learning.* New York, NY: Cambridge University Press.

Sadik, A. (2008). Digital storytelling: A meaningful technology-integrated approach for engaged student learning. *Educational Technology Research and Development, 56*, 487–506.

Shirky, C. (2008). *Here comes everybody: The power of organizing without organizations.* New York, NY: The Penguin Press.

Sweller, J. (2005). Implications of cognitive load theory for multimedia learning. In R. E. Mayer (Ed.), *The Cambridge handbook of multimedia learning.* New York, NY: Cambridge University Press.

HIGHER EDUCATION: A MEDIUM IN SEARCH OF A MESSAGE

Kyle F. Reinson

ABSTRACT

Educators have always blended technology and pedagogy. With written, aural, and visual methods of sharing information optimized over time, the college and university classroom experience became a planned presentation of explicit knowledge through the revelation of course content. A respectable academic space emerged across disciplines where "the sage on the stage" could require textbooks and normalize assessment outcomes because content was decidedly controllable. There is a pedagogical crisis looming in higher education, however, the epicenter of which is student access to educational content that is useful and reliable without the major investment of a four-year degree. This crisis challenges higher education instruction to be less the medium of explicit knowledge (as it has been for decades) and more the dynamic and interactive medium whose mission is improving the thinking capacity of students through sharing and creating explicit and tacit knowledge. This chapter accordingly suggests that a seismic shift toward collaborative, problem-based approaches to learning is in order so that higher education instruction can redefine itself.

Increasing Student Engagement and Retention using Multimedia Technologies:
Video Annotation, Multimedia Applications, Videoconferencing and Transmedia Storytelling
Cutting-edge Technologies in Higher Education, Volume 6F, 17–37
Copyright © 2013 by Emerald Group Publishing Limited
All rights of reproduction in any form reserved
ISSN: 2044-9968/doi:10.1108/S2044-9968(2013)000006F004

INTRODUCTION: THE MEDIUM

Imagine Sally. She is a typical new college student. Far from her home, Sally is adrift in life-changing experiences where she is meeting new people, gearing up for the semester with nervous excitement, and getting accustomed and acclimated to the campus and its amenities. Being away at school is a daunting challenge for many students because they are suddenly separated from what they have always known. In Sally's case, she is able to cope thanks to her smart phone. Sally stays in touch with her family and friends back home via text messaging or social media applications. She finds herself hungry before her first night class of the semester and quickly locates five suggestions for where to get the best slice of pepperoni pizza in her college town by simply entering a ZIP code and the term "pizza" on her mobile Internet browser.

After Sally eats, she makes her way to class using the global positioning application on her smartphone to guide her back to her campus classroom just minutes before the start of the lecture. She takes a seat at the back of the lecture hall and prepares for the arrival of the instructor hoping for a first look at the printed copy of the course syllabus. To pass time, she checks the latest celebrity headlines, sends a few tweets, and makes plans for coffee with her new roommate after class so they can discuss their upcoming weekend of social activities. All part of college living, and technology has made it easier for her to manage her time and her life.

Sally can even catch her favorite television program on her smart phone after class while she waits for her roommate. This device that some might call a distraction enables Sally to constantly keep her head down and pay attention while her fingers and eyes navigate the virtual world in which she resides during many of her waking hours. Just as Sally is rather effectively managing her own life with mobile technology, the instructor enters the classroom and quickly explains that everyone with electronic devices must shut them off now and pay close attention to the first lecture on the basic elements of the course's content. It is clear that Sally will not be engaged in this classroom in the same way she is engaged in her daily life (if she is to be engaged at all).

The great disconnect between the student customer and higher education's message emerges. It manifests itself in each PowerPoint slide the instructor clicks through as Sally struggles to care, scrambles to take down notes, and wonders how this class will ever benefit her in real life, if she can even recall what was presented after the course concludes. Will she drop this class because she is not engaged? Can the university or college expect to retain her as a student if she does not see much benefit in her courses? As more and more reliable content appears online with no financial strings of a four-year degree attached, what is higher education's message? Such serious questions intersect not just in Sally's case, but globally and in the face of increasingly sophisticated technology that is making the content available at less cost, faster, and through media that are arguably better than the medium of delivery higher education is currently prepared to offer its customer.

This chapter suggests that higher education's over-reliance on content delivery in its pedagogy presents a legitimate threat to its own viability as a societal institution. As a social and intellectual space where scholars are producing new knowledge, colleges and universities can improve their methods for transferring that knowledge. Examining questions of content and knowledge is a helpful first step in understanding if and how higher education will adapt to the digital future. A related question to explore might be how higher education instruction, as a medium itself, might facilitate the transfer of knowledge (explicit and tacit) in the process of preparing today's students for today's world. Could collaborative, conversational, and problem-based approaches to pedagogy offer alternatives in the classroom that could build student capacities for knowledge beyond lectures and rote memorization? Would such alternatives improve student engagement and retention? If so, what might improvements to the medium of higher education look like? Can a lecture engage Sally or her classmates as well as her smart phone?

SHOULD CONTENT BE KING?

The introductory scenario represents much of what is already known about the reality of technology in the lives of college students. Many educators may have indeed done just what the instructor of Sally's class did – demand that the attention of students be placed squarely on them. One educator has walked out when students have sent text messages in class, and stated that "(…) what I will not do is tolerate such brazen disrespect for me" (Jaschik, 2008). Students must conform in a lecture setting, after all, because educators have explicit knowledge to impart. Over time, many students have grown up with an acceptance that this is precisely how learning happens. Instructors are paid to develop and share course content, perhaps even shoulder the burden of engaging and entertaining their students, and follow up by assessing students on how well they have paid attention or remembered something about (what for many is) their first exposure to the content in a course that will last only 15 weeks.

Content-driven courses are by far the standard, with educators contemplating reading lists and concepts they feel are the most important for students. Many institutions normalize course content through textbook adoption and learning objectives, potentially limiting the academic freedom of otherwise intelligent people who might prefer to take risks and try engaging learners in new ways. The increasingly common use of adjunct instructors also serves to feed the content is king model. Adjunct instructors now comprise approximately 70% of all faculty appointments (Stratford, 2012). For part-time or non-tenure-track academic labor, using the adopted textbook is just more cost-effective. After all, they will not be paid anything extra for taking risks. At some institutions, tenure-track faculty can be discouraged from worrying too much about teaching while they are focused on collecting publications for their dossier. The system is built on content, but the foundation is beginning to shake as the Internet is supplying increasingly advanced content that stands alone and explains itself.

Lecture halls full of students have simply not been ideal spaces for classroom innovation, and this is possibly because of their size or the embedded nature of the dramaturgical lecture as the instructional method of choice across disciplines. Lecture halls are also lucrative for many institutions, and developing lopsided student–faculty ratios can help cut costs. However, even courses with smaller or more limited enrollments can place an arguably dangerous amount of emphasis on explicit knowledge in the form of course content.

Some instructors rely on textbooks to organize their course content, this can often be an expensive investment for students, and can lead to mistrust. Lewin (2009) reported the average student spends between $700 and $1,100 on textbooks. These artificially high prices seem out of synch with the free content that can be found on the web and can often be as reliable. One group of former college students took their argument against required textbooks to the web to engage college students in a conversation about how much textbooks are actually used in various classes. The website, bookdecay.com, asks students bluntly: "Do Your Professors Use Their 'Required' Textbooks? Stop Wasting Your Money" (BookDecay.com, 2012). Of course, educators know that reading itself is a valuable method of learning and developing one's knowledge, even if students are not tested on the material. However, if students view course readings as superfluous and not central it may be indicative of other problems that exist with learning engagement. Even if students read, does the content that instructors select resonate with every student? So much of this is determined long before the first day of class.

The problem with preparing for content-based courses is that the planning takes place before the course itself begins. There is little or no advance familiarity with the students and their personalities or level of attained knowledge. Learning settings are a mystery, so educators must guess about what pedagogical efforts might work. Imagination can and perhaps should be a central part of curriculum design, but opportunities for student collaboration in that process are often lost when instructors use content as the one-way ticket to meeting course objectives before they have even met the intended audience. McKernan (2008) noted that in college teaching, "since the early twentieth century, the dominant model has been a 'technical' and managerial style of ends-means rational planning, by instructional-behavioral objectives" (p. x). This dominant model was implemented before sweeping changes in mobile and Internet technology redefined how people access and process information.

Content is usually packaged to fit every learner with a one-sized product. Instructors often rely on prerequisites to indicate what familiarity students might have with the content of previous coursework; however, one might imagine the flaw in that logic being that some students may have performed marginally in prerequisite courses while others earned an "A." Students are not unified intellectually by merely being exposed to the same content. Some courses are foundational, but not all courses. Learning is a socially constructed experience, not merely a set of competencies. Students can be unified when they collaborate and instructors guide them through the process of constructivist learning (Vygotsky, 1978), stretching beyond the content is king model. A helpful pathway for scaffolding is explained here by Bransford, Brown, and Cocking (2000) who pointed to engaging and retaining students of the now and of the future by granting more attention to the progress they make, something that is difficult to achieve in typical lecture format:

> There is a good deal of evidence that learning is enhanced when teachers pay attention to the knowledge and beliefs that learners bring to a learning task, use this knowledge as a starting point for new instruction, and monitor students' changing conceptions as instruction proceeds. (p. 11)

The attention span for a typical college lecture is easily eroded by the content available through the devices that students are often forbidden to use in class. Without a balance in the use of class time (less sage, more collaboration), the instructor cannot take stock of any instruction efforts. If students only show up to class to sit through presentations and take notes, opportunities for engagement can be squandered but opportunities for financial gain do emerge. ShareNotes.com is one recent web-based venture that allows students to cash in by sharing and selling their lecture notes in a space where other students may buy them (ShareNotes.com, 2012). While this might signal an entrepreneurial way for students to offset tuition and book fees, it also suggests the college lecture has diminished value because of its content-centric nature. Why go to class when you will only be tested on the content? Simply revealing and later testing students on explicit content may have once been an effective pedagogy. However, when students invest thousands of dollars in a course knowing all along they can just look up the right answer later on a search engine (even after they are done with college), such assessment practices begin to seem illogical.

Wright (2007) explained that information has been freed from its old physical shackles by networks. Today's students embody a generation of pioneers who have enjoyed this shackle-free abundance for much of their lives and a growing number have the technology in their hands to learn collaboratively. One study found that 45% of those 18–29 who use cell phones to go online will use mobile browsing most (Smith, 2012). The social realities of today's undergraduate students are digital, or at the very least greatly enhanced by digital mobile technology, but as Macedo (2000) explained, "teachers must treat students as empty vessels to be filled with predetermined bodies of knowledge, which are often disconnected from students' social realities and from issues of equity, responsibility, and democracy" (p. 5). Also consider that college students have a massive glut of information that is readily available to them through networks that facilitate their decision-making processes all day. They are immersed in spaces and networks that are instantly gratifying to them. They have little or no desire for time-consuming research, listening or waiting on anything. A lecture is a bit of cognitive dissonance.

A basic mental map of decision-making (Fig. 1) about a variety of choices in college life stacks up favorably on the side of technology providing all the answers to a student like Sally in an efficient manner. The college lecture could be as instantly compelling and gratifying, but instructors would have to reach students in creative ways by offering more mobile interaction inside and outside the classroom.

Understandably, educators might prefer to believe they are currently being listened to and understood, or even that students prefer memorizing content modules to being challenged to think critically or even creatively.

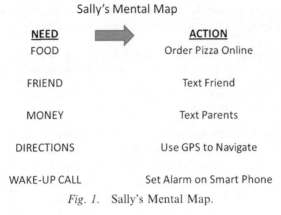

Fig. 1. Sally's Mental Map.

However, as the next generation of learners decides if they should invest in higher education, educators and institutions must be aware that student use of technology will continue to be beyond the control of instructors. Adoption of cutting-edge technologies, therefore, is no longer a choice in higher education but a necessity. Even though content delivery has been an essential hallmark of higher education since its inception, the age of information has shifted that function to the cloud. The abundance of accessible content is a juggernaut confronting the scarcity of a classroom space. Content is a much bigger king than most instructors can manage alone, so perhaps sharing the burden with students is the next phase in a flipped classroom that engages all participants in learning outcomes.

TEXTBOOKS AND CAPITALISM

Thrift (2001) described the "backward gaze" toward capitalism reveals it to be "a constantly mutating entity made up of fields or networks which are only ever partly in its control," and that "no matter how many assets are engaged, it must constantly face the pressure of unexpected events" (p. 376). The economics of textbooks and those in the academic community who publish them often present an expensive problem for students who in a variety of cases can find the same content at their college libraries or online with no cost to them. Economic imperatives operate at the micro level in the higher education classroom and guide how course content is managed. Washburn (2005) argued that corporate influence is one pressure at play.

Textbooks are an expensive manifestation of corporate goals intersecting with learning in an uneven way. Frank and Meyer (2007) explained that:

> Learning techniques grew increasingly codified in specialized organizations, roles, and materials, most obviously in the formalization of pedagogy itself. The textbook commenced its reign as the ultimate carrier of general laws and fixed facts, and the standardized "introductory" course became the sanctioned start of a rationalized pathway from elementary to advanced studies. (p. 305)

The allegiance to content-driven courses is the greatest evidence of capitalism's careful and strategic march toward automation. Textbooks and their content were at once a convenient way to help students process knowledge but have become a palpable liability as students are forced to subsidize a soon-to-be antiquated enterprise. Even as some textbooks become available in digital formats, the question of student willingness to perpetually pay for them remains dubious.

TECHNOLOGY AND TEACHING

Technology can make the mundane more interesting, but it can also make the more interesting mundane. Today's mobile networks and the technology supporting them can speed delivery of content, duplicate and revise it — and in the blink of an eye content can be shared again with millions of people in Internet perpetuity. Technology does not act alone to guarantee student engagement and retention and we should be careful not to mandate that it could or even should. We are, however, encountering a world where multimedia experiences are ubiquitous and global. As communication itself has become a multimedia experience, college-level instruction should at least keep pace with the latest trends. Mobile technology can quickly become a more viable vehicle for instructional delivery, and educators should be open to change rather than seek comfort in more traditional methods like dramaturgical lectures that are unlikely to engage learners much longer.

A new multi-mediated paradigm is clearly upon us. Hierarchies are breaking down and social networks are rising up to replace them, becoming even more effective at organizing people than institutions (Shirky, 2008). McLuhan (1964) noted that "it was not until the advent of the telegraph that messages could travel faster than the messenger" (p. 89), and that "all technologies are extensions of our physical and nervous systems to increase power and speed" (p. 90). Does higher education's message travel faster than it once did? In certain spaces it clearly does. Does higher education fully leverage its power and speed? Does this inevitable power and speed of information signal the official end of seat time being equivalent to learning time (if it ever was)? Learning spaces are very much up for debate in terms of what is best, and what is best may not apply equally to all. As an example of McLuhan's power and speed in action, the sophisticated lectures featured at Apple's iTunes U convey wonderful explicit knowledge about everything from Shakespeare to astrophysics (Apple, 2012). Many colleges and universities have seen this convenient platform as a means of branding and selling their institutions online and offering selected free samples of their (best) college lectures. At the same time, students interested in shorter and less formal content can get "ideas worth spreading" at TED.com and its latest effort launched in 2012 called TED-Ed. TED-Ed is a space where animators and educators create specific learning lessons for open-source consumption (TED Conferences, 2012). The trend apparent in these examples is one of competition for eyeballs online and for better and more accessible ways to help people learn. To be fair, many instructors incorporate content from these sites into their courses already, but when the lights come back on they stand in front of the same classroom and return to the lecture. While TED-Ed appears to have an aim of online instruction, and iTunes U delivers stylized lectures, the cloud can also be a reasonably reliable source. Educators have warned about the accuracy of the content students might find when they trust "the cloud" for reliable information and have threatened to "slash" essays that include Wikipedia as a source (Eisen, 2007). As digitized print and electronic materials share the same spaces online, however, the room for error is getting narrower. What students see in Apple and TED educational spaces is a stylized lecture where the lighting is perfect and all the mistakes are edited out. Even the very best and most engaging live instructors are not perfect in every class session nor are they brilliant all semester. Yet, when higher education falls back on delivering explicit knowledge via a lecture filled with content, students are likely to compare the multi-mediated alternative to what they are getting in the classroom and "wish their professor was more like that." The live lecture is, at current, unable to mutate and adapt to be competitive to more stylized alternatives. While this may be an aesthetic issue, it is nonetheless a driver of student engagement among those students who complain to instructors that they are visual learners and cannot sit still for a lecture. Despite technology, traditional pedagogies still have inertia and they are often emulated out of habit and not necessarily rooted in effectiveness. Reynolds (2012) observed that the delivery model of higher education has remained the same for hundreds of years and in that time, "instruction hasn't advanced much," and that "some professors may use PowerPoint (a dubious improvement), but the basic model of one person standing in front of a bunch of other people talking hasn't really changed." When one person talks to a group they tend to set the group's agenda by default, and the promise (or threat) of a grade is usually the incentive used to engage students to pay attention. Higher education still suffers from what Batson (2009) characterized as the "I tell you" model of rote memorization, regurgitation, and grading. Some students thrive in this environment and others do not.

If a teacher has a substantially different preexisting knowledge set than his or her students (and they often do) there are built-in difficulties, barriers to understanding that are not the fault of instructor or student per se, but characterized by an institution's inertia, technology feeds the inertia. Older technologies, even the effective ones, never disappear completely. Instead, they linger within their social milieu. The undergraduate classroom still has presentation equipment from decades ago despite rapid and recent innovations. Courses are still classified as lecture-based and discussion-based. Class sizes are still very important in terms of the content that can be covered and the interactions that are possible between educators and students.

Change only happens when the timing is right, or fails to happen at all as institutions become obsolete. Technology is now presenting perfect timing to higher education because the learning curve is ongoing, not too steep and, in fact, not really more difficult than creating an account on Facebook. The conversational classroom is on the near horizon and it will liberate both instructors and students to find new ways of seeking, sharing, and creating knowledge.

KNOWLEDGE: EXPLICIT AND TACIT

Technologies of knowledge were much different when Polanyi (1967) brought conceptions of tacit and explicit knowledge into intellectual and management circles 50 years ago, but a look at the differentiation today is helpful for finding new ways that the adoption of cutting-edge technologies can become more pervasive in the medium of higher education instruction. Both explicit and tacit knowledge are important in education, but because tacit knowledge is more difficult to articulate, it remains a virtually untapped source for innovation in higher education pedagogies.

Erden, von Krogh, and Nonaka (2008) and Nonaka (1991) in addition to Polanyi (1967) conceptualized knowledge as both tacit and explicit. Explicit knowledge can be spoken, put into words and into texts that can be visual or text-based. Tacit knowledge is tied to senses of touch, smell, sight, sound, and movements or even experiences that are physical. Intuition and certain "rules" that are implicit are also forms of tacit knowledge (Erden et al., 2008, p. 5). The moment students send a tweet, it becomes explicit in the form of a short literary text that can count as course participation. When students react to both explicit and tacit knowledge it is possible to see how deeply they are considering an idea and how deeply the subject matter is being engaged. Instructors can intertwine tacit and explicit knowledge-building by incorporating technology to get students interacting with each other and the course content, mashing up subjects for greater under-standing. Students can also begin to fashion themselves as subject matter experts (or at least burgeoning experts) when they create Twitter accounts and share their interests. Twitter can make students instant content curators, adding and clarifying context for topics in the course and even the tangential subjects students might want to explore further. Would knowing what really stuck with students make designing final exams easier? With Twitter, instructors have a digital footprint of student engagement and information aggregation that could lead to inclusive exam questions that recognize student centrality to the process.

Information aggregation has given rise to The Daily Me, where news and information can be polarized by one's own human choice (Negroponte, 1995, Sunstein, 2001, 2006). Higher education can probably not win the war of The Daily Me, but it could win battles for The Daily Us (Sunstein, 2006), where social networks serve as opportunities for student engagement, instructor engagement, and most of all: collaboration. The real-time information network Twitter is a perfect example of The Daily Us in action, and instructors are finding new ways to engage students, not by demanding their attention and threatening to leave class, but by taking their busy schedules into account (Reinson & Sodano, 2011).

The Daily Us is contingent upon social networks and the ability of all users to generate, mash-up, and redistribute content in often artistic ways. If an instructor were to create learning environments that foster creativity, collaboration, and critical thinking she or he could remove some of the hierarchy that slows higher education down and replace the college lecture with a set of internal student course processes that mirror how organizations both large and small communicate in the real world. Sunstein (2006) explained insightfully that if "internal processes," like those at play during

NASA's tragic Challenger and Columbia flights, "had been properly structured, those blunders would have been far less likely to occur" (p. 213). Hierarchy is not the goal, but learning is. Organically, student engagement takes on its own new shape where instructors will cede some of their power. The Daily Us could ideally last beyond the confines of a semester, linking previous courses together rather than putting content in silos.

Though research is quite limited on specific assignments that might build both tacit and explicit knowledge, the technological tools are in place. Smart phones in hand, students could tweet during classes. A sample assignment idea for a political science lecture course might entail the *following steps for students* if the instructor is attempting to create the Daily Us experience:

1. Create a Twitter account with a professional photo of yourself and obtain a "handle" that identifies you as a college student interested in social media and democracy. (Sally searches Twitter. Sees that "@sallymedia" is available and creates an account.)
2. When you create your account, follow your instructor on Twitter, and he will follow you back. His handle is "@reinsoncreative." Please follow all of your classmates who are following your instructor. See the "@reinsoncreative" list of followers.
3. Find and follow at least 10 Twitter users who share your professional career interests, then find 20 users who are tweeting about the current presidential election and follow them.
4. Download Twitter's mobile application to your smart phone and tweet daily about the campaign, the course, professional interests, or current news you find that you think would be interesting to either other students or your instructor.
5. Your participation grade for the course will be based on the quality and quantity of your contributions on Twitter during this semester.

This simple five-step process can be modified based on the subject, but in the first week of classes, a space has been created where student participation is no longer optional and is more consistent with how students are experiencing their world. Writing must be concise, professional, and compelling on Twitter. To get a good participation grade, students can show how deeply they understand a subject through the interactivity of hyperlinks supporting their thoughts and opinions. With the right ground rules, the resulting digital texts created by students reveal where they are in terms of learning and foster collaboration that can build tacit knowledge they can apply in professional settings.

Ozmen (2010), who acknowledged that educational organizations are not particularly astute at benefitting from tacit knowledge, sets forth five recommendations for higher education to benefit more from it. She recommended that organizational cultures at colleges and universities support organizational learning through internal cooperation and collaboration, and that they should also create action plans that are inclusive of staff to develop ways of explicating tacit knowledge and facilitate the sharing of such knowledge throughout the organization. She also emphasized the creation of physical spaces and interactions designed to transmit tacit knowledge and she advocated building electronic infrastructures like college portals to collect the outcomes of these actions (p. 1864). Twitter and Yammer are platforms in the classroom that can speak to Ozmen's ideal and facilitate such activity.

GROUP TACIT KNOWLEDGE

Growing the capacity for tacit and explicit knowledge sharing would mean new sharing groups might form around certain areas of expertise within colleges and universities, sharing knowledge freely between students and other students as well as faculty and staff. Zhong and Qu (2012) suggested that while explicit knowledge has been effectively encountered by knowledge management processes, tacit knowledge needs a model of sharing. In the spirit of healthy collaboration, these groups need not be hierarchical, and in fact could constitute a problem-based learning experience of its own by forming groups that have a stake in fixing problems facing the institution or even suggesting new pathways or group-ways for innovation.

Erden et al. (2008) defined "group tacit knowledge" (GTK) and noted that sharing tacit knowledge itself "necessitates the 'here and now' interaction of people" (p. 15). But how does one explain platforms like Twitter and even enterprise social networks like Yammer, Jive, and Chatter becoming more popular with business and enterprise but not yet higher education? Opportunities seem evident for new explorations. The latest innovation by Blackboard, a Learning Management System, is Blackboard Collaborate, which affords spaces for synchronous video and "smart board"-style interaction. Courses based less on content and more on collaboration now have the technical support (via site-based software like Blackboard or open-source alternatives like Yammer and Twitter) to unpack tacit knowledge from faculty, staff, and students that would make the academic experiences more rich. Indeed, student e-portfolios are, in fact,

an outcome that would represent a common space for the assessment
function of an institution and serve the dual role in the personal branding of
students for job searches. The question of, "What did you do for four years
in college?" is suddenly answerable, accountable, and marketable for all
parties. Learning outcomes incorporating e-portfolios clearly demonstrate
progress. GTK could be a powerful way for institutions to remain unique
because of the minds it brings together. Johannessen, Olaisen, and Oslen
(2001) have explored the understanding of the role of tacit knowledge in
knowledge-based society and point to the advantages of collective reflection
as tacit knowledge at the personal level. When tacit knowledge can become
explicit knowledge (for collective reflection) they argue that a "learning loop
between innovations and continuous improvements" has been created
(p. 16). If students are being engaged in these learning loops along with
faculty, they are also being prepared for success in the real world as knowledge workers, which, encompasses almost every profession and career.

Knowledge workers are nearly every worker in the information age, and
today's students and tomorrow's workers will deal in explicit and tacit forms
of knowledge daily. As Davenport and Prusak (1998) noted, "knowledge
management jobs are proliferating rapidly," and these jobs should combine
the "'hard' skills (structured knowledge, technical abilities, and professional
experience) with 'softer' traits (a sure sense of the cultural, political, and
personal aspects of knowledge)" (p. 110). Tacit knowledge skills are
important to knowledge workers because these skills extend the capacity of
their job performance beyond the job description. Skills in digital spaces
become life skills. In both negative and positive contexts, the lives of college
students are already public data. People around the world live in what
Andrejevic (2007) theorized as a digital enclosure where "every virtual
'move' has the potential to leave a digital trace or record of itself," and
"places and activities become encompassed by the monitoring embrace of an
interactive (virtual) space" (p. 2). Curry (2010) explained that:

> When I apply for credit, the bank officer "sees" a digital individual; when a credit card
> company asks Trans Union for a list of prospects, it gets a list of digital individuals; and
> when the local pizza company sends out a mailing, it sends it not to me, but to a digital
> individual, one who shares my name and address. (p. 695)

Although we all exist in real geographies, our footprints are also found in
virtual worlds where our previous work, shopping, and transportation
habits (among other activities) act as an extension of the self. Our thought
patterns, attitudes, and actions are transformed into data just waiting to be
mined.

FREEDOM AND LIBERATION

The words of Charles Horton Cooley (1964) offer an interesting snapshot archiving educational perceptions more than a century ago because they speak to a broad historical moment of change that is similar to ours:

> I can perceive, during my own lifetime, an actual growth of freedom in most of our institutions. Family discipline has become more a matter of persuasion and example, less one of mere authority and rod. In the school, mechanical modes of teaching, enlivened by punishment, have given way to sympathy, interest, and emulation. (p. 427)

For Cooley, freedom was tied to physical controls, yet in the classrooms of higher education it is now often the content delivery controlling the student experience, right down to final exams and other tests that yield ephemeral mastery rather than sustained learning that can be applied toward and continued in one's own life. The subjects are important, but the medium of higher education instruction has settled on just a few best practices for student engagement in them. The lecture and its assumed outcome of rote memorization are fine ways to have something to show for the semester in the form of grades, papers, and test scores for assessment and accreditation, but as the semester ends so does the learning. It is compartmentalized as "over with" in the minds of students who now seek what they really came to college for: enhanced career prospects.

Why should students study for a final exam when their only reward is a letter grade and the end of the course? Those stakes seem so low. Jaffee (2012) boldly suggested that encouraging students to study for tests like a final exam might actually undermine higher education's mission because when faculty emphasize studying for tests it "communicates to students that the process of intellectual inquiry, academic exploration, and acquiring knowledge is a purely instrumental activity – designed to ensure success on the next assessment."

The good news is, both exams and reviewing their results point to promising alternatives that can liberate students and engage them in the building of the "soft skills" they will need for careers in any field. Why not allow students to use an enterprise social network like Yammer during a test so they can share information, speculate what the right answers might be, and perhaps enjoy the process of finding the correct answer through inquiry and reflection or even a spirited argument with fellow students? Keeping the technology away from students might feel like the right thing to do, but technology can also create a vibrant space where conversations of learning are taking place. For liberating even the largest of lecture halls,

Stark (2006) argued that instructors should not "go over" or review exams and instead devote the same time to team exams, which hold administrative benefits like "efficiency," allow for question "validity checks" and a "pleasant mood" for students (pp. 824–825), and he notes that his process benefits student learning in all subjects by producing "accurate feedback," "accurate engagement in learning," and "learning by explaining" (pp. 822–823). Course content is neither the captor nor the liberator, and can be transferred easily enough from person to person without a college professor to manage the process, but who is instead present to facilitate learning outcomes. Large groups can do the work and the learning all-at-once, and ideas like a team exam diffuse so much of the test anxiety that students grapple with on campuses everywhere. Learning should not be a fear-based proposition for students. Instructors must be careful of distraction as well. Unless students can develop a healthy habit of self-regulation as Wei, Wang, and Klausner (2012) have noted, distractions like texting or using Twitter during class can limit learning. In courses where Twitter is used as a convenient tool to capture conversations, the desire to text and tweet could become a student's meaningful contribution rather than a waste of their time and money.

CONCLUSION: NEW SPACES FOR LEARNING

Any profession risks obsolescence and college professors are no different. Automated Teller Machines (ATMs) and online banking have changed the way humans interact with their financial resources. This automation has been at the expense of human interaction, namely with other humans in the bank. Mobile technology has spawned a global citizen journalism that is arguably more effective at "getting the scoop" than legacy journalism ever was. Even the printed telephone book, once the ideal tool for advertisers seeking consumers who were "ready to buy" has ceded its utility to mobile applications and web search that can facilitate the same slice of pepperoni pizza that once required looking in the phone book and making a telephone call. As McLuhan (1964) warned 50 years ago:

> With automation, it is not only jobs that disappear, and complex roles that reappear. Centuries of specialist stress in pedagogy and in the arrangement of data now end with the instantaneous retrieval of information made possible by electricity. Automation is information and it not only ends jobs in the world of work, it ends subjects in the world of learning. (p. 346)

As technology has slowly supplanted human labor throughout industrial history there has been an inevitable shift in how professionals justify their expertise in the face of change. Some bank tellers can transition easily to a complementary profession, but others might deliver pizza. How do college professors embrace change without being offended?

Richards (2005) observed that teachers can be intimidated by cutting-edge technology and Ting (2011) explained that they often "resent the naïve rhetoric of ICT (information and communications technology) integration typically associated with top-down policy imperatives" (p. 147). In her study of urban educators Mouza (2011) found that "many teachers were reluctant to implement technology in complex student-centered ways, despite their ability to design lessons that articulated the connections among technology, content and pedagogy" (p. 23). These are substantial barriers standing in the way of change and developing scholarly networks, and another is the information overload and Mangan (2012) suggested "some scholars who are already feeling overwhelmed by the demands of LinkedIn, Facebook, Twitter, blogs, and e-mail either shy away from the new sites or dabble in them and then let their accounts sit dormant."

It could be suggested that today's college students are the problem, having access to technology at early ages and having grown accustomed to on-demand lifestyles facilitated by computers and mobile devices. The problem could also be defined as a generational change in communication and the slow pace with which higher education moves. Spiraling student loan debt and an uncertain guarantee that a college degree will lead to gainful employment are also factors that build a healthy skepticism about investing tens of thousands of dollars on four years of content that can be found online.

Social media is at the center of students' lives, creating circuits and networks that level the communicative playing field. Selwyn (2012) acknowledged that "tensions remain between those who believe that social media can be used to strengthen and improve the higher education institution in its current form, and those who believe that social media exist to disrupt (and ultimately replace) the university altogether" (p. 4). As this chapter concludes, one important example is well worth noting. A start-up called Udacity bills itself as a space for "Free Classes. Awesome Instructors. Inspiring Community" (udacity.com, 2012). One of its free courses, open to everyone regardless of preexisting knowledge is called "CS101: Building a Search Engine," where students are promised they can "learn key concepts in computer science and build a search engine like google[sic]!" in just seven weeks. Imagine these questions (Fig. 2) being

Can I get an extension on a homework assignment?
There are no deadlines for homework, so there is no need for an extension.
Is there a final exam?
Yes. There will be at least two opportunities to take an exam for this course. One after about 7 weeks and the other approximately 8 weeks later.
The next exam will be available at 23:59 UTC on 27th May 2012. You will have one week to complete the exam. You may submit your answers as many times as you like, but you will receive no feedback until after the closing date. The closing date for the exam is 23:59 UTC on 3rd June 2012. No submissions will be accepted after this time.
How will my final grade be determined?
Your final grade will be determined by your exam grade.
What are the rules on collaboration?
Working with other students is often the best way to learn new things, and we hope students in the class will form vibrant communities, both on-line and in-person, to help each other learn. The key is to use collaboration as a way to enhance learning, not as a way of sharing answers without understanding them.
You are welcome (and encouraged) to view the lectures with others, and discuss and work together on answering the in-lecture quizzes. For the homeworks, you may discuss the questions with other students in the on-line forums and in-person study groups, but everything you submit should be your own work. For the final exam, you are not permitted to work with anyone else, and should only ask clarification questions on the on-line forums which will be answered by the course staff.

(Udacity.com, 2012)

Fig. 2.   A Sample FAQ from Udacity, which features Massive Open Online Courses (MOOCs).

asked and answered in this way on current college and university campuses. How does the medium of higher education currently respond? This is how Udacity responds.

The course closely mirrors the lecture-based environments of the college classroom with short, no credit quizzes and exercises using an online version of Python to teach the basics of computer science. No textbook is required. The course is free.

In formulating a new message for higher education in a changing world, it is clear that educators cannot allow technology to be a barrier. Habermas (1987) argued that the "functions the university fulfills for society must preserve an inner connection with the goals, motives and actions of its members" (p. 3). There is still plenty of hope and opportunity to preserve this inner connection, but the world outside is not waiting for academe to move forward.

Teaching methods like peer instruction appear perfectly suited for web-based social networks even though substantial efficacy research in this area has not yet been published. A study of Harvard students and those at two-year colleges found student engagement and retention was much better in classroom environments where peer instruction was used instead of lecture-based pedagogy (Lasry, Mazur, & Watkins, 2008). Nicol and Boyle (2003) found that peer instruction was even more effective than large group discussions. When innovative educators allow and encourage students to be part of the content creation process in a course students have a stake in a course's success beyond the letter grade they might receive. When students are producing and engaging explicit and tacit knowledge they might just be learning everything they need to be successful in life. Black and Browning (2011) explained that students who are challenged to explore digital creativity "become self-motivated and self-directed, while gaining confidence in their digital creative ability and themselves as teachers" (p. 22). As a medium, higher education has always exuded a message of cutting-edge innovation. Before the technology passes them by, educators should seize the opportunity to accommodate students who may not be speaking a new language, but who have been learning in new ways and with new media to send a message of their own.

REFERENCES

Andrejevic, M. (2007). *iSpy: Surveillance and power in the interactive era.* Lawrence, KS: University Press of Kansas.

Apple. (2012). *The all-new iTunes U.* Apple in Education. Retrieved from http://www.apple.com/education/itunes-u/

Batson, T. (2009, April 1). Can campuses change before obsolesence? *Campus Technology.* Retrieved from http://campustechnology.com/articles/2009/04/01/can-campuses-change-before-obsolescence.aspx

Black, J., & Browning, K. (2011, September). Creativity in digital art education teaching practices. *Art Education, 64*(5), 19–24, 33–34.

BookDecay.com. (2012). Retrieved from http://www.bookdecay.com/splash/

Bransford, J. D., Brown, A. L., & Cocking, R. R. (2000). *How people learn.* Washington, DC: National Academy Press.

Cooley, C. H. (1964). *Human nature and the social order.* New York, NY: Schocken Books.

Curry, M. R. (2010). The digital individual and the private realm. *Annals of the Association of American Geographers, 87*, 681–689.

Davenport, T. H., & Prusak, L. (1998). *Working knowledge: How organizations manage what they know.* Boston, MA: Harvard Business School Press.

Eisen, B. (2007, February 20). Cornell profs slam use of Wikipedia. *Cornell Daily Sun.* Retrieved from http://cornellsun.com/node/21501

Erden, Z., von Krogh, G., & Nonaka, I. (2008). The quality of group tacit knowledge. *Journal of Strategic Information Systems, 17*, 4–18.

Frank, D. J., & Meyer, J. W. (2007). University expansion and the knowledge society. *Theory and Society*, *36*, 287–311.

Habermas, J. (1987). The idea of the university: Learning processes. *New German Critique*, *41*(Special Issue on the Critiques of Enlightenment), 3–22.

Jaffee, D. (2012, April 22). *Commentary: Stop telling students to study for exams.* Retrieved from http://chronicle.com/article/Stop-Telling-Students-to-Study/131622/

Jaschik, S. (2008). If you text in class, this prof will leave. *Inside Higher Ed.* Retrieved from http://insidehighered.com/news/2008/04/02/texting

Johannessen, J.-A., Olaisen, J., & Olsen, B. (2001). Mismanagement of tacit knowledge: The importance of tacit knowledge, the danger of information technology, and what to do about it. *International Journal of Information Management*, *21*, 3–20.

Lasry, N., Mazur, E., & Watkins, J. (2008). Peer instruction: From Harvard to the two-year college. *American Journal of Physics*, *76*(11), 1066–1069.

Lewin, T. (2009, August 13). Textbook publisher to rent to college students. *New York Times*. Education. Retrieved from http://www.nytimes.com/2009/08/14/education/14textbook.html

Macedo, D. (2000). Introduction. In D. E. Macedo (Ed.), *Chomsky on MisEducation* (pp. 1–14). Lanham, MD: Rowman & Littlefield.

Mangan, K. (2012, April 29). Social networks for academic proliferate, despite some doubts. *Chronicle of Higher Education: Technology*. Retrieved from http://chronicle.com/article/Social-Networks-for-Academics/131726/

McKernan, J. (2008). *Curriculum and imagination: Process theory, pedagogy and action research.* London: Routledge.

McLuhan, M. (1964). *Understanding media: The extensions of man.* New York, NY: McGraw-Hill.

Mouza, C. (2011). Promoting urban teachers' understanding of technology, content, and pedagogy in the context of case development. *Journal of Research on Technology in Education*, *44*(1), 1–29.

Negroponte, N. (1995). *Being digital.* New York, NY: Vintage Press.

Nicol, D. J., & Boyle, J. T. (2003). Peer instruction versus class-wide discussion in large classes: A comparison of two interaction methods in the wired classroom. *Studies in Higher Education*, *28*(4), 457–473.

Nonaka, I. (1991). The knowledge-creating company. *Harvard Business Review*, *69*(6), 96–104.

Ozmen, F. (2010). The capabilities of the educational organizations in making use of tacit knowledge. *Procedia Social and Behavioral Sciences*, *9*, 1860–1865.

Polanyi, M. (1967). *The tacit dimension.* London: Routledge & Kegan Paul, Ltd.

Reinson, K. F., & Sodano, T. (2011, January 5). *Student engagement with Twitter.* Retrieved from http://sjfcvideo.wordpress.com/2011/01/05/student-engagement-with-twitter/

Reynolds, G. (2012, May 5). *Sunday reflection: What comes after the higher education bubble?* Retrieved from http://washingtonexaminer.com/opinion/columnists/2012/05/sunday-reflection-what-comes-after-higher-education-bubble/572421

Richards, C. (2005). The design of effective ICT-supported learning activities: Exemplary models, changing requirements, and new possibilities. *Language Learning & Technology*, *9*, 60–79.

Selwyn, N. (2012). Social media in higher education. In *The Europa World of Learning*. Retrieved from http://www.educationarena.com/pdf/sample/sample-essay-selwyn.pdf

ShareNotes.com. (2012). Retrieved from http://www.sharenotes.com/sharenotes-features-and-rewards/index.php

Shirky, C. (2008). *Here comes everybody: The power of organizing without organizations.* New York, NY: The Penguin Press.

Smith, A. (2012, June 26). *Cell internet use 2012.* Retrieved from http://www.pewinternet.org/Reports/2012/Cell-Internet-Use-2012/Key-Findings.aspx

Stark, G. (2006). Stop "going over" exams! The multiple benefits of team exams. *Journal of Management Education, 30,* 818–827.

Stratford, M. (2012, February 19). A simple spreadsheet strikes a nerve among adjuncts. *Chronicle of Higher Education.* Retrieved from http://chronicle.com/article/Accidental-Activist-Collects/130854/

Sunstein, C. R. (2001). *Republic.com.* Princeton, NJ: Princeton University Press.

Sunstein, C. R. (2006). *Infotopia: How many minds produce knowledge.* Oxford: Oxford University Presss.

TED Conferences (2012). *TED initiatives.* Retrieved from http://www.ted.com/pages/initiatives_ted-ed

Thrift, N. (2001). Perspectives on new political economy: Chasing capitalism. *New Political Economy, 6,* 375–380.

Ting, Y.-L. (2011). Introducing new technology to teachers: A pilot evaluation. *International Journal of Technology in Teaching and Learning, 7,* 136–151.

Udacity.com. (2012). *Introduction to Computer Science (CS 101): Building a search engine – Overview.* Retrieved from http://www.udacity.com/overview/Course/cs101/CourseRev/apr2012#q1

Vygotsky, L. S. (1978). *Mind in society.* Cambridge, MA: Harvard Press.

Washburn, J. (2005). *University, inc.: The corporate corruption of higher education.* New York, NY: Basic Books.

Wei, F.-Y. F., Wang, Y. K., & Klausner, M. (2012). Rethinking college students' self-regulation and sustained attention: Does text messaging during class influence cognitive learning? *Communication Education, 61,* 185–204.

Wright, A. (2007). *Glut: Mastering information through the ages.* Ithaca, NY: Cornell University Press.

Zhong, X., & Qu, K. (2012). Research on the model construction of teachers' tacit knowledge sharing based on social software. *Procedia Engineering, 29,* 223–228.

PART II
APPLICATION OF MULTIMEDIA TECHNOLOGIES

USING TECHNOLOGY AND DIGITAL NARRATIVES TO ENGAGE DOCTORAL STUDENTS IN SELF-AUTHORSHIP AND LEARNING PARTNERSHIPS

Sean Robinson

ABSTRACT

As educational institutions continue to call for greater accountability and learning outcomes take center stage, faculty, administrators, and institutions alike must assume a broader, more holistic approach to teaching and learning. As outlined in this chapter, technology and virtual spaces, when utilized well, can radically shift how graduate faculty can help doctoral students become critical and reflective thinkers, to develop or refine a professional identity, and help them to transform their assumptions about their knowledge and about themselves, a process that Kegan (1994) and Baxter Magolda (1999) call self-authorship. Using digital narratives as part of a technology-mediated classroom that is built around learning partnerships and principles of self-authorship is one way to accomplish this. Such an approach can lead to innovative practices in the

Increasing Student Engagement and Retention using Multimedia Technologies:
Video Annotation, Multimedia Applications, Videoconferencing and Transmedia Storytelling
Cutting-edge Technologies in Higher Education, Volume 6F, 41–65
ISSN: 2044-9968/doi:10.1108/S2044-9968(2013)000006F005

classroom, deeper, more reflective learning for students, and greater overall success for our institutions. By combining multimedia tools and technology with an adult learning-centered pedagogy built around self-authoring practices of student development, faculty can more effectively organize doctoral education to engage and involve students in the process and to truly cultivate a new generation of doctoral students as scholars, researchers, and practitioners.

INTRODUCTION

Constructivist theory maintains that student participation and interaction are keys to the learning process (Phillips, 1995). Over time, notions of constructivism in the field of education have ranged from Dewey's (1938) notion of experience to Vygotsky's (1978) zone of proximal development (ZPD) to Lave and Wenger's (1991) community of practice. According to social constructivism, learning only occurs when students can share their background knowledge and participate in collaborative and cooperative activities (Harland, 2003; Palinscar, 1998). In this way, social constructivism theory places the emphasis on students rather than instructors. Research by Alexander and Murphy (1998) has shown that students gain more from instruction when they can take control of, and are involved in, their own learning.

In the past decade or so, higher education has seen a proliferation in various forms of technology used within the classroom, and that serve as a unique method of facilitating a dynamic and collaborative learning environment. These online learning communities (OLC), or virtual learning environments (VLE), are a growing element in the field of education and can trace their roots to social constructivism. In this approach, learning is conceptualized "as a collective and participatory social process in which a series of layered communications mediate the exchange of knowledge" (Ke & Hoadley, 2009, p. 488). In practice, online learning communities are increasingly used for professional development and for students in formal schooling (Chang, 2003). At their best, these communities can be effective online communities of practice (Lave & Wenger, 1991) or knowledge-building communities (Scardamalia et al., 1992). At their worst, they can impede groups of users or lead to persuasive but unproductive ideas if interactions are disrespectful or unequal (Linn & Burbules, 1993).

In higher education, information technology can provide those structures that support learners in both making sense of their own experiences and participating in a larger community. Within doctoral degree programs, the utilization of technology, including online learning platforms, blogs, podcasts, video conferences, wikis, and, as specifically outlined later in this chapter, digital narratives can provide the space and tools for students to delve deeper into their own intellectual development and meaning-making – the hallmarks of doctoral education; this in turn can strengthen the theory – practice connection. This is especially important for students in doctoral programs, since these individuals are learning how to become scholars, researchers, and practitioners within their chosen fields.

One of the purposes of doctoral training is specifically to produce scholars, and in many programs, practitioners who can conceptualize and conduct their own research (Austin & McDaniels, 2006; King, 2003). These skills are important for graduates of doctoral programs who wish to pursue faculty jobs, work in policy development, or further their administrative career. Several studies have shown that both limited collaborative work or experiences ultimately limit the intellectual growth of students during doctoral training, and provide limited career opportunities post graduation (Maher, Ford, & Thompson, 2004; Weidman, Twale, & Stein, 2001).

Technology is changing the way we teach and learn. In most higher education settings, it is rare to find a class where technology is not used by a faculty member to develop or present material, or by the students to complete assignments, communicate, and collaborate with others in the classroom, or search for information. Technology is seen as promoting student-centered learning in that its use emphasizes collaboration, increased social interactions, situated cognition, increased opportunities for problem-based learning, and flexible access to information and resources (President's Committee of Advisors on Science and Technology, 1997). As a result, emerging classroom practices suggest that technology can serve to ameliorate a number of problems in higher education, such as large class sizes or static materials or instruction (Grineski, 2000). While there is evidence that learners believe technology is beneficial to them, there still remains limited evidence of its effectiveness, particularly at the graduate level (Lowerison, Sclater, Schmid, & Abrami, 2006; Shuell & Farber, 2001). As outlined in this chapter, when utilized well, technology in general, and specifically digital narratives (also sometimes referred to as digital story-telling), can radically shift how faculty can help doctoral students become critical and reflective thinkers, to develop or refine a professional identity, and help them to transform their assumptions about their knowledge and about themselves, a process that Kegan (1994) and Baxter Magolda (1999) call self-authorship. By combining specific forms of technology-based media with an adult learning-centered pedagogy built around self-authoring practices of student development, faculty can more effectively organize doctoral education to engage and involve students in the process and to truly cultivate a new generation of scholars, researchers, and practitioners.

DOCTORAL STUDENTS AS ADULT LEARNERS

In today's world, doctoral students experience a fractured world of life realities, juggling competing demands to be both an engaged doctoral student while pursuing other key life role commitments. Few doctoral students today are solitary scholars; indeed, few live in academic monastic life of the mind focused solely upon intellectual research pursuits. Today's doctoral students are more diverse and are engaged in a complex set of life commitments beyond the academy. As we consider the role of technology in graduate education, there are two primary areas we ought to keep in mind that can help us to consider the holistic nature of these complex and diverse students: adult learning theories and student development theories. These foundational perspectives undergird effective doctoral preparation and offer scaffolding opportunities that support the dynamic complexity of doctoral program goals related to identity development, knowledge creation, and professional preparation. Furthermore, when viewed from the lens of learning partnerships, these two perspectives can offer insight into how technology and corresponding learning activities, such as the creation of digital narratives, can be used as a mediating vehicle for creating opportunities and experiences for self-authorship, as well as personal and professional growth.

According to the Council of Graduate Schools (1990) the doctoral degree "is designed to prepare students to become a scholar, that is, to discover, integrate, and apply knowledge as well as communicate and disseminate it" (p. 10). Part of this preparation for the student generally includes mastery of content in the chosen field of study and, given the research focus of the doctorate, the demonstration of independent scholarship. With this definition in mind, the doctorate is paramount to higher education and society, as it influences not only the students who enroll in such programs, but also the faculty they work with, the students that they teach, the larger disciplinary context to which they contribute, and the society with which they will practice their skills and disseminate their knowledge. Three key perspectives from the research and literature of adult learning offer a rich frame for understanding teaching and learning within doctoral education and include (1) the importance of self-directed learning, (2) the impact of forming and reforming social and personal identities for transformative learning, and (3) the significance of multiple and diverse communities of practice, as they also influence doctoral student participation.

Doctoral programs have historically been viewed as an apprenticeship of immersion experiences based on observation, collaboration, scaffolding, and assessed demonstration of key expectations, generally centered on creating research and scholarship. These expectations are often viewed by students as risk-taking behaviors and attitudes that are guided by expert mentoring faculty within the scholarly community. Often, however, doctoral faculty are not cognizant of, or quite possibly do not remember, just how unsettling these expectations and corresponding risk-taking behaviors are for doctoral students; nonetheless, this new world of studies places doctoral students into uncharted territory. Most doctoral students face disjunctures between their sense of self as an adult, their placement between being a novice and developing into an expert, and the development of their new identity as scholar and knowledge creator. In addition, the disciplinary world of doctoral studies is evolving. As suggested by a number of prominent authorities, graduate education is being revisioned with new paradigms, expectations, and possibilities for doctoral preparation. In this new climate, one of the key challenges for faculty and doctoral students is to both open intellectual and social boundaries for the exploration of new learning and research investigation, and to provide support and encouragement for developing confidence and self-efficacy, risk-taking toward innovation, and self-direction.

One of the hallmarks of success in these new challenges is the ability and actions of doctoral students to be self-directed learners: being able to pursue learning beyond their mentors, to engage in critically reflective examination of knowledge and disciplinary assumptions, and to join the scholarly cohorts of their doctoral faculty and mentors. Although the concept of self-directed learning has significant historic roots explicating the nature of autodidactic learners, current learning theory suggests that the key skills and attitudes of self-directed learning are critical for the success of adults in doctoral studies. Grounded in innovative research exploring how students learned a foreign language for their competency exams, early work by Tough (1979) uncovered what he called self-directed learning, which focused upon the forms and processes of learning within students' own goals and control, and their taking the master planning role of defining and directing the learning experiences either alone or in collaboration with others.

More recent research on self-directed learning reflects two new refined perspectives of this phenomenon based on interdisciplinary understandings. The first is represented in Garrison's (1997) meta-cognitive model integrating self-management, self-monitoring, and motivation within self-directed learning. Adding to interdisciplinary understandings of self-directed learning, Brown (2003) considered learning within a social culture as an aligned perspective of self-directed learning efficacy. He suggested, "Learning is a remarkably social process. In short, it occurs not as a response to teaching, but rather as a result of a social framework that fosters learning ... knowledge is inextricably situated in physical and social context of acquisition and use" (p. 65). The development and understanding of both individual efficacy of learning-how-to-learn strategies and a socio-cultural environment supporting self-directed learning skills is pivotal for successful doctoral students.

Building upon the generic self-directed learning model of Grow (1991), critical reflective engagement is also an essential skill requirement for doctoral students as part of their self-directed learning competence. Doctoral students need to understand and identify the key values, assumptions, and beliefs that have shaped their experiences thus far, and will continue to shape their possibilities for attention, intention, and active doctoral scholarship. As scholars pursue research questions, they often identify dilemmas of multiple definitions, understandings, and ways of being, a significant set of alternative responses, including the ambiguity of conflicting consequences, and the routine uncertainty of the nature of our current world (Bernstein, 1983; Schon, 1983). A critically reflective stance in these self-directed investigations represent a purposeful, thought-out stance among contested understandings of the epistemology of knowledge and the nature of truth within academic disciplines and knowledge domains (Brookfield, 2000). This suggests that doctoral students should have the capacity and intellectual space to critique and question analyses and theories, and to also engage in reframing key assumptions and perspectives of knowledge and action. Thus, critically reflective students engage in praxis of action and analysis, engage in research and learning, and finally act upon the knowledge and understandings in its varied forms and processes – whether in books, blogs, stories, mainstream journals, or even challenging the traditional modes of thinking and discourse of one's field. Moreover, the self-directed, critically reflective learner must also acknowledge key responsibilities of being a collaborative member of the disciplinary community and supportive colleague in such uncharted intellectual water. Thus, self-directed learning and critically reflective engagement are pivotal areas of development for doctoral students; these areas will influence both their future success and the success of their disciplinary contributions.

STUDENT DEVELOPMENT THEORY, SELF-AUTHORSHIP, AND LEARNING PARTNERSHIPS

A recurring topic of study in doctoral education focuses on the student experience overall. Through understanding the pathways to, through, and from the doctoral experience, scholars hope to assist in the recruitment, retention, and graduation of doctoral students. In the quest to describe the doctoral student experience, scholars have utilized many different approaches and frameworks. However, more than any other, socialization has become the common theoretical lens through which to better understand the complexity of the doctoral student experience (e.g., Austin & McDaniels, 2006; Bragg, 1976; Gardner, 2007; Golde, 1998; Weidman et al., 2001). While socialization has been the predominant lens through which to understand the role of the doctoral student, certain limitations exist in viewing students solely within this context. Indeed, while undergraduate students are viewed as changing and growing cognitively, interpersonally, personally, morally, and professionally (Evans, Forney, Guido-DiBrito, Patton, & Renn, 2010), doctoral students have generally been seen only through a professional preparatory lens.

Student development has been described as "the way the student grows, progresses, or increases his or her developmental capabilities as a result of enrollment in an institution of higher education" (Rodgers, 1990, p. 27). To explain the development students undergo, scholars have posited various stages and periods. Taken together, student development theory has become a leading force in higher education programs, counseling efforts, and is one of the major tenets of the student affairs profession. When viewed collectively, these theories can be categorized into several main areas that assist us in understanding the totality of the student development experience overall, and the doctoral student development experience in particular.

McEwen (2005) describes three categories of student development theory. The first is psychosocial development, exploring growth and change related to student self-perception of their own abilities, their relationships with others, and future life directions. Second, cognitive structural development deals with how students think, moral development, and how students interpret the world around them. Third, McEwen highlights social identity development which explores how students make sense of their social identities. Development, at any level, occurs as a result of a particular set of conditions, challenges, and support (Sanford, 1966).

According to Sanford, when individuals are presented with a challenging situation or experience that has not previously been encountered, a response emerges, resulting in developmental growth. However, if too many new situations emerge without the appropriate support to mitigate these challenges, an individual may actually digress in his or her development. Therefore, it is the optimal balance of challenge and support that underlie student development. It is the focus upon challenge and support within the psychosocial, cognitive-structural, and social identity realms that makes self-authorship, and by extension learning partnerships, a useful frame to consider when working with doctoral students in a technology-mediated arena.

Self-Authorship and Learning Partnerships

According to Baxter Magolda (1999), theories of learning and development must do more than coexist in parallel paths. Instead, they must become part of a set of holistic educational and learning practices that situate student development, learning, and meaning-making as part of the same path and trajectory. Drawing on Kegan's (1994) early work on learning and self-authorship, Baxter Magolda uses the term to refer to the process of questioning, clarifying, and finally enacting one's goals, beliefs, and values. In this way, Baxter Magolda views self-authorship as an orientation to knowledge construction and evaluation based on balancing an understanding of the contextual nature of knowledge with intrapersonally grounded goals, beliefs, and values. This can occur best in a highly collaborative arena in which students are both challenged and supported by their faculty as well as by their peers.

Doctoral students are expected to manage complexity and engage multiple perspectives. They are expected to gather and judge relevant evidence from others to make decisions by an internal set of values and beliefs without being consumed by pleasing everyone. They are expected to act in ways that benefit themselves and others equitably and contribute to the common good. The learning partnership model (Baxter Magolda, 2001), introduces learners to these expectations by portraying learning as a complex process in which learners bring their own perspectives to bear on deciding what to believe and, simultaneously, sharing responsibility with others to construct knowledge. Because this vision of learning is a challenge to authority-dependent learners, the learning partnership model helps students meet these challenges by validating their ability to learn, situating learning in their own experiences, and defining learning as a collaborative exchange of perspectives.

The learning partnerships model (Baxter Magolda, 2001) is the result of a 17-year longitudinal study of young adult development. This model is a means of blending guidance and enabling responsibility to promote self-authorship. Implementation of these partnerships demonstrates how developmental maturity and context-specific learning goals can be achieved simultaneously. The learning partnerships model enables the shift from authority-dependence to self-authorship by challenging learners to see the composition of reality in complex terms and supporting the coordination of their beliefs, ideas, and interpersonal loyalties. The model demonstrates how to achieve the balance between guidance and empowerment in ways that help diverse learners develop self-authorship. Learning partnerships model contains the three core assumptions about learning: (1) knowledge is complex and socially constructed, (2) one's identity plays a central role in crafting knowledge claims, and (3) knowledge is mutually constructed by the sharing of expertise and authority. Assuming that knowledge is mutually constructed emphasizes the shared responsibility between faculty and student, and between students themselves, thereby engaging multiple perspectives in the formation of new knowledge and social and personal identities. All three assumptions emphasize personal responsibility for learning, while simultaneously emphasizing connection – the necessity to connect to one's own (intrapersonal) and others' (interpersonal) perspectives.

Learning partnerships support self-authorship via the three principles: validating learners' capacity as knowledge constructors, situating learning in an individual's own experience, and defining learning as mutually and collaboratively constructing meaning. Validating students' capacities to learn and construct knowledge is necessary for them to realize that they can always go back to the drawing board and start anew. Situating learning in their experiences instead of the experience of authority (e.g., a faculty member) gives them a context in which to bring their own personal and social identity to the learning arena. Defining learning as the mutual process of exchanging perspectives to arrive at particular knowledge claims supports their participation in the social construction of knowledge. The three principles model autonomy through encouraging students to bring their own experiences, constructs, and perspectives to the learning arena, be it a classroom, research lab, internship, symposium, or the like. The principles model connection by encouraging students to form connections between their own and others' experiences and ideas.

Validating the Student as Knower
Kegan (1994) maintains that faculty must offer "welcoming acknowledgment to exactly who the person is right now and [who] he or she is"
(p. 43). This acknowledgment is essential for doctoral students to realize
that they have a voice, whether in person or virtual, and that they have
permission to express themselves as part of their learning process. Respect
for students is an essential component of their feeling comfortable in
working with faculty members. According to Chickering and Reisser (1993),
it is the frequent and friendly interaction with faculty that promotes student
intellectual and identity development.

Changing the pedagogical relationship from the professor talking *at* the
student, as is typical in a lecture-based course, to talking *with* the student
can serve to validate him or her as a knower. Furthermore, by connecting
course content, information, and ideas to a student's own experience,
faculty can validate a student's opinions and ideas while helping her feel less
intimidated and more open to sharing her ideas as a way to learn. Teaching
strategies in which instructors reward students for taking risks at thinking
and offering up ideas can offer a bridge that facilitates student cognitive
growth. Faculty member's concern for the student, respect for the student as
a person and learner, and a willingness to engage in a relationship of mutual
respect will allow students to feel validated as knowers. It is this holistic
acknowledgment of who the student is that enables her or him to risk more
complex ways of meaning-making and knowledge construction.

Situating Learning in Students' Own Experience
Another aspect of validating students is to include their experience (both
their life experience and their meaning-making activities) into the learning
process. Many students leave their life experience at the classroom door,
thinking that it is irrelevant to academic learning. Many faculty reinforce
this view by never connecting learning to students' experiences. However, as
Baxter Magolda's (2001) study suggests, students who are able to use their
own experience when learning new material or ideas, thereby connecting
something familiar with new learning, are able to view themselves as more
capable of self-authorship.

Using language and examples directly from students is one basic, yet
substantial way of respecting and validating their prior experiences and
helps to situate students' learning in a meaningful way. Advocates of using
narrative in learning (e.g., McEwen & Egan, 1995) address this principle as
does Freire's (1970/1988) idea of generating themes directly from students'
lives. Connections between students' experiences and a particular area of

knowledge can also be accomplished by creating real-life learning environments to generate experiences and create new knowledge students do not
already possess.

Noting real-life examples, sharing stories, and engaging in real-time
learning can validate and situate students as knowers. Using narratives and
stories can help promote self-authorship because students can learn to
analyze their own and others' perspectives. Participating in real-life learning
experiences can promote self-authorship because students have to analyze
data and take responsibility for decisions that affect real people. This type of
learning can support students in relating to the content, investing in
learning, and feeling valued as knowers and meaning-makers.

Learning as Mutually Constructing Meaning
Inherent in this principle is the assumption that educational interactions
shape both students and faculty − that the meaning made will result from a
dialogue in which both voices are considered. This interaction allows a
process in which the faculty and the students engage in mutual active
knowing and re-knowing of the ideas under study. In order to do this and to
avoid imposing her or his own knowledge, that faculty must move away
from the position of omnipotent authority. This does not mean that the
faculty gives up his knowledge; rather, he introduces it in the context of
students' perspectives, bringing it to interact with dialogue, but not imposing it unilaterally.

All too often faculty usually prepare their thoughts and lectures in
private, only to go to class prepared to speak from this previously
considered and developed perspective. When this occurs, students see only
the final version of the faculty's thoughts and perspectives, not the process
of creating them. Furthermore, faculty more often than not ask leading
questions in an effort to get students to the conclusions already conceived of
by faculty. This does not allow for the mutual meaning-making and
knowledge construction necessary for development of self-authorship skills.
Within a learning partnerships framework, the faculty should draw out
students' ideas, which then shape their own ideas, which then demonstrate
that both ideas (and both individuals) are important. Bruner (1986)
contends that this process allows the student to "become party to the
negotiatory process by which facts are created and interpreted. At once the
student becomes an agent of knowledge making as well as a recipient of
knowledge transmission" (p. 127). King and Kitchener (1994) advocate
bringing students into this process by "familiarizing students with
ill-structured problems with [one's own] discipline or areas of expertise"

(p. 233). Offering students the opportunity to struggle with such problems creates situations in which different viewpoints can be examined, and students can be encouraged to make judgments and explain what they believe, and on what evidence. This then, according to King and Kitchener, fosters complex thinking and development.

Sharing knowledge creation can lead students to believe that they have a valuable contribution to make in the learning process. Participating in dialogues with students is essential to accessing their world and building bridges between their thinking and the material at hand. Learning as mutually constructing meaning encompasses validating students as knowers and situating learning in students' own experience. By inviting students to join in a genuine dialogue and sharing in knowledge creation, faculty members can validate students as knowers. Situating learning in students' experience is a necessary part of helping doctoral students participate in knowledge creation, as well as knowledge dissemination. Mutually constructing meaning requires validating students' capacity as knowers in helping students explore relevant evidence for constructing an informed perspective. Mutually constructing meaning requires situating learning in students' experience and simultaneously introducing interpretations and knowledge claims that experts in the discipline have advanced, so that students can link the two. Validating the student as knower, situating learning in the student experience, and learning as mutually constructing meaning all meet Chickering and Reisser's (1993) criteria for an educationally powerful curriculum: they are relevant to students' experiences, recognize individual differences, create encounters with diverse perspectives that challenge current assumptions, and provide opportunities for students to integrate diverse viewpoints. According to Chickering and Reisser, such a curriculum "encourages the development of intellectual and interpersonal competence, identity, purpose, and integrity" (p. 270). Using the three principles of the learning partnerships model as an underlying structure for teaching and learning is not a matter of using techniques; it is, rather, a matter of transforming one's assumptions about teaching and learning, about student engagement, and about the constructing of knowledge. In short, these three principles simply represent a different perspective on knowledge instruction, learning, teaching, and student development.

The blend of challenge and support in the learning partnerships model provides guidance and empowerment simultaneously, modeling the blend of connection and autonomy present in the nature of self-authorship. Coordination of beliefs, values, and interpersonal loyalties require complex integration of autonomy and connection. Self-authorship is that capacity to internally define a coherent belief system and identity that requires mutual engagement with the larger world. This internal foundation supports the capacity to actively listen to multiple perspectives, critically interpret those perspectives in light of relevant evidence and the internal foundation, and make judgments accordingly. Grounding in the internal foundation counteracts the need for approval, giving openness to new possibilities and diverse others. It enables what Jordan (1997) calls mutuality in which each person is able to "represent her or his own experience and relationship, to act in a way which is congruent with an inner truth and with the context, and to respond to and encourage authenticity in the other person" (p. 31). Thus, self-authorship, in its intricate blend of autonomy and connection enables meaningful, interdependent relationships with diverse others, grounded in an understanding and appreciation for human differences and the cultural practices and values that these differences reflect. Collaborative learning partnerships directly and meaningfully engage learners in these interdependent relationships.

THE ROLE OF TECHNOLOGY AND DIGITAL STORYTELLING IN FOSTERING SELF-AUTHORSHIP

Technology and various multimedia tools provide an ideal means for collaborating, creating learning partnerships, enhancing self-authorship, and encouraging professional and personal identity formation to occur in both synchronous and asynchronous formats. Learning platforms such as Blackboard, Web-CT, e-College, and numerous others, allow for an open space in which students can experiment, take risks, reflect, think, write, collaborate, and give or receive constructive feedback. By adopting a learning partnership model and through viewing courses and curriculums as collaborative, mutually rewarding partnerships, technology no longer needs to be simply an add-on for one-way classroom instruction, but becomes a true means for increasing opportunities for learning and enriching the overall experiences of students (Salomon, Perkins, & Globerson, 1991; Weigel, 2002). The technology becomes both the mediating space and the individual tools for both faculty and student. Faculty are facilitators of learning whose main purpose is to empower students to take ownership of their own learning and meaning making. In doctoral education, "owner-ship" of a disciplinary knowledge base and of one's opinions related to that knowledge is central to developing and maintaining the identity of scholar, researcher, and practitioner bestowed upon graduates of doctoral programs.

Similar to the traditional classroom setting, within a technology-mediated learning environment, over the course of hours, days, weeks, or even months, a community takes shape. Within this community, cognitive, interpersonal, and intrapersonal capacities can be presented, explored, disassembled, and then reformed as students gain new content knowledge, as they have a context for both themselves and others within their new knowledge base. Online technologies and activities, particularly asynchronous ones, allow for extended "give and take" among everyone. Using technology creates the potential for the continuous merging of individual meaning-making, social construction of knowledge, and discipline specific knowledge dissemination or creation, all of which can lead to a new professional identity as scholar, researcher, and practitioner. Interactive discussion boards, chat rooms, online journals, and other text-based spaces and mechanisms give students the opportunity to take in knowledge, reflect upon it, and then create their own meaning or knowledge. This can then be put back out there for others to critique and reflect upon, in an iterative mutual meaning-making cycle. In the online world, knowledge can be seen to be both existing and evolving. Faculty and students can share their ideas in the context of existing knowledge, coming to understand that knowledge, and then critically reflecting on the underlying assumptions or meanings that can lead to further knowledge creation.

More than simply a common meeting space online, the learning community in a technology-mediated course allows the mutual exploration of ideas, a safe place to reflect on and develop those ideas, and a collaborative, supportive approach to academic work. Engaging in collaborative learning and the resultant reflective practice involving transformative learning is necessary in a virtual learning community and offers power to individuals in the learning process. Gunawardena, Lowe, and Anderson (1997) believe that the process in which online learning communities socially construct knowledge, using collaboration and reflection, goes through five phases. The first phase involves sharing and comparing information. This is the time early in the course where students test each other out, share experiences and expectations, and determine what strengths and knowledge each person brings. The second phase involves the discovery of areas of potential disagreement, dissonant, or inconsistency of ideas. Based on the testing of ideas that goes on in the first phase, and the disagreement that may occur in the second, Gunawardena et al. propose that the group moves into the third phase in which the negotiation of meaning begins to occur. This phase foresees the group testing their new syntheses of ideas against facts; facts that may be presented in text or readings, proposed by the faculty, or may be what the participants have experienced in their daily lives. Phases one through four create the disorienting dilemma that Mezirow (1991) describes in his theory of transformative learning. By comparing current knowledge against what has always been known, the door opens to the development of new knowledge creation and meaning-making. Phase five, then, is illustrated by the emergence of metacognitive statements on the part of students that illustrate that their thinking around a particular topic or idea has changed. When designing and facilitating technology-mediated courses, the inclusion of personal meaning activities, collaborative activities and the ability to reflect on one's own and other's perspectives can help form and sustain learning communities, and promote the development of self-authoring capabilities. Paying attention to and facilitating student movements through the five phases can help both individual students and the class achieve specific learning outcomes, attain higher levels of cognitive, interpersonal and intrapersonal development, promote satisfaction in educational experiences, and help solidify professional identities.

Active involvement and engagement by both faculty and students, supported by collaboration enhances learning outcomes and reduces the potential for learner isolation that can occur in an online virtual environment. By mutual interaction and engagement in a virtual learning community, faculty and students alike have the opportunity to expand and deepen their learning experience, take risks by testing or sharing new ideas with a supportive group, and receive critical and constructive feedback. The likelihood of successful achievement of learning objectives, as well as self-authoring capabilities, increases through collaborative engagement. Conrad and Donaldson (2004) state, "The collaborative acquisition of knowledge is one key to the success of creating an online learning environment. Activities that require student interaction and encourage the sharing of ideas promote a deeper level of thought" (p. 5). As Baxter Magolda has demonstrated (1999, 2001), such activities can also extend beyond cognitive development to the development of greater inter and intra-personal skills, all of which are necessary for graduate students.

Digital Narratives and Storytelling

In most technology-mediated learning communities, asynchronous discussion boards have been the primary means of engagement, collaboration, and learning. Yet too often this type of activity leads to primarily a transactional type of exchange between faculty and student, and the pure text-based technology can be a barrier to social interaction, co-constructed knowledge, or intra- and interpersonal development. As mentioned earlier, stories and narratives can help validate students' experiences, connect individuals together, but they can also encourage dialogue and reflection, and offer a change to take a risk, and can provide both a means of challenge and support for others. Although stories and storytelling are powerful strategies for teaching and learning, generating, creating, and sharing stories can be a challenge in the online environment. But digital narratives and storytelling offer a way to break down traditional barriers of text-only technologies prevalent in most technology-mediated class-rooms. Digital storytelling was initially introduced into the classroom as a technique to encourage and embed student reflection on the activities in which they were engaged, recognizing that reflection can be enhanced as a collaborative process (McDrury & Alterio, 2003). But stories can go beyond merely reflection; they can allow for new forms of knowledge and meaning-making to occur. McDrury and Alterio contend that "it does seem that sharing stories encourages a reflective process, especially when storytelling is accompanied by dialogue and occurs in formalized settings" (p. 111). Thus, the reviewing of the multimedia digital stories in a classroom could help "bring about thoughtful and reasoned change to practice" (McDrury & Alterio, p. 59).

Stories help us make meaning out of experience; experiences, and the stories created to make sense of those experiences, are the keys to learning (Bruner, 1996; Schank, 1990; Zull, 2002). Stories also help build con-nections with prior knowledge and improve memory (Schank, 1990). Finally, storytelling helps people connect to others by disclosing personal thoughts, feelings, and beliefs and by relating to each other's experiences (Lowenthal, 2008). Digital narratives and storytelling is a newly emerging form of more traditional storytelling. Using advances in technology and multimedia tools, one can reinterpret the act of storytelling by delivering the same in-person engaging and impactful narrative using photographs, music, voice-overs, and video delivered in an asynchronous format. At its most basic level, a digital narrative is a story told in a digital format that offers up a particular point of view, usually that of the storyteller (Lowenthal, 2009). Digital stories are essentially personal expressions and experiences with a purpose. Using personally meaningful visual and auditory elements (photos, music, narration, interviews, etc.), the digital storyteller delivers a relevant lesson, usually based on personal experiences, and that often extends beyond the personal into a more general human experience. Using digital narratives throughout a class builds a sense of collaboration and deepens social ties, so that "as stories are shared, the sense of community itself is strengthened" (Freidus & Hlubinka, 2002, p. 24). Additionally, by creating and sharing digital stories – sharing experiences, feelings, beliefs, including discussions of problems and barriers – both students and faculty can tap into "a system of psychological support" (Freidus & Hlubinka, p. 16). As Ackermann (1996) puts it, "to know is to relate and ... to know better, or gain deeper understanding, is to grow-in-connection" (p. 25). And this is part of the goal of learning partnerships, which can ultimately lead to the development of self-authorship and new ways of thinking and being in doctoral students.

Digital narratives and storytelling, when used thoughtfully as part of a course that is technology mediated can connect students and faculty to one another and make experience more meaningful. Students can be asked to develop a narrative around a key idea or theory that brings to life that very concept in the student's own world. Such storytelling brings faculty and students together as co-learners, gaining perspectives from others, offering new ideas, co-constructing new knowledge, and learning ways of being. As co-learners and collaborators in the process, students and faculty can relate past experience to present actuality in order to project more meaningful futures together. By engaging their creativity and imagination, students engaged in storytelling processes merge images of each other's life experiences and begin to see new social, personal, or even professional identities. Sharing stories can engage them in co-creational processes of telling, listening, retelling, and ultimately con-structing new knowledge and learning. Some examples might include the following:

- Sociology students studying gender might be asked to document over the course of a single day the various ways that their spaces (home, office, class, etc.) and activities (gym, dinner with friends, sporting event, etc.) are in fact "gendered."
- Architecture students might be asked to do a walk-through of a building and offer a narration of both the theoretical constructs of the building, and the way the student actually experiences that building (What does she notice? What does she feel or think? What are her reactions or perceptions of parts of the building? How are other people "experiencing" the building?).
- Marketing students might be asked to document in photos or videos particular forms of advertising in a city along with reactions and

perceptions of those advertisements; students might also interview folks on the street about their perceptions of those same materials.

Students can post these digital narratives and stories for others to react to, thereby creating a new dialogue that is situated around a more 3-dimensional experience. Together, students and faculty can unpack the experience, interrogate it, and create new meanings and knowledge around those narratives.

Experience can link storytelling with learning (Pfahl, 2003); storytelling activities such as those listed above can serve as a medium for faculty to help students view human experience to find and construct meaning. Critical incidents that are existential happenings, theory-in-action, turning points, or events recounted in narratives hold significant meaning and implications for action. Constructing alternative scenarios, reflecting upon assumptions behind them, and contemplating meanings of their implications for the future can offer students freedom to explore and take-risks and help them to gain a renewed sense of self and enhanced capacity to act in more meaningful ways. These are necessary for doctoral students who are embarking on new roles as practitioners, scholars, researchers, and critical thinkers.

Narratives are one way people organize their experiences into "texts" or stories; therefore, storytelling can become an interpretive vehicle to look backward across the distance of time to reflect upon what has happened and to find future possibilities implicit in the present. Using storytelling in this way helps identify "praxis, meaningful action taken in the world" (Freeman & Robinson, 1990, p. 62). By talking about lived experiences that have not been "accorded the amount or quality of conscious attention necessary to fully appreciate their worth, meaning, or scope" (p. 63), students can further understand how workings of society and the psyche create unintended blinders in the form of unquestioned assumptions and meaning.

Freeman and Robinson (1990) suggest that narrative may be an ideal process in that it characterizes movement of development toward some future end: rewriting the self. In making this suggestion, they imply that narrative has transformational potential. Characteristics of this process include refusal to order life according to discrete ends and acceptance that there are better and worse ways of being in the world. Freeman and Robinson argue for an interpretive rewriting process by identifying its limitations and possibilities:

> Alongside the revision of ends, it follows that development entails a process of reconstructing one's past and the self in which it has culminated. This is simply because

for every new end that is figured in the course of one's life, old ends are superseded, which in a more general sense can be taken to mean that the "text" of one's life, one's narrative, is being rewritten. (1990, p. 61)

Focusing on and questioning narratives of experience can lead students on journeys through a process that Freeman and Robinson (1990) characterize as four moments in time: *recognition* of disjuncture and contradictions between what exists and what is more desirable, *distanciation* to begin to divest existing modes of experiencing for new ones through processes of objectifying and separating the self from the self, *articulation* to identify problems, and then *appropriation* to internalize differences articulated between the old and the new as one's own vision. This kind of development from within, conceptualized as a passage through four moments in time, constitutes a way of constructing knowledge and learning. Although there is not a linear alignment, passing through these "times" does allow a student to engage in the self-authoring process. Students are acknowledging their own values, beliefs, and feelings, and begin to question them. They become open to sharing their own and listening to others' perspectives and ideas. They take risks related to their social and personal identities. In this way, digital narratives can create a mutual process of transformation among both faculty and students. This becomes especially important in those text-based virtual arenas where most online learning occurs.

The use of digital narratives in a technology-mediated classroom invites and creates a new type of social ecology and interconnectedness in such a virtual world. Digital stories and narratives can allow students to see, hear, and experience their peers not as external objects, but as true subjects with different experiences worthy of time, energy, and attention; this also shows students that the world is not an isolated, insular space. For Daloz and his colleagues (1996), this bigger picture involves contributing to the creation of new connections and knowledge, which extend beyond one's self and holds the potential to change and enlarge personal thoughts, feelings, beliefs, and meanings by embracing others. Taylor (1991) calls for the "ethics of authenticity" to be self-creative and fulfilled in relationship to others. Identity, once created, "requires recognition by others" (p. 47). Taylor argues that "ethics of authenticity" and "politics of recognition" are two parts of the same project: we must not only voice who we are, but also recognize the other and come into a relationship of acceptance with the other by finding ways to acknowledge and to integrate difference. The creation of digital narratives offers up the possibility of accomplishing that kind of integration by telling one's own story and by listening to those of others. This kind of mutual give and take is at the heart of intra- and interpersonal development necessary for self-authoring to occur.

Finding and using one's voice in "learning our way out" has powerful effects on both faculty and students as they engage in collective endeavors of calling forth and listening to their stories. In bringing together a group of students to share experiences and create meaning, the goal "is to interpret from as many vantage points as possible ... the ways there are of being in the world" (Greene, 1988, p. 120), creating kaleidoscopic views of human experience. Digital narratives allow for possibilities for both self-directed learning, since students can be free to tell a particular story from a particular vantage point and critical reflective practice as they analyze their own narratives and respond to feedback and ideas from their peers.

To use storytelling as a meaningful learning process, in addition to creating conditions conducive to using narrative, faculty need to become aware of conditions and factors that support knowledge construction and learning from a self-authoring mindset. The conditions Mezirow (1991) identifies as important to critically reflective learning with potential to become transformational for individuals include providing accurate and complete information; being free from coercion and self-deception; having the abilities to weigh evidence, to evaluate arguments, and to be critically reflective; being open to alternative perspectives; having equal opportunity to participate; and being willing to accept an informed, objective, rational consensus to test legitimate validity. These are also those skills and abilities that doctoral students need as they move into new roles and assume new identities as scholars, teachers, practitioners, policy makers, and leaders in the 21st century.

Stories and narratives can change distorted points of view; they illuminate how the vision of the eye of a collective beholder can become more acute as individuals first engage in processes of rewriting the self and then transfer some of the same narrative thinking to extended contexts by trying different lenses. Not only can outcomes become more meaningful, but they also hold possibilities for transformational change as points of view become "more inclusive, differentiated, permeable (open to other points of view), and integrated ... through rational discourse" (Mezirow, 1991, p. 7). Such a discourse that respects thoughts, cognitions, feelings, attitudes, and values as intrinsic parts of relational thinking encourages storytelling, knowledge creation, and learning, and thus can lead today's doctoral students on a new journey of self-authorship.

CONCLUSION

Technology-mediated learning can offer a chance for both critical thinking and reflection as well as content learning. Technology positions the faculty and learners in an environment where all can present and explore primary literature, knowledge and data, uncover deeper, provocative questions framed within students' own experiences, and learn processes to inform those questions. Such an approach allows students to see knowledge as something that is not absolute, and provides a mechanism for them to have their own interpretations, thus allowing self-authorship to occur within the context of a relevant disciplinary knowledge base. The ability to integrate meaning making, the process of disciplinary inquiry and knowledge creation, and the emergence of new social and professional identities and roles are a few of the hallmarks of doctoral education. The ability to take these to a deeper level can be greatly enhanced by technology, if such education is seen as a learning partnership, not as a place where the sage on a stage simply hands down generations of knowledge. In a rapidly changing world, soft skills such as the ability to collaborate, communicate skillfully, engage in lifelong learning, create and disseminate knowledge, and problem-solve, will enable doctoral students to respond to the changing demands of a global workforce as scholars, researchers, policy-makers, practitioners, and leaders. Such globalization requires graduate students to be able to work in a multitude of environments, conducting and disseminating research, sharing ideas, working across time zones, cultures, space, and geography, communicating electronically, and solving an array of unknown problems and challenges in their specific disciplines. Universities educating doctoral students to respond to these challenges can do so, not just in traditional face-to-face classroom practices, but through strategic use of online communities and virtual environments, and specific tools and activities such as digital narratives.

The use of digital storytelling in higher education is still in its infancy but does offer new ways for students to present their ideas, research and scholarship, and to reflect upon it. As McDrury and Alterio (2003) note "students find stories appealing if they connect with their own experience" and the use of digital narratives does offer an opportunity to enable this (p. 47). The digital nature of these stories makes them ideal for storage and easy retrieval, thus making them available for review at regular intervals to make personal and group development explicit, and become part of an organized collection of evidence of reflection and growth. This would encourage the acquisition of "learning-about" and "learning-to-be" skills

(Brown, 2005) for lifelong learning and the development of a new breed of doctoral students.

Developing and supporting a community of doctoral students built around a learning partnership model can meet many of these demands, but the pedagogy and course design must support student learning through this new model. It should not merely continue down the path of the traditional paradigm. In the rush to offer online education or courses, faculty and administrators often overlook or misunderstand the concept of a learning community sharing experiences, knowledge and skills amongst its members, and acknowledging both shared and different learning goals. Developing a new type of learning community is more than just adding technology, and requires more than just a text-based set of materials and activities. Students must be able to learn through jointly constructing knowledge by sharing their own experiences in ways that make sense to them. By engaging in dialogue with other students and with faculty around digital stories, in a supportive but challenging environment, they become active participants in their own learning process, even in virtual spaces. This active participation, along with opportunities to critically reflect on their own learning and behaviors to validate new ideas and use them in context, is in line with adult transformative learning, student development, social construction, and self-authorship.

As educational institutions continue their calls for greater accountability, and learning outcomes take center stage, faculty, administrators, and institutions alike must assume a broader, more holistic approach to teaching and learning. Using a learning partnerships model, thinking of ways to engage students in self-authorship, and using new multimedia tools for learning is one way to accomplish this. Such a paradigm can lead to innovative practice in the classroom, deeper, more reflective learning for students, and greater overall success for our institutions. Furthermore, research along these dimensions aimed at examining this model might serve to highlight specific conclusions regarding the nature of facilitating constructivist approaches to teaching and learning for doctoral students as they continue their journey from student to scholar, researcher, and practitioner within their own disciplines.

REFERENCES

Ackermann, E. (1996). Perspective-taking and object construction: Two keys to learning. In Y. B. Kafai & M. Resnick (Eds.), *Constructionism in practice: Designing, thinking, and learning in a digital world* (pp. 25–36). Mahwah, NJ: Lawrence Erlbaum Associates.

Alexander, P. A., & Murphy, P. K. (1998). Profiling the differences in students' knowledge, interest, and strategic processing. *Journal of Educational Psychology, 90*(3), 435.

Austin, A. E., & McDaniels, M. (2006). Preparing the professoriate of the future: Graduate student socialization for faculty roles. In J. C. Smart (Ed.), *Higher education: Handbook of theory and research* (Vol. 21, pp. 397–456). Netherlands: Springer.

Baxter Magolda, M. B. (1999). *Creating contexts for learning and self authorship.* Nashville, TN: Vanderbilt University Press.

Baxter Magolda, M. B. (2001). *Making their own way: Narratives for transforming higher education to promote self-development.* Sterling, VA: Stylus.

Bernstein, R. (1983). *Beyond objectivism and relativism: Science, hermeneutics, and praxis.* Philadelphia, PA: University of Pennsylvania.

Bragg, A. K. (1976). *The socialization process in higher education.* Washington, DC: George Washington University.

Brookfield, S. (2000). The concept of critically reflective practice. In A. Wilson & E. Hayes (Eds.), *Handbook of adult education and continuing education* (pp. 33–50). San Francisco, CA: Jossey-Bass.

Brown, J. S. (2003). *Learning in a digital age.* Retrieved from http://net.educause.edu/ir/library/pdf/FFPIU015.pdf

Brown, J. S. (2005). *New learning environments for the 21st century.* Retrieved from http://www.johnseelybrown.com/newlearning.pdf

Bruner, J. (1986). *Actual minds, possible worlds.* Cambridge: Harvard University Press.

Bruner, J. (1996). *The culture of education.* Cambridge: Harvard University Press.

Chang, C. (2003). Towards a distributed web-based learning community. *Innovations in Education and Teaching International, 40*(1), 27–42.

Chickering, A., & Reisser, L. (1993). *Education and identity* (2nd ed.). San Francisco, CA: Jossey-Bass.

Conrad, R. M., & Donaldson, A. (2004). *Engaging the online learner: Activities and resources for creative instruction.* San Francisco, CA: Jossey-Bass.

Council of Graduate Schools. (1990). *The doctor of philosophy degree: A policy statement.* Washington, DC: Author.

Daloz, L. A., Keen, C. H., Keen, J. P., & Parks, S. D. (1996). *Common fire: Lives of commitment in a complex world.* Boston, MA: Beacon Press.

Dewey, J. (1938). *Experience and education.* New York, NY: Simon & Schuster.

Evans, N., Forney, D., Guido-DiBrito, F., Patton, L., & Renn, K. (2010). *Student development in college: Theory, research, and practice* (2nd ed.). San Francisco, CA: Jossey-Bass.

Freeman, M., & Robinson, R. E. (1990). The development within: An alternative approach to the study of lives. *New Ideas in Psychology, 8*(1), 55–72.

Freidus, N., & Hlubinka, M. (2002). Digital storytelling for reflective practice in communities of learning. *SIGGROUP Bulletin, 23*(2), 24–26.

Freire, P. (1970/1988). *Pedagogy of the oppressed.* New York, NY: Continuum Press.

Gardner, S. K. (2007). "I heard it through the grapevine": Doctoral student socialization in chemistry and history. *Higher Education, 54*, 723–740.

Garrison, D. (1997). Self-directed learning: Toward a comprehensive model. *Adult Education Quarterly, 48*, 18–33.

Golde, C. M. (1998). Beginning graduate school: Explaining first-year student attrition. In M. S. Anderson (Ed.), *The experience of being in graduate school: An exploration* (pp. 54–64). San Francisco, CA: Jossey-Bass.

Greene, M. (1988). *The dialectic of freedom.* New York, NY: Teachers College Press.

Grineski, S. (2000). I've a feeling we're not in Kansas anymore: The commercialization and commodification of teaching and learning in higher education. *Bulletin of Science, Technology & Society, 20*(1), 19–28.

Grow, G. (1991). Teaching learners to be self-directed: A stage approach. *Adult Education Quarterly, 41,* 125–149.

Gunawardena, C. L., Lowe, C. A., & Anderson, T. (1997). Analysis of a global online debate and the development of an interaction analysis model for examining social construction of knowledge in computer conferencing. *Journal of Educational Computing Research, 17*(4), 397–431.

Harland, T. (2003). Vygotsky's zone of proximal development and problem-based learning: Linking a theoretical concept with practice through action research. *Teaching in Higher Education, 8*(2), 263–272.

Jordan, J. (1997). A relational perspective for understanding women's development. In J. V. Jordan (Ed.), *Women's growth in diversity: More writings from the Stone Center* (pp. 9–24). New York, NY: Guilford.

Ke, F., & Hoadley, C. (2009). Evaluating online learning communities. *Educational Technology Research & Development, 57*(4), 487–510.

Kegan, R. (1994). *In over our heads: The mental demands of modern life.* Cambridge: Harvard University Press.

King, M. F. (2003). *On the right track: A manual for research mentors.* Washington, DC: Council of Graduate Schools.

King, P. M., & Kitchener, K. S. (1994). *Developing reflective judgment: Understanding and promoting intellectual growth and critical thinking in adolescents and adults.* Jossey-Bass Higher and Adult Education Series and Jossey-Bass Social and Behavioral Science Series. San Francisco, CA: Jossey-Bass.

Lave, J., & Wenger, E. (1991). *Situated learning: Legitimate peripheral participation.* New York, NY: Cambridge University Press.

Linn, M. C., & Burbules, N. C. (1993). Construction of knowledge and group learning. In K. G. Tobin (Ed.), *The practice of constructivism in science education* (pp. 91–119). Washington, DC: American Association for the Advancement of Science (AAAS) Press.

Lowenthal, P. R. (2008). Online faculty development and storytelling: An unlikely solution to improving teacher quality. *Journal of Online Learning and Teaching, 4*(3), 349–356. Retrieved from http://jolt.merlot.org/vol4no3/lowenthal_0908.htm

Lowenthal, P. R. (2009). Digital storytelling: An emerging institutional technology? In K. McWilliam & J. Hartley (Eds.), *Story circle: Digital storytelling around the world* (pp. 252–259). Oxford: Wiley-Blackwell.

Lowerison, G., Sclater, J., Schmid, R. F., & Abrami, P. (2006). Student perceived effectiveness of computer technology use in higher education. *Computers & Education, 47*(4), 465–489.

Maher, M. A., Ford, M. E., & Thompson, C. M. (2004). Degree progress of women doctoral students: Factors that constrain, facilitate, and differentiate. *Review of Higher Education, 27*(3), 385–408.

McDrury, J., & Alterio, M. G. (2003). *Learning through storytelling in higher education: Using reflection and experience to improve learning.* London: Kogan Page.

McEwen, H., & Egan, K. (Eds.). (1995). *Narrative in teaching, learning, and research.* New York, NY: Teachers College Press.

McEwen, M. K. (2005). The nature and uses of theory. In M. E. Wilson & L. Wolf-Wendel (Eds.), *ASHE reader on college student development theory* (pp. 5–24). Boston, MA: Pearson Custom Publishing.

Mezirow, J. (1991). *Transformative dimensions of adult learning.* San Francisco, CA: Jossey-Bass.

Palinscar, A. S. (1998). Reciprocal teaching and questioning. In A. Woolfolk (Ed.), *Educational psychology.* India: Pearson Books.

Pfahl, N. L. (2003). *Raising the bar for higher education: Using narrative processes to advance learning and change.* Unpublished doctoral dissertation, Teachers College, Columbia University.

Phillips, D. C. (1995). The good, the bad, and the ugly: The many faces of constructivism. *Educational Researcher, 24*(7), 5–12.

President's Committee of Advisors on Science and Technology. (1997). *Report to the president on the use of technology to strengthen K-12 education in the United States.* Washington, DC: GPO.

Rodgers, R. F. (1990). Recent theories and research underlying student development. In D. Creamer & Associates (Eds.), *College student development: Theory and practice for the 1990s* (pp. 27–79). Alexandria, VA: American College Personnel Association.

Salomon, G., Perkins, D. N., & Globerson, T. (1991). Partners in cognition: Extending human intelligence with intelligent technologies. *Educational Researcher, 20*(3), 2–9.

Sanford, N. (1966). *Self and society: Social change and individual development.* New York, NY: Atherton Press.

Scardamalia, M., Bereiter, C., Brett, C., Burtis, P. J., Calhoun, C., & Smith Lea, N. (1992). Educational applications of a networked communal database. *Interactive Learning Environments, 2*(1), 45–71.

Schank, R. (1990). *Tell me a story: Narrative and intelligence.* Evanston, IL: Northwestern University Press.

Schon, D. (1983). *The reflective practitioner: How practitioners think in action.* New York, NY: Basic Books.

Shuell, T. J., & Farber, S. L. (2001). Student perceptions of technology use in college courses. *Journal of Educational Computing Research, 24,* 119–138.

Taylor, C. (1991). *The ethics of authenticity.* Cambridge, MA: Harvard University Press.

Tough, A. (1979). *The adult's learning projects: A fresh approach to theory and practice in adult learning* (2nd ed.). Toronto: Ontario Institute for Studies in Education.

Vygotsky, L. S. (1978). *Mind in society: The development of higher psychological processes.* Cambridge, MA. Harvard University Press.

Weidman, J. C., Twale, D. J., & Stein, E. L. (2001) Socialization of graduate student and professional students in higher education: A perilous passage? ASHE-ERIC Higher Education Report No. 28, ASHE, Washington, DC.

Weigel, V. (2002). *Deep learning for a digital age: Technology's untapped potential to enrich higher education.* San Francisco, CA: Jossey-Bass.

Zull, J. (2002). *The art of changing the brain: Enriching the practice of teaching by exploring the biology of learning.* Sterling, VA: Stylus Publishing.

LEARNING AND TEACHING AS COMMUNICATIVE ACTIONS: TRANSMEDIA STORYTELLING

Scott J. Warren, Jenny S. Wakefield and
Leila A. Mills

ABSTRACT

Transmedia – a single experience that spans across multiple forms of media – is still a new media in the educational landscape and therefore may pose a challenge to educators wanting to create opportunities for interactive media communications in their classrooms. In this chapter, we share an instance in which a university professor introduced transmedia to support graduate student learning to encourage inquiry, critical thinking, problem solving, creativity, contemplation, and critical discourses. Further, we examine how two of the graduate students took their learning a step further by designing and creating a model transmedia lesson tailored for the 6th grade Social Studies classroom. This chapter provides a theoretical framework within which transmedia may be used: Learning and teaching as communicative actions theory – LTCA.

Increasing Student Engagement and Retention using Multimedia Technologies:
Video Annotation, Multimedia Applications, Videoconferencing and Transmedia Storytelling
Cutting-edge Technologies in Higher Education, Volume 6F, 67–94
ISSN: 2044-9968/doi:10.1108/S2044-9968(2013)000006F006

INTRODUCTION

The iGeneration Is Here – How Do They Learn?

To engage and motivate our students in education today, we are increasingly asked to design learning activities that include technology as part of the instructional design process (Abrahams, 2010). Our current media landscape is disrupted by many new technologies such as social networking, mobile computing, augmented reality, and transmedia (Pence, 2012) allowing for a near ubiquitous media convergence. It has been suggested by the U.S. Department of Education that this new technology convergence should be incorporated into education to accommodate and immerse the new generation of learners (Ccabell, 2011) that Rosen (2011) reported are born 1980 and thereafter, and interchangeably are labeled as *Generation Y*, *Net Generation*, *Millennials*, or the *iGeneration*. These students are increasingly technology savvy and are multitaskers. Rosen additionally noted that "[t]o them, the smart phone, the Internet, and everything technological are not 'tools' at all – they simply are" (p. 12). It remains to be uncovered how to best allow for technology diffusion to accommodate learning for such students. We believe that this depends not only on the specific learning experience students have, but also the inclusion of a distributed narrative, information shared over a range of modalities, and covering many sources as this may help many students to a richer learning experience and "more complex mental representations of the material" (Rosen, 2011, p. 14). Transmedia allows for such learning to occur through communicative actions and allows instructors and students to embed and embody learning experiences within motivating stories and contexts.

Learning through Story
Learning through stories is not new; that is, we often remember stories uniquely and they have impact on us and evoke lasting emotional responses. Stories help us build intersubjective understandings. As Norman (1993) stated: "[they] are important cognitive events, for they encapsulate, into one compact package, information, knowledge, context, and emotion" (p. 129). Narratives help us connect new learning to existing personal knowledge as the patterns of narrative form connections to earlier knowledge in the brain, and are contextualized by existing social norms and values. We analyze stories subjectively and by spending time with them, which helps make them become more memorable and easily retrievable. Daniel Pink suggested that "[s]tory is just as integral to the human experience as design" (2005, p. 101).

Lebrecht (2010) explained transmedia as a variation of social media. It is a term he attributes to Marsha Kinder and her 1991 book *Playing with Power in Movies, Television, and Video Games: From Muppet Babies to Teenage Mutant Ninja Turtles.* The popularization of the term "transmedia," however, is credited to Henry Jenkins who crafted the theory of *Transmedia Storytelling.* In this storied landscape, the use of media across multiple platforms gives a narrative meaning through collaboration used to solve problems ranging from fictional to real world problems (Warren, Dondlinger, McLeod, & Bigenho, 2011).

Jenkins (2010) noted that students seek out content through active hunting and gathering processes while crisscrossing various media platforms and Lamb (2011) added that transmedia environments not only help students seek out and explore information, but also allows for interactive evaluation of ideas with other learners. In this sense, transmedia is a thoughtful blend of story characters and narrative layered into play (and, in this case, learning experiences); further, the interactions are extended through the use of media channels. A successful implementation of a transmedia-based lesson within a class should provide students with an interesting task as well as the guidance to select various media platforms from which to embark on an immersive multimodal transmedia learning experience.

Each technology tool used for transmedia learning contributes an important aspect to story. Students must decide if what they find "belongs," while concurrently weighing the reliability of content and unifying their overall story (Jenkins, 2010) or their understanding of the topic. The nature of individual – subjective – perception leads students to compare their story with those of others. Objectively expressing their subjective understanding of the topic – or a story within which the topic may be embedded or embodied (Barab et al., 2007) – in a dramaturgical or performative manner – extends and confirms students' understanding. Each transmedia story is essentially never-ending, as it is continuously reshaped with the help of peer and audience constative feedback. At the same time, the story, or learning experience, intersects several, carefully chosen, technology platforms. In this manner, transmedia contributes to a continuous learning process where linear learning is no more. Instead multimodal experiences allow learners to seek, weigh, and communicate answers. Knowledge is found socially constructed based on existing knowledge.

Past educational transmedia learning experiences involve critical thinking, problem solving, creativity, contemplation, and discourse (Warren et al., 2011). Transmedia can be explained as a single experience that spans across multiple forms of media. These various platforms may include tools such as social media, email, digital video, podcasts, content management systems, multiuser virtual environments (MUVEs), interactive Flash, videos, and many others brought together in a coherent, interrelated larger system to guide the user's experience.

Transmedia provides students with the opportunity to be deeply immersed in a topic. Further, they concurrently use technology tools for exploration as they develop narrative and characters that will provide others with a learning, as well as play, experience. Expression of subjective understanding is an objective means of providing students with opportunities to demonstrate their learning and growth. Students learn to critique those knowledge artifacts that result from this process.

The learning and teaching as communicative actions (LTCA) theoretical framework, proposes that the interplay among four communicative actions function as a basis for human learning. This theory guides the transmedia learning model that we present in this chapter with a specific example in which a university professor introduced both the concept of cognitive conflict and a transmedia learning experience to his graduate students. LTCA theory, as defined by Warren and Stein in 2008 and expanded upon by Wakefield, Warren, and Alsobrook (2011), provides a framework by which an instructor can gauge student development of knowledge in the context of supporting effective human communication, creative self-expression, and collaborative knowledge construction. It is through this process that students and instructor understand established truths that are open to critique, which allows the emergence of new knowledge. We also provide an illuminative example of how LTCA theory was applied through the experiences of two graduate students as they took the transmedia learning a step further by designing a Social Studies transmedia assignment for the 6th grade classroom. We begin with an overview of LTCA theory.

THEORETICAL FRAMEWORK: LEARNING AND TEACHING AS COMMUNICATIVE ACTIONS THEORY (LTCA)

Theories about how we learn have been proposed and argued among philosophers, educators, and scientists as they have brought forward their various views. One current, leading theory suggests that learners construct knowledge either socially or individually. Though social constructivists generally agree to the outcome of learning being a social product – a shared creation generated through active actions and interactions between learner and instructor rather than an individual enlightenment – some disagree about the basic process leading to knowledge (Prawat & Floden, 1994.) What truth is has also shifted within cognitive science resulting in contrarieties depending on particular foci. This has resulted in disparity and combative views as set forth through relativist, contextualist, and objectivist views. It has been suggested by Wakefield et al. (2011) that truth should be examined holistically instead of through one narrow lens. This is because, for example, viewing a learning experience from only a relativist perspective is often unconstructive, because as such one may only view truth as always specific to the individual's mind and perceptions. When one views that no absolute truth exists, coming to understand multiple perspectives on learning becomes futile. It is from that perspective that learners and instructors experience the social world in all its complexity. As such, any learning experience should include a means by which students and instructors can understand relationships as overlaps among the three above mentioned worldviews (Wakefield et al., 2011).

The pragmatic framework of learning and teaching as communicative actions (LTCA) theory supports this more holistic approach. It proposes that learning and teaching do not take place in isolation, not solemnly through an acquisition model, not only in context, not just relative to a particular student's frame, or only as objective reality external to the mind. Instead, meaningful learning stems from communicative actions and interactions, ardent inquiry, and critical thinking, leading to knowledge construction. For educators, the improvement of "human communication towards instructional and learning goals" (Warren, Bohannon, & Alajmi, 2010) lies at the core of LTCA theory, helping shape our point of view as to what it is to learn, teach, assess, and design instructional activities. Further, it proposes a means to guide learners and instructors toward reaching and improving understanding through effective human communication in the 21st century within the learning and teaching framework (Warren, 2011).

The original framework for LTCA builds on German pragmatist Jürgen Habermas' theory of communicative actions (1981[1984]). The four actions guiding LTCA, which we shall explain in context of a transmedia assignment, were originally and fully defined by Habermas in 1998. They are *normative, strategic, constative*, and *dramaturgical* communicative actions. Fig. 1 presents the pragmatic, iterative framework that includes the specific communicative actions, ardent inquiry, and critical thinking, which are

Fig. 1. A Pragmatic, Iterative Framework of Communicative Actions, Including Ardent Inquiry, and Critical Thinking Leading to Knowledge Construction.

expected to lead to new knowledge construction. LTCA theory guides in the design of transmedia learning – a new model of active learning.

Normative Communicative Actions

Communication shapes today's classrooms and it is a critical life skill that we must incorporate within our classrooms and model for our students. Classroom experiences should begin with a sharing of *normative communicative actions*. Such norms help guide classroom management, fairness, and guide effective communication and convey the kind of behavior to which a community member is entitled (Habermas, 1981[1984]). Normative communicative actions may be negotiated among students and instructor and are constructed through discourse leading to consensus and binding intersubjective agreements. For example, project objectives and individual student outlines can be developed as a result of social negotiation and students can use a rubric for self, and peer evaluation, allowing for active participation which empowers students to take ownership of the learning process.

Strategic Communicative Actions

Lectures are often seen as a sharing of objective, reified knowledge; that is to say, knowledge that has been socially validated over time and contains accepted facts, that is, "transmission of culturally stored knowledge" (Habermas, 1981[1987], p. 63). These truths are deemed *strategic communicative actions* and are the most common actions employed in educational settings today. Students may be directed to listen, take notes, and read weekly assigned textbook chapters as part of an instructor's instructional methods. These actions are not negotiable; however, students may choose to transgress and therefore reject this. By their nature, strategic communicative actions are explicit in their expectations and directives. Strategic actions forms the foundation for the students' knowledge construction and allow instructors to provide learners with an entry point to knowledge from which they may further explore and critique established facts and truths.

Transmission of the culturally accepted knowledge is thus a strategic communicative action that scaffolds learners' academic growth. However, transmission of hierarchically organized knowledge "is opposed to the way that humans naturally think. Throughout history, the dominant methods for communicating and conveying ideas has been to tell stories" (Jonassen, 2004, pp. 92–93). Denzin (2001) has noted that "[e]xperience, if it is to be remembered and represented, must be contained in stories that are narrated" (p. 59).

Constative Communicative Actions
To illustrate such actions as mentioned above, we will provide an example in which the instructor embedded an activity that required students to explore a transmedia environment over the web through *inquiry*. This activity was used to spur interest and to initiate *constative communicative actions*, that is, classroom discussion and discourse that was then carried beyond the classroom walls through related reading, exploration, and reflection assignments.

It is through such interactions that students *think deeply* and *critically* about the use of, and then design with transmedia, to support their own learning and teaching purposes.

Constative communicative actions are dialogues between or among interlocutors. This back-and-forth sharing of meaningful expressions, arguments, and validity claims allow students and instructor to engage in discursive argumentation and construct new truths through reaching social consensus. Sharing past and current intersubjective understandings objectively allows for an open critique of independent thinkers' understandings as thoughts are put forward and shared with peers, instructor, and the public. Peers, instructors, and experts (if applicable) all help construct new valid truth through this process (Wakefield et al., 2011).

Dramaturgical Communicative Actions

Transmedia learning experiences involve creativity, contemplation, and integration of multiple modes of media along with the expression and discussion of the shared story as a demonstration of learning. Further, these experiences allow for the emergence of an expression of individual student identity. Using various platforms to search for materials, evidence, share, and express understanding is part of the *dramaturgical communicative action*. This involves the expression of an intersubjective understanding in an objective way through creative and artistic means. Such manifestations may include artwork, graphic design, reflective writing, demonstration, and presentation including personal identity and utterances indicating individual truths. Dramaturgical communicative actions are open to thoughtful critique to help the learner improve on understanding and design.

These four communicative actions – normative, strategic, constative, and dramaturgical – all in concert with inquiry and critical thinking within the learning experience – provide a framework that allows for the creation of new opportunities for expression of understanding of complex issues in a collaborative and communicative environment.

Guided by LTCA theory, we now introduce our two case studies in which we seek to illuminate how transmedia was incorporated into a higher education learning experience as well as a Kindergarten through 12th grade K-12 learning experience and inform how such experiences may unfold. As we begin our first case, a professor's lecture provides the starting point. A lecture may be seen as a convergence of spoken and written forms, sharing transcripts and text while conducting "authorial performance" and "textually enabled dramaturgical effect" (Friesen, 2011, p. 101). Students were asked to deeply explore a story what was presented to them. In the process, they were expected to inquire, communicate, engage with building shared understanding, and answer questions including *who, why, what, when,* and *how* about the unfolding story. What was presented was, however, of ill-structured nature; that is, many possible solutions to what it was and what it was for were possible.

INTRODUCING A TRANSMEDIA CLASSROOM EXPERIENCE: A CASE STUDY

Last night in my class, I tried to get them to think more deeply about how transmedia may be used to target affective and higher order thinking skills and not just to spur content acquisition (....) I worked pretty hard to move them off the content acquisition model of learning for a while and into how it might be used to engage learners in higher order thinking such as critical and creative thinking and problem solving as well as seeking to get learners comfortable with abstraction and affective components they may be struggling with in their learning environment. (Warren, February 16, 2011)

This higher education experience occurred in a course teaching graduate students about theory of instructional technology implementation. The course examines traditional and present-day research on technology implementation in schools and informal settings. It has the main goal of increasing student awareness and understanding of the issues and implications that large and small-scale technology implementations may engender. Further, the course sought to explain how interactive multimedia technologies in particular may affect cognition in different educational environments and modes (online, hybrid, and face-to-face settings). A take-away from this course is that as we design learning environments, we need to take into consideration aspects of cognitive functioning and consider the impact of "overload" some learners are dealing with when bombarded by ubiquitous technology stimuli resulting from interactions with social media and connected technologies.

Related to this, I wanted students to start thinking about how stimuli can be both positive and negative. A few days prior to this class session I had posted on Twitter, my blog, and on Facebook a comment and a link to an experience that I had come across on the Web. The Adobe Flash™ animated web experience included embedded videos and interaction with a visual environment that appeared to have no directions or identifiable goals. I wanted to share this with those following my accounts to hear their thoughts on what this experience could be about and what it meant for cognition as they each reacted to it.

In a class session later in the week with my doctoral students, I brought up the experience again. The class session was tailored to introduce students to the concept of cognitive conflict and how this may and, indeed, should occur in learning experiences. This commonly arises as we are exposed to things that are puzzling, unexpected, or do not make sense to us. When encountering such experiences, instructors must think and rethink the consequences and learning possibilities of a digital experience. Because they engage and pose a certain kind of difficulty, these experiences also contribute to cognitive growth and knowledge construction. My major learning goal was to provide students with an experience they could work through, to be conflicted about elements of the experience, and engage in deep reflection. I hypothesized that this would allow them to generate and communicate their understandings to their peers and instructor. This should allow development of personal theories about how cognitive conflict can be built into learning, fostering increased hypothesis creation and discursive, argumentative communication toward testing their hypotheses, and developing evidence to support their claims to truth about why and how people can learn from or with transmedia.

In this experience, the visitor enters an animated virtual forest through the computer screen into a created reality. Students began class by spending 15 minutes exploring the virtual woods seeking answers to what the experience was intended to be. In the simulated woods, visitors can travel in several directions. As a player does so, different actors and musicians are encountered through the embedded videos connected to the forested environment in which students find themselves. These people tell their story only if the visitor takes the time to stop and listen to the unfolding narrative. In some instances, phrases appear in the woods like "We will complete the movie together," but there is no real context. In other spaces, one is posed puzzles in which players are asked to fill in letters to continue the experience by building new words and unlocking new spaces. The act of listening and struggling with meaning challenges each to decipher what is being shared. It is thus up to the visitor to make sense of the experience, stories, and social interactions.

As students were exposed to the stimuli each generated hypotheses to share with peers what the experience was and how it related to the topic of cognitive conflict. Actors and musicians ranging from Terence Howard and Debra Winger to Moby and Yoko Ono appeared in the short videos and each tells something they are afraid of and pose questions intended to draw the player deeper into the woods and to ask questions. As students ventured through the experience, I monitored them for body language, expressions, and peer communications, to gauge their curiosity and relative levels of irritation with what is, effectively, an ill-structured problem with no clear strategic communication. Some students wondered aloud as to why such high profile actors and musicians would participate in such a project and why there were no clear goals as to what they were supposed to be doing, which frustrated them because they wanted to know what to do so they could reach set goals and milestones as one might do in a video game. At the conclusion of their exploration, some students put in their email addresses and received messages from the transmedia system, though they, too, were vague and invited further exploration.

At the conclusion of the in class experience, one student gave his vivid description of the experience:

> It was intentionally ill-defined from the outset. The music was ominous and the leaves falling in front of bare winter trees amplified the feeling of uncertainty. The spoken words were ambiguous, provocative, and often dark. It was sprinkled with celebrities throughout of context. There were mini-puzzles embedded, but there were not a lot of clear game mechanics – leveling up, ultimate reward, etc. – and yet there was plenty to keep one digging.

He went on to say that it was more than a simple puzzle or filmic game and instead

> It has an interactive online multimedia journey that seemed designed to take an individual on an inward journey of the mind as much as through any game-based alternative reality. It was about thinking and how we come to understand what is reality, which aligned well with one of the outcomes of the course, which was developing our own nascent theories of implementing instruction in technology.

His comments provided the sense that, despite the ill-structured nature of the experience, students were learning through their interactions in the space without being provided specific strategic direction. They became curious because of how the material was presented and each constructed their own understanding of the experience, especially as they sought to apply the concepts already discussed that semester related to cognition and theoretical development in the context of large-scale technology use for learning. This was also one of the major goals of the course.

Another student, new to the program, said afterwards that she had a positive experience, despite being apprehensive at the outset, a feeling she perceived that the other students shared.

I could tell I was not the only one in the classroom that knew this was something that we had never done before and that we would be gaining something completely new from this experience that would open our minds to new things. It was a bit scary and altogether very exciting at the same time.

Ill-structured problems, which are at the heart of both David Jonassen's framework and LTCA, can be challenging for students when they first encounter them as their past experiences have traditionally been different. For example, a public school educator, originally from another culture said:

I had the opportunity to learn different from what my foundations were. We were taught to "assimilate" and "regurgitate" for the purpose of passing our exams but I learned during this experience to see what I was being taught in concrete terms as opposed to abstract and imagination. Never in my earlier education spanning over 30 years had I gone through this innovation in learning. The difference in understanding and knowing the content of the subject is amazing when placed side by side with how I've been used to learning in the past.

He later concluded that

If learning is a change in behavior as some people say, then I really learned a great deal. If I have another opportunity to do it again, I will try to go to the next level by exploring the environment – finding out what works and what does not work. The only rational way to do this is by experimenting, try it out and practice.

One of the things we can use stimuli for is to engender the kind of cognitive conflict that my students experienced here. This is because many learning paradigms require learning, or require cognitive conflict in order for learning or knowledge construction to occur. My initial questions to students after their experience included how can we, as educators, use broad questions that have no one right answer, for learning? We can generate a lot of hypotheses around the purpose. We can try to construct as a group what we think might be happening. We can try to generate some sort of solution. However, how can we find out for sure what this experience is about? What are some of our available options?

Students engaged in discourse around the meaning of the adventure and, further, how such cognitive experiences could be incorporated in education. Other facilitated questions included:

- What is the primary goal that we have with educational technologies for school?
- What does learning mean?
- What kinds of positive changes do we want to make in learners?
- What types of stimuli might we want to use to get to some other types of outcomes than behavior outcomes?

- What role does "thinking" play in society today?
- Stimuli can be used to engender cognitive conflict. Many learning paradigms require cognitive conflict for knowledge construction to occur. How can we use cognitive conflict and ill-structured problems when we think about what might be happening in an experience like this?

Exercises like this are ill-structured, open-ended, and are developed to spark a number of cognitive and social outcomes. These include goals such as increasing learner curiosity, interdependence among learners; discourse based on collected knowledge; and improved information seeking. Employing such strategies, students learn more about the experience and sharpen their skills while concurrently encountering or constructing rich knowledge. Through discourse, students engage in problem solving, hypotheses generation, develop solutions, and evaluate provided information based on different criteria: Is it good or bad? Is it meaningful? Does it fulfill a purpose? Is there evidence to support the claims made in the hypothesis?

In Fig. 2, I sought to have the doctoral students brainstorm and identify the major influences from psychology, educational theory, and daily

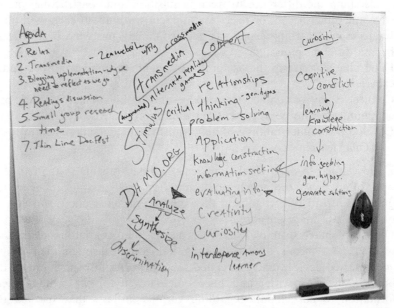

Fig. 2. Teacher and Students Proposed Transmedia Model Developed in Class.

classroom teaching practices that were present in their assorted transmedia experiences during the evening.

Transmedia, because it traverses several platforms, may be seen as noisy and difficult to navigate for some users. This is because the experience involves traversing various technologies that the learner is unfamiliar with and must learn in order to be successful. Transmedia, however, is also a single adventure that spans across many forms of media – a cross-platform media experience that allows story elements to emerge and this can be very engaging. Using such technology tools, I feel may allow instructional professionals to make learning more personal, engaging, spark student curiosity, and perhaps even be tantalizing. This is also expected to allow for building bridges between reality and story, while also allowing for discourse. Lance Weiler (2011) noted that "[t]here are no rules anymore in terms of how you can create." The interactive web experience that I introduced to students, called *In the Woods* (http://itwpathway.com), conformed to this notion.

My learning goals for the lesson included those from LTCA theory:

- Construct and communicate a personal or group-constructed definition of learning that can be connected to transmedia
- Understand the difference between acquisition and constructing knowledge and either accept or reject the inherent truth about each method
- Immerse in a learning experience that communicates what it is to learn from a different paradigm
- Determine as a group the usefulness of cognitive conflict in open-ended experiences
- Connect cognitive conflict, transmedia, and problem-based learning and communicate it to peers for critique and improvement of concept
- Develop own understanding of how transmedia can be designed to reach particular learning goals

I also wanted to open up the awareness of the students to the fact that people often focus too much on technology itself and its influence on cognition, instead of recognizing the communication it allows for, which should be its primary purpose.

One such shared example was when a particular ubiquitous media tool was used as a means of coordinating individuals through their smart, interconnected devices, and associated tools to foster discourse among the group. Tools like Twitter and Facebook allowed for up-to-the-moment information to participants regarding various protests that sparked the Egyptian revolution in 2011. Transmedia has similarly been used to bring a focus on educational topics by simulating epidemics. From this, it has been employed to engage learners in dialogues about real-world scenarios. One such instance is Weiler's (2011) New Frontier location-based alternate reality game (ARG) called *Pandemic*. ARGs are a subset of transmedia that use the distributed and open source nature of the Internet to develop game experiences that take people through video, audio, text, and mundane experience to develop a context for play that closely mirrors the real world with a few, important changes that bring focus to a particular problem that the instructor or designer seeks to expose the learner to. The communication aspect of the experience is what we need to focus on, not the technology. My theory is thus that transmedia benefits curiosity, problem solving, and information-seeking behaviors. Each of these engenders cognitive conflict in learners, which is necessary to successful learning.

> Many transmedia projects are constructed as ill-structured problems with no one correct answer and are intended to get players to engage more deeply similar to the way that several theorists including Savery and Duffy and Jonassen have proposed with problem-based learning and constructivist learning environments. (Warren, February 16, 2011)

In my own work, I encourage students to become familiar with transmedia projects, because I teach topics such as instructional design and the use of related technologies and emergent theory. My notion is that instructional design students who will be seeking instructional design positions after graduation should be familiar with this new trend and develop strong portfolios showing that they can create innovative and engaging 21st century learning experiences. Companies are moving toward using transmedia to support the launch of products, and it is expected that the field of education will follow because transmedia experiences are inexpensive to develop because the tools already exist.

My belief is that, over the course of the next five years, transmedia will become more accepted and adopted, both in the private industry and in education. The next generation of learners will benefit from being more creative, better thinkers, and better overall communicators. Sometimes focusing the iGeneration's attention may require a pique of their curiosity with the intertwined narrative of most transmedia. As such, these components are mainly about communication: visual, auditory, textual, or other relevant channel. Each may be used to communicate directive where there need only be a binary choice: accept a statement/fact as true or do not (strategic); rule-setting where there remain questions (normative), argument where the truth or knowledge remains in question (constative); or perform a task that shows the learner's or small groups' particular understanding of truth or knowledge (dramaturgical). Each, of course, remains open to critique, which should lead to a better knowledge construction or improved mental modeling.

Inspired by their professor's thoughts on transmedia and interested in expanding on their learning as well as portfolios, two of the graduate students, concurrently enrolled in the professor's instructional design class, designed and modeled their own transmedia experience for the 6th grade social studies classroom. Continuing from this example, we next illuminate how K-12 students engaged in learning about the Holocaust in a lesson design that provided students with a transmedia expression of under-standing reflections project (Fig. 3).

MODELING A TRANSMEDIA CLASSROOM EXPERIENCE: A CASE STUDY

When building our model transmedia social studies assignment for the 6th grade classroom, we considered several issues. These included the importance of culturally accepted truths, learning through reflection, and learning through story. We recognized that our storytelling assignment needed a foundation in a real, familiar character – yet this character needed to be unfamiliar enough to make it relevant and exciting for students to explore (Vance, 2011). We settled on the real-life story *Anne Frank: Diary of a Young Girl* as we felt it held the necessary components of engaging story, history, culture, people, climate, and setting. The story of Anne Frank is of a young Jewish girl hiding from the Gestapo. She lives in a secret annex of a warehouse in Amsterdam, Holland, together with seven other people during World War II Fig. 4 shows the social studies teacher introduce the Anne Frank assignment.

Further, we wanted the LTCA framework to be at the core of our assignment (Table 1) because we sought to ensure students' active engage-ment in communicative actions throughout the assignment. Broadly, LTCA communicative actions (normative, strategic, constative, and dramaturgical actions) pertain to behavior for individuals, groups, institutions, and society and lead to agreement about what truth or knowledge are among individuals in a group, such as a classroom. We shall explain these in the context of our model lesson.

Transmedia Lesson Plan

Themes from Anne Frank:
Social awareness of an era dominated by a culture of fear

Lesson Outcome
Facilitated by using learning and teaching as communicative actions (LTCA) theory to design instruction, students are guided to express learning mastery through transmedia. Student selection of media to include communication technology with traditional media allows students to experience and express lifeworld change through a story developed in response to guided instruction.

Grade Level: 6-8

Learning Objectives
Using classification levels of Bloom's Taxonomy each student will:

1. *Discuss* [Comprehension] possible transmedia projects for Anne Frank unit, *decide on* [Evaluation] and *identify* [Analysis], in collaboration with the instructor, a for the student, suitable project.
2. *Demonstrate* [Application] ability to create Reflection Project in response to themed questions and points of discussion (using media).
3. *Participate* in reading and reflective discussion with peers [Synthesis] and *practice* [Application] necessary skills for transmedia story development and communication.
4. Individually *apply* [Application] learned skills by *designing / developing* [Synthesis] individual reflections through media.
5. *Experiment* with [Analysis] and *solve* [Application] construction problems while creating Reflection Project.
6. *Prepare* [Application], *summarize* [Synthesis] and *explain* [Evaluation] design project during a presentation session open to assessment by peers, instructor, and [if applicable] a global audience. All students present individual story projects.

Materials
1. Access to classroom art supplies for drawing, painting and, sculpting.
2. Access to classroom technology for presentation and multimedia software e.g. MS PowerPoint, Prezi, Hyperstudio, etc.
3. Access to classroom digital technology to include cameras, flip and/or other creative video options such as machinima.
4. Technology support for development of skills with digital and computer media tools.
5. Access to Internet, websites, e-mail, and various social media for announcing, posting, training sessions, and final showcase event information and channels for receiving anonymous feedback.

Assignments
1. Students will keep an Anne Frank Reflective Journal.
2. Students will participate in classroom discussion, which will culminate in selection / submission of a presentation topic and organized outline.
3. Students will provide peer comments/feedback to classmates on class projects.
4. Students will develop and present a final transmedia presentation.
5. Students will participate in self-assessment, and peer-assessment of final presentations.

Fig. 3. Lesson Plan.

Fig. 4.   The Social Studies Teacher Introduces Students to Anne Frank: A Diary of
a Young Girl.

Table 1.   LTCA Theoretical Framework.

Employing learning and teaching as communicative actions (LCTA) theory lesson design will
provide opportunities for classroom interaction to include four levels of communication:
1. *Normative communicative actions* establish rules pertaining to behavior for individuals and
   groups within the classroom and school system.
2. *Strategic communicative actions* convey the educational and cultural truths which are
   conveyed as hierarchically organized knowledge.
3. *Constative communicative actions* allows learners opportunity to voice critique of learning,
   textbooks, instruction, and to engage in peer-to-peer feedback, and evaluation wherein
   heuristic techniques facilitate dialogue and discourse.
4. *Dramaturgical communicative actions* exist in a two-worlds perspective allowing for subjective
   interpretation of meaning for the objective, physical world, as well as the second internal state
   the – *lifeworld* – which provides ability to visualize and give evidence of learning as the
   expression of change in internal state.

*The Holocaust – Themes from Anne Frank: Social Awareness in an
Era Dominated by a Culture of Fear*

As our transmedia experience began, we first shared norms with students. In
our classroom community, the *normative communicative actions* conformed
to the behavior we expected from students and the steps in the learning
experience that we had set. This included deadlines for various parts of the

assignment, what measures needed to be met for achieving a certain grade, but also general classroom behavior etiquette, that is, an entitlement measure.

Knowing that "[s]tories can be used effectively as instructional design support systems helping people learn to solve problems" (Jonassen, 2004, p. 93), we continued by setting the outcomes and objectives of the learning sequence within the *strategic communicative actions*. In our case this conformed to the book we had chosen and wanted students to read. The diary of Anne Frank provided an initial understanding of time, place, character, and events, which served as the point of entry for students' further exploration and learning on the topic which we called: *Themes from Anne Frank: Social Awareness in an Era Dominated by a Culture of Fear*.

We asked students to keep a reflective journal for reactions to daily readings, vocabulary words, and topics they might later want to refer to, asking them to also note particular events, and major incidents. The journal was further used as an asynchronous communication channel. This allowed for student–teacher discussions as we could spend time with students discussing individual entries assessing their subjective understanding as well as their progress toward a goal of developing intersubjective, shared understandings among the whole classroom group. We also provided reflection topics for students' journal entries. These included "student topic selection" and "student project organization" and were graded. Keeping a journal spurred classroom discussion as students shared with each other their topic selection and ideas for narrative and story development.

As the students' holistic inquiry into the story and their understanding of the Holocaust related events unfolded, students were asked to select media that would help them share and transmit their story and allow them to share their understanding with others. Used in this way, transmedia experiences allow for social interaction and are also immersive, bringing the learner into contact with multiple sensory experiences that help make a story feel authentic. Transmedia experiences involve creativity, contemplation, and integration of multiple modes of media with the expression and discussion of the shared story as a demonstration of learning. A demonstration of a transmedia assignment was also initially given to students to spur ideas and peer-to-peer support and sharing was encouraged.

Feedback on students' stories was provided through *constative communicative actions*, which allow learners an opportunity to voice critique toward what is being communicated by the instructor, peers, or textbooks. In this context, learning is advanced through techniques where learners open up a dialogue that leads to *discourse*. Habermas explained discourse as a give and take of reasons – arguments – between participants (Finlayson, 2005) and students in a classroom provide counter claims and evidence that may change the original claims made by classroom participants, opening a healthy dialogue. Meaningful constative discourse allows student growth and takes place in the social environment of the classroom as students discuss passages with the instructor and peers allowing opportunity for clarification (feedback). We incorporated this as students took turns reading aloud from the Anne Frank's diary using paperback books, the Kindle, or iPads to facilitate discussion of students subjective understanding of the readings as we went along asking questions such as *What do you think is going on here? Why do you think that? Does anyone else have a different view? What do you think of xx's idea?* In particular, we spent a class session discussing the topic of "living with fear" after in-class reading toward the end of the book. The quote below is an excerpt from this emotionally filled reading. It sparked strong classroom discussion where individual interpretations of the text and mutual understandings emerged as students engaged in constative communicative actions.

> It's really a wonder that I haven't dropped all my ideals, because they seem so absurd and impossible to carry out. Yet I keep them, because in spite of everything I still believe that people are really good at heart. I simply can't build up my hopes on a foundation consisting of confusion, misery, and death. I see the world gradually being turned into a wilderness, I hear the ever approaching thunder, which will destroy us too, I can feel the sufferings of millions and yet, if I look up into the heavens, I think that it will all come right, that this cruelty too will end, and that peace and tranquility will return again. (Frank, 1952, p. 237)

In *Seven Habits of Highly Effective People*, Stephen Covey (1989) argued that important life skills include being able to express oneself, communicate, and argue. In our design, we wanted students to have ample opportunity to participate in discourse. This helps students grow into effective communicators and learn the skill of respectful critique when reviewing peers' work – valuable skills in the 21st century. The *dramaturgical communicative actions* provides an opportunity for this type of critique. Here the subjective personal identity, disposition, intentions, and understanding gets a forum in the objective world (Habermas, 1981[1984]) through creative and artistic means such as through poetry, painting, working with graphic design, writing a paper or a blog post (Wakefield et al., 2011), holding a presentation, or as in our modeled assignment, through storytelling using participatory media tools – transmedia. For students, dramaturgical communicative actions provide a way to visualize and express change in internal state – *lifeworld* – evidence of growth. They also allow for a learner's work to be thoughtfully critiqued. From this critique, students receive important feedback allowing them opportunity to improve and grow.

Benjamin Bloom (1968) found in his research on *Mastery Learning* that there are few things as important for making learning occur than *time on task* and *application of learning*. To become successful, students need to immerse themselves in academics and apply what they have learned as often as possible and also think critically. With the growth and use of technology in education we now more than ever communicate with one another over the Internet and over various electronic devices. This interaction contributes to a free-flowing communication in our connected world (Warren & Wakefield, 2012). Dreyfus and Dreyfus (1986) proposed that learning and understanding are a continuous process whereby learners go through stages on their way toward expertise – gradually the learner matures from novice, to advanced beginner, competence, proficiency, and finally into expertise. We concur with this view and accept that the learning process may be slow. Teachers, however, should act as facilitators, scaffolding learners through communicative actions throughout this learning process providing them opportunities to express their learning.

Within the context of LTCA, dramaturgical communicative actions allow students to spend time on task and reflect upon content, and then express their internal understanding of the materials they have studied as they communicate their understanding and learn mastery. Furthermore, transmedia communication through story extends to a virtual audience beyond the classroom if student presentations are shared on the web. This way a global audience may critique, extend, and participate in development of not only a lesson but also students' learning. Transmedia expressions provide students (and teachers) an outlet and opportunity to exhibit a creative reaction to learning and teaching.

The Reflections Project

The *Reflections Project* was the dramaturgical expression assignment we gave students. Student responses were to be developed via transmedia. In the process, students had choice of presentation media, and were supported in their creative expression to express lifeworld experience in reaction to classroom presentation, reading, discussion, and reflection. Lamb (2011) noted that nonlinear transmedia learning may include linked resources such as "print materials; documents; maps; web-based clues; mobile apps; cell phone calls; social media connections; activities and games; and media such as, audio, video, or animation" (p. 15). The media tools we suggested for students in the model experience included Popplet, Prezi, Storify,

HyperStudio, video capture, photography tools, audio and video podcasts, blogs, shared spaces such as, wikis, or other available and commonly accessible Google tools. Through audio, for example, a learner may experiment with communication as a narrator or interviewer; post a podcast on an Internet blog where listeners may leave comments allowing for interactivity. Fig. 5 lists some materials instructors may consider for a transmedia experience such as ours. As students worked on their cross-platform, multimodal media assignments, they engaged in dramaturgical expressions of their understanding and awareness of what was going on in the time of the Holocaust. This form of communication shows their internal knowledge construction, but remains open to critique by outside people such as the teacher so that their understanding can be improved.

One of our students contacted a college professor her mother knew who was of Jewish decent. The professor offered images from his family tree to help improve her unfolding story as she assembled a Prezi for classroom presentation at the end of the assignment period. The Prezi tool is one that allows for mashups, that is, inclusion of media from other platforms. In her Prezi, she included not only the images, but also YouTube videos such as the Secret Annex Tour (http://youtube/GTpXf5Np3Pw) and other Anne Frank related artifacts she found online. The Prezi allowed for feedback both in the classroom and over the Prezi platform and also from a global audience. This

Fig. 5.   A Student's Transmedia Classroom Presentation.

global component emerged as she tweeted the Prezi presentation's existence linking to it for others to view. As an extension, Prezi could also further be captured together with any anonymous feedback using screen capture software. The resulting images would be posted to another media platform, for example, TeacherTube for critique. This would further extend the story to yet another platform and a new audience Fig. 5 shows one of the students presenting to class.

For high school students, a convergence of social media and Smartphone apps can help the transmedia story unfold in a common space. This happens when students create a class Facebook page (or group) where they "collect" and mash-up artifacts and advance their story development using resources such as YouTube videos and Flickr photos they find online. This constructed, shared space can then be linked to and from, for example, Twitter for further reach. Together with the students' shared narrative on their Facebook page, this contributes to a learning space – a social learning community.

The common tools we suggest in a transmedia assignment are those that allow for creative outlets and provide a vehicle for sharing expressions with a wider audience. It is these outsiders that can help shape the story and improve it through critique. Such tools should include a feedback system to support discourse for the dramaturgical communicative action. These acts generally emerge through content distribution and expression of a student's internal lifeworld, resulting in outcomes such as documentary and web media creations. They can be shared and distributed on the Internet through social tools such as blogs, Twitter, Facebook, MySpace, and YouTube/ TeacherTube which open up thoroughfares for visualization to a broad audience and for sharing and thoughtful critique.

Transmedia Evaluation

We linked our transmedia lesson with LTCA theory, which guides collaborative, problem-based, active learning through communicative actions. Because of this, we do not think that teachers need to be overly grade oriented; instead, what is needed is a blend of formal and informal assessment along with a focus on discourse, collaboration through communication, creative endeavor with the finished product, and good presentation. To grade a transmedia experience, we suggest a peer review based on given guidelines, without being too explicit. Freedom to shape the story must remain so as not to stymie creativity. A rubric such as the one we provide in Table 2 may be helpful toward reaching this goal. It provides

Table 2. Transmedia Reflections Project Rubric.

	1	2	3	4	Total
Topic selection	Topic is related to the reading assignment.	Topic is related to reading assignment, and illustrated with examples.	Topic is related to reading assignment, illustrated with examples, and extended by student reflection.	Topic is related to reading assignment, illustrated with examples, and extended by student reflection in collaboration with other student(s).	
Organization	Project organization incorporates 1–2 forms of media.	Project is logically organized, and includes 3 forms of media.	Project is logically organized, and includes 3 forms of media to include Internet technology.	Project is logically organized and uses more than 3 forms of media to include technology and non-technology based media.	
Presentation	Student presents an "on topic" transmedia project presentation, 5–8 minutes in length.	Student presents an "on topic" transmedia project presentation, 5–8 minutes in length, which includes an introduction.	Student collaborates with another student to present an "on topic" transmedia project presentation, 8–10 minutes in length, which includes an introduction.	Student collaborates with two or more other students to present a well-organized and "on topic" transmedia project, 8–10 minutes in length, which includes an introduction, and closing/wrap-up.	
Participation	Student submits project self-assessment.	Student submits one self-assessment, and one peer assessment.	Student submits one self-assessment, one peer assessment, and participates by completing comment/feedback form for one other class project.	Student submits one self-assessment, two peer assessments, and participates by completing comment/feedback form for two other class project.	

Total:

point values for topic selection, organization, presentation, and participation. The first two items relate to the reflective journal. The items that follow relate more to evaluation formally and informally in an ongoing, participatory manner where students play a role as well.

Using knowledge sharing through social media, and supported by the LTCA theory, teachers may express their teaching and learning experience with the 21st century learning model of facilitation. Such a technique incorporates new modes of guidance of learners, communication, and self-expression as assessment and allows multiple forms of classroom discourse that can guide learners toward effective human communication that should result in learning. We feel the technology infused 21st century classroom is a new blend of dialogue and expression.

DESIGNING WITH TRANSMEDIA

Any participant in a learning community, whether instructional designer, teacher, or student, may create a transmedia learning experience. While transmedia use "will cause a teacher to lose some control of the educational experience" (Pence, 2012, p. 136), it also has the benefit of allowing the learner opportunity to explore, control how to engage with the artifacts they find, and reflect. Documenting a learner's thought processes helps as

> (…) it provides a stage from which both teachers and students may observe the learning process, make note of the strategies being used, and comment on the developing understanding. The visibility afforded by documentation provides the basis for reflecting on one's learning and for considering that learning as an object for discussion. In that way, documentation demystifies the learning process both for the individual as well as the group, building greater metacognitive awareness in the process. For teachers, this reflection on students' learning functions as assessment in the truest sense of the word. (Ritchhart, Church, & Morrison, 2011, p. 39)

Each transmedia learning experience is collaborative. When designing transmedia learning experiences, it is therefore important that the learner is provided guidance in the form of a framework. By modeling and providing appropriate tools, the instructor provides a stage on which the learner can paint and present the scene they want to show their audience. Students missing satisfactory ideals may be unconstructive and unsuccessful. This is undesirable as communication, constructive critique, dialogue, and discourse are each in the heart of the LTCA theory and the communicative actions the theory requires. Supportive scaffolding must be included, and in a safe environment, because students will share their personal views.

Transmedia blends together with the communicative actions to provide situated computer-based learning while freeing instructors from the constraints of a single medium. Instead, teachers may combine activities and tools such as hypermedia, cell phones, and videos containing a compelling narrative. It is these that form the basis of transmedia storytelling in a 21st century learning model. One word of warning we share with Lamb (2011) is that when using transmedia, instructors should seek to avoid the technological elements that divert attention from what it is we want students to attend to and learn. For example, one should avoid adding redundant audio and hypertext links to a transmedia experience when still images or video alone are sufficient to convey necessary information efficiently. Providing additional, distracting media may simply increase cognitive load to a negative level and do more harm than good.

CLOSING DISCUSSION

Some educators may fear the introduction of new media into the classroom. They may suspect that lesson development will become overly complex or the implementation too time consuming and if done incorrectly, that is possible. However, immersing students in new experiences using transmedia allows them to engage in meaningful modes of higher-order classroom learning through story, which can support engagement. As Norman (1993) noted, "The stories we tell not only explain things to others, they explain them to ourselves" (p. 129). Meaningful learning stems from *communicative actions* and *interactions*, *ardent inquiry*, and *critical thinking*, leading to *knowledge construction*. The lessons presented in this chapter depicted situated instructional designs and knowledge construction with transmedia storytelling guided by the LTCA theory. This framework emphasizes communicative actions where through intellectual work students are able to individually, as well as collectively, arrive at social knowledge construction. It provides a way to design opportunities for students to immerse themselves in and engage with a meaningful story context while thinking deeply about a topic, discussing, developing a personal learning narrative, critiquing for understanding and growth, and sharing in today's technology rich landscape.

In these case studies, we presented models where students both learn and teach each other using a cutting-edge methodology. We have introduced the LTCA framework as a structure for learning and teaching through transmedia. The four communicative actions in the theory provide a framework within which an instructor can gauge student development of knowledge in the form of effective human communication and creative self-expression. It is these communicative acts that orient learners toward understanding of established truths that are the foundation upon which new knowledge may effectively be built. Over the next few years, we foresee that the technology-rich educational landscape will grow and expand to include more transmedia learning and the theories that support its use will evolve as well.

REFERENCES

Abrahams, D. A. (2010). Technology adoption in higher education: A framework for identifying and prioritizing issues and barriers to adoption of instructional technology. *Journal of Applied Research in Higher Education*, *2*(2), 34–49.

Barab, S., Zuiker, S., Warren, S. J., Hickey, D., Ingram-Goble, A., Kwon, E.-J., & Herring, S. (2007). Situationally embodied curriculum: Relating formalisms and contexts. *Science Education*, *91*(5), 750–782.

Bloom, B. (1968). Learning for mastery. Instruction and curriculum. Regional education laboratory for the Carolinas and Virginia, topical papers and reprints, number 1. *Evaluation Comment*, *1*(2). Retrieved from ERIC database. (ED053419). Available at http://www.eric.ed.gov/ERICWebPortal/search/detailmini.jsp?_nfpb = true&_&ERICExt Search_SearchValue_0 = ED053419&ERICExtSearch_SearchType_0 = no&accno = ED053419

Ccabell. (2011, April 21). *Why use transmedia in early learning?* [Web log post]. U.S. Department of Education. Retrieved from http://www.ed.gov/oii-news/why-use-transmedia-early-learning-0

Covey, S. (1989). *7 habits of highly effective people*. New York, NY: Free Press.

Denzin, N. K. (2001). *Interpretive interactionism*. Thousand Oaks, CA: Sage Publications.

Dreyfus, H. L., & Dreyfus, S. E. (1986). *Mind over machine*. New York, NY: Free Press.

Finlayson, J. G. (2005). *Habermas: A very short introduction*. New York, NY: Oxford University Press.

Frank, A. (1952). *Anne Frank: The diary of a young girl*. New York, NY: Doubleday & Company, Inc.

Friesen, N. (2011). The lecture as a transmedial pedagogical form: A historical analysis. *Educational Researcher*, *40*(3), 95–102.

Habermas, J. (1981[1984]). *The theory of communicative action* (Volume 1: Reason and the rationalization of society) (T. McCarthy, Trans.). Boston, MA: Beacon Press.

Habermas, J. (1981[1987]). *The theory of communicative action: Lifeworld and system* (T. McCarthy, Trans.). Boston, MA: Beacon Press.

Habermas, J. (1998). *On the pragmatics of communication* (M. Cooke, Trans.). Cambridge: The MIT Press.

Jenkins, H. (2010, June 21). *Transmedia education: The 7 principles revisited* [Web log post]. Retrieved from http://henryjenkins.org/2010/06/transmedia_education_the_7_pri.html

Jonassen, D. H. (2004). *Learning to solve problem. An instructional design guide.* San Francisco, CA: Wiley.

Kinder, M. (1991). *Playing with power in movies television, and video games. From muppet babies to teenage mutant ninja turtles.* Los Angeles, LA: University of California Press.

Lamb, A. (2011). Reading redefined for a transmedia universe. *Learning & Leading with Technology, 39*(3), 12–17.

Lebrecht, T. (2010, July 24). *Old spice and the return of ad-power: Are "transformats" the future of marketing?* [Web log post]. Retrieved from http://bit.ly/dfBBTl

Norman, D. A. (1993). *Things that make us smart: Defending human attributes in the age of the machine.* Reading, MA: Perseus Books.

Pence, H. E. (2012). Teaching with transmedia. *Journal of Educational Technology Systems, 40*(2), 131–140.

Pink, D. (2005). *A whole new mind. Why right-brainers will rule the future.* New York, NY: Penguin Books.

Prawat, R. S., & Floden, R. E. (1994). Philosophical perspectives on constructivist views of learning. *Educational Psychology, 29*(1), 37–48.

Ritchhart, R., Church, M., & Morrison, K. (2011). *Making thinking visible: How to promote engagement, understanding, and independence for all learners.* San Francisco, CA: Jossey-Bass.

Rosen, L. D. (2011). Teaching the iGeneration. *Educational Leadership, 68*(5), 10–15.

Vance, B. (2011, March). Transmedia storytelling: Constructing compelling characters and narrative threads. Paper presented at the annual South by Southwest (SXSW) Conference in Austin, TX.

Wakefield, J. S., Warren, S. J., & Alsobrook, M. (2011). Learning and teaching as communicative actions: A mixed methods Twitter study. *Knowledge Management & E-Learning, 3*(4), 563–584.

Warren, S. J. (2011). *Learning and teaching as communicative actions.* Retrieved from http://www.ltca.us/LTCA_Theory.html

Warren, S. J., Bohannon, R., & Alajmi, M. (2010, April). Learning and teaching as communicative actions: An experimental course design. Paper presented at the annual meeting of The American Educational Research Association, Denver, CO.

Warren, S. J., Dondlinger, M., McLeod, J., & Bigenho, C. (2011). Opening the door: An evaluation of the efficacy of a problem-based learning game. *Computers & Education, 58*(1), 397–412.

Warren, S. J., & Stein, R. (2008). Simulating teaching experience with role-play. In D. Gibson & Y. Baek (Eds.), *Digital simulations for improving education: Learning through artificial teaching environments* (pp. 273–288). Hershey, PA: IGI Global.

Warren, S. J., & Wakefield, J. S. (2012). Learning and teaching as communicative actions: Social media as educational tool. In K. Seo (Ed.), *Using social media effectively in the classroom: Blogs, wikis, Twitter, and more.* New York, NY: Routledge.

Weiler, L. (2011, Feb. 6). *This is transmedia* [Video interview]. Retrieved from http://trulyfreefilm.hopeforfilm.com/2011/02/this-is-transmedia.html

TECHNOLOGY AND THE CHANGING NATURE OF NARRATIVES IN LANGUAGE LEARNING AND TEACHING

Felix A. Kronenberg

ABSTRACT

Two different types of technology-enabled stories that can help expand the notion of narratives are discussed in this chapter. The narratives found in digital storytelling and video games offer new possibilities and advantages for language learners and instructors. They are multimodal, immersive, and authentic; they offer significant motivational benefits and allow for agentive, situated, and participatory learning. Both forms, DST and video games, exemplify new modes of relating meaningful narratives. Media creation and sharing as well as gaming are familiar domains for today's learners. Thus, if these authentic practices are part of the learner's everyday experiences, it makes sense to utilize their potential for educational purposes. As the review of some applications in this chapter indicates, there is an area of convergence that is of particular interest for language learning purposes and may lead us to contemplate a redefinition

Increasing Student Engagement and Retention using Multimedia Technologies:
Video Annotation, Multimedia Applications, Videoconferencing and Transmedia Storytelling
Cutting-edge Technologies in Higher Education, Volume 6F, 95–119
ISSN: 2044-9968/doi:10.1108/S2044-9968(2013)000006F007

of these narrative forms. In addition to more traditional narratives, these new and emergent forms can and should be represented in language learning curricula.

INTRODUCTION

Stories are an important component of foreign or second language learning and teaching. Reading texts, generally the classics, in the foreign or second language (L2) is one of the pillars of the first formal language teaching method, the grammar and translation method. With the possible exception of the audio-lingual method's rote memorization and drilling exercises and its often disconnected and artificial content, stories are a part of most language teaching methodologies and approaches, and are therefore found in almost all modern language textbooks. The traditional textbook is still the predominant format of content delivery in formal second language curricula. Also many supplemental materials, such as videos or audio narratives, contain stories. Using narratives for language learning and teaching is hardly anything new. But they are not always an ideal way to teach languages. The medium itself forces a certain type of narrative. In traditional books, stories are written texts, sometimes illustrated by images, but the format does not enable sounds, moving images, or interactive elements to be a part of the narrative.

Most of these stories are provided by someone other than the learner – they were created by professors, accomplished authors, editors, writing professionals, or teachers. Not only may these stories be difficult to relate to, they are also passive in that there is no meaningful two-way interaction with the text itself. With the exception of post-reading tasks, such as discussions or questions and answers, the text itself remains unchanged. It is not a participatory artifact, but a static one. Many stories we find in modern educational media are difficult for learners to relate to. An example of such a story can be found in the modern American textbook for college-level introductory German, *Kontakte* (Tschirner, Nikolai, & Terrell, 2012, p. 56): In the first chapter, college students are introduced to Herr Wagner, an adult, who performs various tasks that differ sharply from many American college students' realities. He works all day, he goes grocery shopping while smoking a pipe after work, and for evening entertainment he goes for a walk by himself, again smoking his pipe. The story is drawn as a cartoon and contains short sentences that describe each image. Not only is the narrative misleading – in no German-speaking country can you smoke inside a grocery store – it is also difficult for its audience to identify with.

In order to make the material and content memorable, the learner should be able to relate to the story, to emotionally experience and engage with the narrative. A learner's identity is a crucial component of learning in constructivist theory: "Through personal experience and critical reflection on their beliefs about the world in which they live and the domains in which they hold affective agency, learners come to know themselves and what they are becoming" (Begg, Dewhurst, & Macleod, 2005). Today's learners relate to narratives through multiple modes of communication, which are increasingly digital and interactive (Kress, 2003). If it is the goal to enable the learner to communicate in a meaningful way, then the stories – and communication modes – surrounding the learner have to reflect his or her reality and be authentic. After all, "stories are all about meaning" (Alexander, 2011, p. 4). Especially for language learning purposes, narrative content is only limited by the learners' imagination. Seemingly trivial, everyday stories are important building blocks for beginners, followed by increasingly complex themes and topics for intermediate and advanced students. As Toolan (2001) points out, stories help us "make sense" of things:

> Everything we do, from making the bed to making breakfast to taking a shower (and notice how these combined – in any order – make a multi-episode narrative), can be seen, cast, and recounted as narrative – a narrative with a middle and end, characters, setting, drama, (difficulties resolved), suspense, enigma, 'human interest', and a moral. (...) From such narratives, major and minor, we learn more about ourselves and the world around us. Making, apprehending, and then not forgetting a narrative is making-sense of things which may also help make sense of other things. (p. iix)

In this chapter I will examine two different types of technology-enabled stories that can help expand the notion of narratives. The first is that of digital storytelling (DST), a form of communication that enables anyone, even those with limited communicative skills and experience, to create a compelling, authentic narrative that can be shared through various distribution channels. The second type of narrative I will discuss are stories found in computer or video games. Rooted in contemporary popular culture, these interactive narratives are increasingly used for language learning and teaching purposes not only for their motivational factors but also their immersive and multimodal advantages. "Gaming, digital forms of communication and participation as well as programming and content creation" Drotner (2008) argues, "are among the dominant, domestic engagements, many of which involve narrative engagement with unknown others" (p. 67).

Research and examples in this chapter focus on higher education, but many of the concepts and examples are applicable for secondary education as well. I chose these two different yet related types of new narratives because they complement each other. DST on the one hand is an active process of creation with a finished product. Games, on the other hand, can constitute interactive storytelling that the user connects with, reacts to, and consumes. Both are relatively new forms for which technology is essential. The two examples overlap in many ways, for example in certain software applications described below as well as a form of DST called *machinima*, which is DST through screen-captured sequences from video games. The visuals and sounds are appropriated for a new narrative, not that of the game but one that the gamer creates outside of the game through editing and voice-overs. Both forms, DST and video games, exemplify new modes of relating meaningful narratives.

DIGITAL STORYTELLING

DST is a vague term, which traditionally has been defined rather narrowly as a "short, first person video-narrative created by combining recorded voice, still and moving images, and music or other sounds" (Center for Digital Storytelling, n.d.). This view suggests a close relationship to video and film. Other terms often used for DST, such as multimedia writing or photo films, indicate a closeness to more familiar narrative concepts. This limited view has been increasingly challenged due to the emergence of new forms of digital narratives. For example, Alexander (2011) defines DST as follows: "Simply put, it is telling stories with digital technologies" (p. 3). He argues that DST encompasses other forms, which may not necessarily include the deeply personal content or the linearity which have traditionally defined digital storytelling. Both the more confined view as well as a more open reading of DST, which may include games, Twitter feeds, blog posts, or Facebook discussion threads, utilize a range of communicative modes. Multimodal stories contain visual and auditory elements, and new mobile interfaces offer the possibility of tactile interaction with the narrative. The use of multiple modes can increase the effectiveness of language learning by providing relief and support: an image may illuminate a voiced description, or a written word may define a voiced sentence. Hull and Nelson (2005) argue in general that "a multimodal text can create a different system of signification, one that transcends the collective contribution of its constitutive parts" (p. 225).

The multimodality of a digital story, as compared to, for instance, a written narrative, can also create a new level of meaning and comprehension for language learners and allows for different ways of readings of, or rather interactions with the text. On a more basic level, multimedia helps to bridge language learners' comprehension when their language proficiency may limit their understanding of a text. Krashen (1989), for example, notes that the visual narrative of comic books can offer "clues that shed light on the meaning of an unfamiliar word or grammatical structure" (p.402). Similarly, sounds or moving images in addition to written text can provide further clues that may lead to a lowered cognitive load for L2 learners.

Media Creation

DST is interesting for our purposes not only as consumed media, but especially as created media. These aspects are not necessarily separate from one another, quite to the contrary. It is the interaction between the two that creates creative synergies and learner comprehension. Couldry (2008) argues that the "aim of digital storytelling is not to produce media for broadcast but to produce 'conversational media'" (p. 54). Thus, the outcome is not a finalized product that is merely consumed, but one that creates two-way information flows. Kress (2003) argues that new technologies led to a change from unidirectionality to bidirectionality of communication (p. 6).

DST is a media device which allows learners to create meaningful, tangible language communication and outcomes. The use of multiple modes can not only lead to a better understanding of a narrative, as discussed above, but also to increased communicative effectiveness. "[T]hat which may be invisible or inaudible in imagery and sound may be rendered visible and audible" through multimedia creation, Nelson (2006) argues, which he attributes to the "relative concreteness that is attendant to multimedia communication" (p. 71). DST enables learners to project their own voice, when that voice is not often heard. This constructivist approach not only opens up the boundaries of traditional learning environments, it is also learner-centric and focuses on the implementation of achievable tasks. DST can be used for both frequent, brief assignments – what I would refer to as digital micro-narratives – as well as extended project work and within a community-based educational framework. This allows students not only to create content – they do that frequently by writing essays or dialogues – but it empowers them to create meaningful and even artistic content that may surpass content created by an instructor or a publisher. For example, our story of Herr Wagner was created by a team of textbook authors, and it reflects what they think might be best for the learners, whether that is the case or not. The story in a book can no longer be changed, it is final, but digital stories can be altered or enhanced by their creator or often their consumers. They allow for previously unimagined creative, professional, and polished products. A student may continue working on a story and perfect it. As an alterable construct it can improve and is much less immediate than direct face-to-face interaction.

In a language classroom, the teacher is usually the person with the vastly greater linguistic competence, appearing to be omniscient and thus completely in power. Through the democratic process of allowing the learner to provide content, power asymmetries in the classroom are lessened. Wolff (2011) advocates that we must pay attention to individual learner differences:

> Despite all the progress that has been made in foreign language teaching during the last 20 years, despite the introduction of communicative language teaching and its different models, the mainstream language classroom is still determined by a form of classroom discourse that English foreign language theoreticians describe – somewhat mockingly – as teacher-controlled interaction, a form of discourse which is planned and directed by the teacher and gives the students only the opportunity to react. (p. 4)

Providing opportunities to act, rather than solely react, are crucial for creative engagement with a second language. Nelson (2006) speaks of a "potential leveling effect" (p. 71) of multimodal communication. If we want to teach communicative skills, then our approach must take into account that we only communicate fully when we contribute, when we create language, when we produce meaning.

Why is this not commonplace in the language classroom, as Wolff (2011) thinks it should be? The answers range from the technical and mundane to the ideological. Allowing students to create meaningful media artifacts requires preparation, time, resources, and knowledge. Minimal technical requirements, such as a mobile device or computer and a microphone must be met. Teachers must be trained and receive ongoing support. The curriculum may not encourage or even allow such creative work, and institutions might not reward teachers because other learning goals have a higher priority. And certainly another possible reason is the fear of losing control, of not being more competent than the learners. For teachers, "losing face" is a common inhibitor of technology use, but ironically it is DST that allows its creators to not lose face. Professional development, good support structures, and the sharing of best practices are avenues through which teachers might adopt these or similar ways to encourage a less teacher-focused and a more learner-centered learning environment. Language centers, the successors of language laboratories, are an excellent way to foster and support these types of activities and provide training, hardware and software for students and faculty (Kronenberg, 2011).

Individualization, Learner Differences, and Identity

L2 learners, especially beginners, are relatively powerless and voiceless, while the instructor is all-knowing. This can lead to deep insecurities, especially for younger people or in language learning contexts that are not voluntary. The insecurity can create a high barrier and render a student literally speechless. In order to help students develop an identity in the target language and find their voice, the teacher may encourage experimentation with multiple identities in order to decouple the actual self and the L2 self. Hull and Katz (2006) suggest that the "process of constructing agentive identities, then, can be viewed as a linguistic ideological struggle to make others' words one's own – to create what Bakhtin calls an internally persuasive discourse, perhaps through an orchestration of voices from multiple discourses and social worlds" (pp. 45–46). Teaching strategies, such as language students choosing their "target language name" or role play have a long tradition in the language classroom. DST, too, allows its producers to project their own voice through another persona. The use of an alter ego or an avatar protects the actual self and allows for playful and uninhibited experimentation with language. The threshold for risk is lowered not only because of the imagined distance but also the creative agency of the creator. "Narratives have to have a teller, and that teller, no matter how backgrounded or 'invisible,' is always important" (Toolan, 2001, p. 5).

The language learner can consume and interact with her or his peers' stories. DST represents a transition from mass media to more "personal media" (Erstad & Wertsch, 2008, p. 32). When we speak of "the language learner" we do not have a single entity but different persons with very different learning styles, strength, and strategies. According to Dörnyei (2005) "ID's [individual differences] have been found to be the most consistent predictors of L2 learning success" (p. 2). Some students thrive in the traditional classroom, but others may feel intimidated or are not good communicators in face-to-face conversations. DST is one possibility of giving some of these students a more effective way to communicate in the target language.

By setting parameters and clarifying expectations, students can creatively and individually work within the given framework. A rubric specifying how the stories are evaluated demystifies how a teacher might judge the work, and should be supplied beforehand. Even a simple storytelling task, such as "Tell me what you did last weekend" can yield incredibly creative results and astonishingly different stories, but a provided framework of expectations and evaluation criteria will lead to more focused and sensible content. Other forms of assessment may also be used with DST, such as peer-review, reflections, or portfolios.

Agency and Participatory Learning

Digital stories allow for various levels of participation. On the most basic level, creators participate in a media dialogue, and do so as equals. This creates a certain group identity among the creators and encourages conversations around a shared, genuine interest. These may happen in face-to-face communication or through digital interactions: users can leave comments or rate the creations of others. The narratives themselves may include a collaborative component when they are co-produced. For example, *VoiceThread*, a modern, collaborative Web 2.0 tool, enables its users to control who can add to the story and who can merely comment or view it. Collaborative DST provides an asynchronous framework for learners to negotiate meaning. They can interact with each other's work, for example, by commenting, rating, asking questions, or adding to the story.

According to Murray (1997), agency "goes beyond both participation and activity." It is rather "an aesthetic pleasure" and "an experience to be savored for its own sake" (p. 128). DST, then, is not merely authoring a digital text but an aesthetic sensation and a creative process that goes beyond the technical and the practical. "To articulate internal experiences by means of words, images, and sounds," Nyboe and Drotner (2008) argue, "makes these experiences visible to others, and articulation thus involves both visibility and exchange. Aesthetic production is a particular form of articulation, as we have seen, because it involves manipulation of existing signs and co-production of new signs" (p. 172).

Telling digital stories can make language production not a forced chore but transform it into a tool of self-realization and self-expression. Language learners, who are barely able to produce a few, basic sentences in face-to-face communication, can thus produce immensely creative work by not solely relying on speech alone. Empowering the learner to actively participate in a meaningful, relevant dialogue in the second language helps create a community and a shared experience rather than solely a dialogue imposed and controlled by external systems and norms, such as grammar rules, institutions, classification systems, and instructors.

Practical Considerations and Examples

New multimedia creation software and hardware has sparked an incredible increase in production of user-generated multimedia narratives. In recent years digital narratives have entered the mainstream, both in the media as well as education. Software applications range from simple and straightforward tools like *Photo Story 3*, *Comic Life Deluxe*, or *Pulp Motion* to sophisticated editing software such as *Final Cut Pro*. There are countless Web 2.0 offerings like *VoiceThread*, a web-based and mobile storytelling platform for collaborative and individual narratives, and an ever increasing number of mobile apps, like *StoryKit*, *Storyrobe*, *SonicPics*, or *Toontastic*. Some of these combine gameplay and collaborative elements. For instance, the *Story Wheel* app allows multiple players to spin a virtual wheel, which then will land on a picture. The picture is animated when touched. The player who spun the wheel then proceeds to record a narrated voice-over, which should correspond to the animated image. The mobile device is passed on to the next player, who continues the story in the same fashion, and so on until the story is finished and published. Another example of the convergence of storytelling and games is the *StoryLines* app, which allows its user to choose a saying and draw it on a mobile device. This drawing is passed on to another player, either virtually or by passing the device, who then tries to title the drawing. The next player creates another drawing based on this last title, and so on. Storytelling can be a social game, just as a game can tell stories.

There are many different forms of digital stories, which include photo stories, claymation, brickfilms, stopmotion films, cartoons, graphic novels, manga, and interactive films, just to name a few. They all take digitized media, such as scanned drawings, image sequences, designed documents, video footage, music or recorded voices, and combine them or repurpose them in manifold ways. Part of the aesthetic and narrative pleasure lies in the new possibilities that digital creation, mixing, and remixing provide.

Hardware generally requires a computer with a microphone and a camera or a mobile device such as the iPad. From a technical standpoint, the trend has been toward easier, cheaper, and more mobile production possibilities.

The vast variety of possibilities in itself makes technical assistance difficult, and pedagogical and curricular support is a key component to successfully integrating DST in a meaningful way. For example, if too much time is spent on technical issues, on troubleshooting or on technical details, then the actual, primary goal of language learning may not be achieved.

As these tools enable such a plethora of possibilities, only a few ideas of successful curricular integration shall be mentioned here. Short narratives for beginners may include stories encompassing elementary categories, such as food, likes and dislikes, family, work and careers, or travelling. These topics are common components of many early language programs and will provide individual practice and communicative self-expression. Aided by multimedia, learners can create meaningful stories after only a few weeks of language instruction. Students may be asked to describe a day in their lives, or tell a funny anecdote they experienced during their first day of school (e.g., http://www.rhodes.edu/languagecenter/20635.asp).

An example of larger scope for more advanced learners is project-based storytelling. Generally, learners work on their narrative over a prolonged time period, and other non-storytelling activities are often attached to the project. For example, in one University of Maryland storytelling project, immigrants' voices are conveyed through DST created by language students (http://www.umbc.edu/blogs/digitalstories/2009/12/digital_stories_from_german_30.html). Similarly, in a grant-funded project at Rhodes College, language students interview immigrants in the community in the target language and then edit the raw media and condense the essence into short digital stories (http://www.rhodes.edu/languagecenter/24235.asp). The focus of these exercises is not on the final product, but the act of creation fills the interviews with meaning and forces the learner to critically examine the content.

GAME NARRATIVES FOR LANGUAGE LEARNING

Are games stories? The debate between narratologists and ludologists has been a prominent topic in the field of game studies for some time. Alexander (2011) describes this debate as the "old divide between those who see games primarily as mechanisms for narrative delivery and those emphasizing gaming's mechanical operations beyond stories" and continues that "[s]uch a reiteration is not especially necessary for our purposes" (p. 91). It is evident that games are not the same as traditional narratives, for instance a novel or a movie. Compared to viewing a film, video game play requires input: "physical action of some kind" (Wolf, 2002b, p. 13). It is the interactive characteristic of gameplay that seems to be at odds with narrative, which is "all about predestination" (Mateas & Stern, 2006, p. 643). The plot of a game, which can be described as "multiform" (Juul, 2005, p. 241), offers a level of participation and immersion that makes it so appealing to its users. Rather than simply providing a prefabricated, finalized story, games are "story-enabling" (David Perry, as cited in Krawczyk, 2006, p. 89).

Indeed, games contain multiple stories due to the large number of possibilities of choices and story-lines, a characteristic of narrativity that also makes DST so compelling. "In an interactive narrative," Wolf (2002a) argues, "different sets of actions and consequences are available to the same player-character and can be experienced on a subsequent playing of the game" (p. 109). Jenkins (2004) talks about "micronarratives" (p. 125), which are part of a larger narrative. This author agrees that some games do contain narratives, even though their form may differ from more traditional forms of narrative, and that each iteration of gameplay may provide a different narrative for each individual user. As described above, new forms, such as *machinima* or the apps *StoryLines* or *StoryWheel*, show the convergence of games and storytelling.

Immersion and Agency

Through games we become participants and agents in another world that may or may not resemble our own; it is a separate, fictional space, a "dramatic *storyworld*" (Crawford, 2005, p. 56), which has different rules and parameters. The consequences of actions are contained in this world in most cases. Still, "in games, just as in real life, the outcomes (winning, losing) are real and personal to the experiencer, unlike in stories" (Aarseth, 2004, p. 366). This immersion is a "key aspect of game-based storytelling," according to Alexander (2011, p. 92). Games and game-like environments that share this immersive quality offer individualized experiences that are accessible and relatively cost-effective. Bogost (2011) argues that because games, in contrast to other media, are so immersive, they force "us to become practitioners of their problems rather than casual observers" (p. 141). Nothing happens in a game if there is no input, it is the game that merely reacts. It does not act, it only prompts the user to do something or offers the possibility to interact with its content. Our attention may be captured even more as games are becoming increasingly social, be it through direct social input or through communication with others through social media outside of the game environment. Gee (2004) refers to spaces for social interaction and user communication, which may be wikis, blogs, discussion boards, etc., as "affinity spaces." He distinguishes between games with a small "g," which are the software, and Games with a capital "G," which are the "combination of the game (software) and the meta-game (social interactional system)" (Gee, 2011, p. 226). Much of the communication happens outside of the games, and games (or rather *Games*) in education should include such social, interactive spaces.

The story that the player experiences differs from the one created by the game writer, as McDaniel, Fiore, and Nicholson (2010) argue. The user's "immediate-level story," in contrast to the intended "high-level story" (DeMarle, 2007, pp. 77–78) is deeply personal. It is being part of the story or stories and its world rather than being a mere observer that creates this immediacy and leads to intense engagement with the medium. Players experience a sense of self-direction, and thus a story that is unique and personal.

Motivation

Motivation and learner attitudes are important criteria for successful second language acquisition (Dörnyei, 2005; Dörnyei & Ushioda, 2010; MacIntyre, 2002). Games are a creative sandbox that may ideally lead to a state of flow (Csikszentmihalyi, 1990), in which the player is fully immersed in the domain and is highly focused on the current tasks and narrative. This heightened form of intrinsic motivation allows the player to experience the game with fully focused cognitive and emotional attention to the task at hand. Flow makes actions that are technically work seem to be effortless. For instance, moving the mouse to the same position and clicking repeatedly on the left mouse button is an activity that may be boring or laborious when performing certain computer tasks. But gamers willingly do the same over and over again, with complete focus and generally a sense of excitement, up to a point when their wrists may physically hurt because of such an action. Thus, flow is an ideal for educators because the learner will try to work hard without any external rewards, and even despite external penalties. It is the opposite of apathy. Egbert (2003) concludes in his study of flow experiences in the language classroom that it "seems clear that flow exists in language classrooms, but it is also clear that cannot fully explain it" (p. 513).

In order to achieve this state of mind, the user has to be or feel in control and has to possess and believe in her or his competency. The narrative in games can be one way of eliciting flow, just as a novel, DST, or a theater play might result in experiences of flow. The goals of the game must be achievable, at least in the mind of the user. The content must be something outside of the ordinary; again, even if the game is played by millions of others, it is seen as personal, extraordinary, and unique to the gamer. Games "transport us to another reality" (Tews, 2002, p. 175). Learners feel that the content is not forced upon them, but instead that the experience is worthwhile for its own sake.

Language Learning Benefits

In addition to the motivational, immersive, and creative advantages, video games may offer further benefits for language learners. They provide a framework for collaboration and create a context for learning. Video games generate opportunities for inquiry and may lead to incidental learning. Bogost (2011) sees them as "models of experiences rather than textual descriptions or visual depictions of them. When we play games, we operate those models, our actions constrained by their rules" (p. 4). The player has the ability to make choices and see the results. Ryan (2004) argues that the "secret to the narrative success of games lies in their ability to exploit the most fundamental of the forces that move a plot forward: the solving of problems" (p. 349). And Aarseth (2004) asserts that in games "everything revolves around the player's ability to make choices" (p. 366). Choice is an important L2 communicative learning component. As opposed to behaviorist views like the audio-lingual method, communicative learners must be able to not merely reproduce but to actively and creatively produce language. They must be able to respond in a meaningful way to authentic challenges. Games allow for playful and imaginative testing of fictional situations. Risk-taking is important for L2 learners as much advancement happens through trial and error, and the game can provide a context for this without serious consequences.

Video games reflect many learners' realities more accurately than more traditional media as games have become a cultural mainstay. They create opportunities for repetition, a key component of L2 competence development, without being boring. Automating language processes with the help of computer games, which are infinitely patient, is another strength of computer games. As already mentioned above, connecting language to images, actions, and dialogues creates connections and taps into existing schemata and previous experiences and knowledge. The task-based nature of games gives the user the feeling and satisfaction of smaller but frequent success, something Gee (2003) refers to as the "Achievement Principle": for "learners of all levels of skill there are intrinsic rewards from the beginning, customized to each learner's level, effort, and growing mastery and signaling the learner's ongoing achievements" (p. 67). Good games create a feeling of never-ending success and a constant flow of rewards and visible improvements, making them quite addictive. In role playing games, for example, players can "level up" or find ever better items and artifacts. They make something abstract − like knowledge, wisdom, experience − into something tangible and understandable. Success and progress are difficult to measure for language learners and even teachers on a smaller and ongoing scale. L2 learners reach a new standardized proficiency level every few semesters, but nobody tells or shows them every five minutes how they are progressing. Games can combine the motivating feeling of success and constant rewards with meaningful content that the traditional classroom often cannot.

GAMES FOR LANGUAGE LEARNING

The state of computer gaming in language education is still an experimental one. The body of research and game analyses for computer games for L2 learning and teaching purposes is small but growing. Among the games examined are those that were produced for educational purposes, such as *Mingoville* (Meyer & Sørensen, 2009) and the interactive fiction game *Ausflug nach München* (Neville, Shelton, & McInnis, 2009). Also commercial, off-the-shelf video games are increasingly the object of academic study, such as *Parappa the Rapper 2* (deHaan, Reed, & Kuwada, 2010) and the multiplayer role playing game *EverQuest II* (Rankin & Shute, 2010). Peterson (2010) reviews seven studies on specific gaming environments: *MOO* environments, *Simcopter*, *Sim City*, *Active Worlds*, *World of Warcraft*, and *Tactical Iraqi*. He concludes that "[t]aken together, these findings suggest that the use of stand-alone games combined with carefully designed support materials may be an effective means to develop vocabulary as a supplement to regular coursework" (p. 87). The recent focus and interest indicate that the research field L2 learning and video games is growing. But only a few games have been studied, and we do not have much data that would indicate how effective computer games are for language learners and teachers.

Mentioned below are successful or potentially successful game categories and examples. Certain categories of games lend themselves better than others to the learning of languages, so only some are discussed here, while others are left out completely for various reasons. For instance, 3-dimensional shooting games or sports games are generally not productive games due to their focus, content, and tasks at hand. That being said, almost all games may offer insignificant learning possibilities or contain small amounts of language, for example cut scenes, which are video sequences in-between gameplay segments, or on-screen instructions. They may also be used as an object of discussion. But as these games will not fit into the majority of teaching situations, we shall not discuss them further. There is not an agreed-upon list of genres (for a good overview, see e.g., Ensslin, 2011, pp. 45–47), so the following examples may belong to other or differently named genres. These discussed genres and games were chosen because of their salient narrative content: educational games, small games, adventure games, and narrative games.

Educational Games

Educational games, sometimes derided as edutainment, are games specifically created for learning purposes. Development and content are driven primarily by learning goals and curricular content. Many games are small and rather simple games, such as vocabulary builders in which the player has to correctly type or match words in order to get points or defeat an enemy. These games are very similar to workbook exercises but are presented in a game-like format.

There are also more complex game narratives in which the player follows a character through a story that often contains familiar categories, such as traveling, food, information requests, or geography, which are also topics in other instructional materials like textbooks. Examples are the interactive fiction game about an excursion to Munich, *Ausflug nach München* (Neville et al., 2009) for computers and the recently released mobile game *Adventure German – The Mystery of the Sky Disk (Lernabenteuer Deutsch – Das Geheimnis der Himmelsscheibe)* by the *Goethe Institut* (http://www.goethe.de/lrn/duw/lad/enindex.htm). In *Ausflug nach München*, learners take on the role of an American exchange student in Germany, who travels to Munich for a weekend trip. They interact with the game through keyboard input, which is a common method in text adventure games. Tasks resemble those found in many textbooks, such as buying food or a train ticket and finding the right train platform, but are presented in an interactive, game-like format. *The Mystery of the Sky Disk* makes use of new technological innovations by adding tactile sensations and a new level of interactivity and immediacy by allowing users to swipe and tap their fingers directly on the screen. This free game for iOS and Android devices as well as through a web-based interface also makes use of embedded multimedia resources, such as animations, images, films, interactive maps, audio recordings, hypertext, etc. The user plays an art expert, Vincent Mirano, who investigates a possible theft or forgery of the 4,000-year old Nebra Sky Disc. The mystery allows the player to travel to various locations in Germany in order to collect clues and perform small tasks. The mini-games that can be found throughout the adventure include tasks such as listening exercises or word ordering.

Another educational game form is that of the web quest. Part scavenger hunt, part web exploration, it is a task-oriented exercise that provides tasks and guidance for its users. It is a very flexible format and does not require a particular format or system. Templates and authoring tools (see, e.g., http://webquest.org/index-create.php) provide an optional technical framework. Results can easily be presented in the form of a digital story.

Another example of successful implementation of gaming technology are the *Operational Language and Culture Training Systems* simulations (http://www.alelo.com/tactical_language.html), which were developed for language and culture training for the U.S. military. The titles, which include the initial Tactical Iraqi and the subsequent Pashto, Dari, French, and Indonesian programs, let the player complete tasks in a realistic 3-dimensional environment. The missions are relevant to the learners, military personnel in this case, and provide achievable, meaningful tasks (Chatham, 2011). The user interacts by moving around in the environment and conversing with non-player characters through speech input. A green "plus" sign appears above a computer character's head if the conversation was favorable, which is a familiar concept also found in the highly successful *Sims* series. The simulation follows an instructional unit and thus allows the learner to showcase and try out what he or she has learned.

Small Games

Small games have seen an immense proliferation in recent years and penetrated various media. They can be free flash games embedded on blogs, aggregation web sites, or social media platforms like Facebook. In the form of mobile apps, they are increasingly available and played anywhere, often in a casual way. Game duration can be short and mechanics deceptively simple. They seem to be mindless and without a narrative. Not all games tell stories (think, e.g., about Minesweeper, or some of the vocabulary games mentioned earlier). But according to Alexander (2011) "[t]hose dual consciousnesses, that character development arc, happen largely off-screen, in the player's body and mind. The most accomplished storytelling effect of casual gaming is therefore invisible" (p. 101).

Small games are an important category for education, however, because of their manageable scope, shallow learning curve, and their accessibility. Fitting into a single lesson, they can create conversation opportunities and prompts. The 20 questions game (http://www.20q.net), derived from a traditionally non-digital game, provides an always present conversation partner and lets users seek an answer individually or collectively. Players imagine a word and the computer tries to figure it out – it's a man versus machine contest that can create a collective in-group identity.

Another small game genre is that of narrative puzzle games. Even though they are often not language-based, they provide a narrative that allows users to retell the story they experienced, to discuss their strategy and progress, or to write up a walkthrough. For example, in the game *Grow Cube* (http://www.eyezmaze.com/grow/cube), players have to activate 10 items in the correct order to create a series of events that generate a small world out of the initially barren cube. In *Quest for the Rest* (http://amanita-design.net/games/the-quest-for-the-rest.html), users click on objects on a screen in order to help a group of protagonists travel through their world. Ryan (2004) reports that a player's performance is the source of satisfaction when playing games, rather than the plot. She continues, however, that when players recount their experiences they do so by telling them as stories (p. 349). Thus, games may simply be the narrative source rather than the narrative itself. They create a shared experience among a group of learners and provide grounds for storytelling. The users have a clearly identified goal, and with careful guidance and scaffolding they must use the target language to complete the tasks together. Such games fit into a single course session or short period of time and create manifold possibilities for meaningful interaction and storytelling.

Adventure Games

Adventure or quest games are one of the oldest computer game genres. Initially they were completely text-based and were part game, part interactive novel. The player typed commands to advance the narrative, for example "go east" or "pick up stick." As games became increasingly graphical, text was replaced and interactive mouse gestures were introduced. Games and game franchises like *Myst*, *The Secret of Monkey Island*, or Sierra's *Quest* Series (e.g., *King's Quest or Space Quest*) created compelling and immersive experiences, and the genre continues to evolve. Aarseth (2004) sees this genre situated in the middle of the narrative debate: "Clearly, games and game engines can *also* be used to tell stories, but this is probably an extreme end of a spectrum that runs between narration and free play, with rule-based games and quest games somewhere in between" (p. 375). The genre, which may include role playing games by some definitions, is a popular choice for educational purposes, as the previously discussed *The Mystery of the Sky Disk* and *Ausflug nach München* show. Van Eck (2006) sees adventure games as narrative-driven open-ended learning environments, "which are likely to be best for promoting hypo-thesis testing and problem solving" (p. 22). But games in this genre can also contain rather linear sequences of events. Alexander (2011) explains that "[o]ne of the earliest notions of game-based storytelling was the 'story on rails,' a narrative that users would play through. Like being on a railroad car, we would see scenery (events, characters) pass by. We could change our vantage point, slow down the car a bit to linger, but could never really alter the train's course" (p. 111).

There are varying degrees of allowed freedom in adventure games. Some do not follow a prescribed path as Alexander (2011) refers to, but instead allow for some components of the game to be of interchangeable order, but with largely the same trajectory. The recently launched educational game *Mission US* (http://www.mission-us.org/) provides two separate scenarios. In the first, *For Crown or Colony?*, the player takes on the role of Nat Wheeler, a printer's apprentice in 1770 Boston. The second mission *Flight to Freedom*, features Lucy, a 14-year-old slave in Kentucky, as the protagonist. The player performs tasks to advance the story and has to make decisions that affect the game's progress. The narratives are interspersed with histo-rical background knowledge and make history more immediately felt. The two missions do not only provide English language learners with authentic language output, but also with cultural knowledge and practice. Similarly, the browser-based game *Das Siegburg-Spiel: Die geheimnisvolle Anno-Truhe* (http://www.tourismus-siegburg.de/web/tourismus/00710) invites the player to solve the mystery surrounding a treasure chest by finding two keys in the German town of Siegburg. By doing so, the gamer learns more about the real city and its heritage and culture. Although the player can roam the city's streets, which are 2-dimensional representations of chosen locales, most steps are to be completed in a fairly sequential order. Nonetheless, since the game was produced for tourists and those interested in visiting the town, it is an authentic experience that language learners can experience as a native speaker would.

But the genre is not a static one, and new developments create a more affective and engaging environment. Two examples shall be mentioned here to illuminate possibilities of future developments, even though they may not be ideally suited for language learning. The first game, called *The Path* (http://tale-of-tales.com/ThePath/index.html), is an independent game, or rather a simulation. The user has no time pressure and is free to roam the game-world. There are no particular challenges to frustrate the player, who can instead experiment with, experience, and enjoy an aesthetic experience. Most activities are completely voluntary and optional. The goal is simple: the player takes on the part of six sisters, who are called to visit their grandmother, one by one. Based on the fairytale *Red Riding Hood*, the player knows that she or he should not leave the path leading to the grand-mother's house. Needless to say, the player is instantly tempted to leave the path and experience what lies beyond. This horror game is more of a journey of introspection and self-reflection than a game in the tradi-tional sense.

Playing various characters is also a characteristic of *Heavy Rain*, a console game for the PlayStation 3, in which the player takes on the role of various characters. The engrossing narrative has tactile qualities through vibration and motion sensing technologies and makes the user become part of the crime story. The player can influence the story, but even mistakes simply lead to a different outcome. Even the death of a character does not end the game, as is usually the case in computer games, but simply shifts the focus to another character. There are numerous plot-lines, and subsequent playings lead to different stories. It is a rather violent game, which affects its usefulness in the classroom, even though most actions are mundane, such as walking through a mall or shaving. It is an immersive and interactive movie, controlled by the player, who is faced with difficult decisions and is emotionally engaged.

Narrative Games

This category is not generally found in genre lists because narrative games are a hybrid form of multimedia narratives and games. One example is *Dear Esther*, which shows that there are no clear-cut lines between DST and games. The player has no tasks to complete or goals to achieve to advance to the next level, which is actually referred to as a chapter. He or she rather roams a remote island in the Hebrides and listens to bits of fragmented narratives, which are triggered when the player reaches certain areas on the island. These subtitled readings are not the same each time the game is played, so the overall narrative and experience differs for each player and each iteration. The experience is quite immersive and seemingly personal. *Dear Esther* is an interactive novel, but one that is experienced rather than purely read. The player can roam the game world as she or he pleases. Language is the clear focus, as the experience would be worthless without listening to the spoken words or looking at the subtitles. If used in a classroom setting, learners could recreate an account of the narrative. Since none of them have all the fragments, they would have to cooperate.

The storytelling game *Sleep is Death* (http://sleepisdeath.net) marks another interesting example of convergence of both gaming and DST. Two human users define a story by playing together. The first person is the player or actor, the other the controller, who sets up and manipulates the game environment and who tells the actor what to do. The actor has three actions available during a limited time frame. It is a storytelling environment with game elements; narrative pleasure is at the heart of the experience. It is driven by the creativity of its players rather than artificial intelligence or programmed algorithms. The game, however, is unsuitable for several reasons: game controls take very long to learn and it is graphically rather simple and looks outdated. But it offers some interesting possibilities for language learning purposes, and with more intuitive controls, simpler rules, and better use of multimedia resources and graphics design, this might be a very interesting and adaptable, game-based, narrative learning platform. *Sleep is Death* is a product in the tradition of MUDs (multiuser dungeon) and MOOs (MUD, object oriented), which were promising language learning gaming tools that have somewhat lost their prominence in recent years. Modern versions of multiuser virtual environments, such as *Second Life*, "create new narrative structures" and "digital storytelling becomes a central form of mediated communication in such worlds" (Erstad & Wertsch, 2008, p. 35).

A very promising development is the convergence of games and the physical world, which has become possible by recent technological inno- vations in consumer products, such as mobile devices with multimedia capabilities, augmented reality features, QR codes, GPS, and digital compass technology. ARIS, a platform for mobile games and interactive stories, provides teachers and learners the opportunity to create and experience a "hybrid world of virtual interactive characters, items, and media placed in physical space" (http://arisgames.org/). It is a storytelling game engine that allows for adapted and self-created content, with which the players engage in the physical world in conjunction with a mobile device. GPS coordinates, text input, or QR codes may trigger certain events, such as videos, audio content, or text. The user can also record content, for example, through the built in camera function. One current and promising project is augmented-reality, situated learning game *Mentira*, which is set in a Spanish-speaking neighborhood in Albuquerque, NM (http://www.mentira.org).

Implementation Hurdles

Traditional games have long been a part, albeit not a large one, in many language learning curricula. But computer games are still not very commonplace within language learning environments, even though they have existed for several decades. The computer has become "a new culture industry" and "one of the major institutions of contemporary visual culture" (Darley, 2000, p. 30). The video game industry produces billions in revenue and video games are a common fact of life in many societies. But this trend has not had a notable impact on formal language learning curricula.

There are technical, financial, and logistical hurdles for educational institutions: the hardware that games require needs maintenance and support. Short development cycles and frequent innovations may render hardware and software less useful after short periods of time, making investments risky. New games may not work on older systems, and newer systems may not play older ones. Games in foreign languages may not be available locally and have to be purchased abroad as not all software is shipped internationally. The heavy upfront investment necessitates thorough research, expertise, and experience.

But there are more fundamental reasons for the reluctance to increase the use of games for language education. For one, "play" is often seen as an opposite to "work" and "study" in modern society (Cook, 2000, p. 186). There is still a prejudice against games as silly and childish, as something of little value and meaning, as only mindless and violent. Part of this may be generational; as more gamers become teachers, professors, and administrators, general acceptance of the medium will grow. We are already witnessing increased approval of games and simulations, as well as "digital game-based learning (DGBL)" (van Eck, 2006).

CONCLUSION

The narratives found in DST and video games offer new possibilities and advantages for language learners and instructors. They are multimodal, immersive, and authentic; they offer significant motivational benefits and allow for agentive, situated, and participatory learning. At first these two new narrative forms seem to be separate concepts, but as the review of some applications has shown, there is indeed an area of convergence that is of particular interest for language learning purposes.

Some examples discussed above, like *The Path* and *Heavy Rain*, show that the adventure genre provides increasingly engaging and immersive experiences. Three-dimensional technologies, tactile feedback, gesture-based commands, and motion-sensing capabilities are just some examples of cutting-edge technologies that will lead to more realistic and natural interactions with the game environment. Games are becoming less artificial and are better at mimicking real life, thus making them seem more authentic and less awkward and artificial. Speech input, which the *Operational Language and Culture Training Systems* described above already provides, is quickly becoming a reality in consumer devices (e.g., Apple's *Siri*). Spoken language input that can be processed on remote servers opens up new possibilities not only for computer games but also those played on mobile devices.

Some applications discussed do not fall into either DST or video games. These examples, such as *Dear Esther*, *Sleep is Death*, *StoryLines*, *StoryWheel*, or the *ARIS* platform, show the related nature of "digital storytelling" and "video game," and may lead us to contemplate a redefinition of these narrative forms. Machinima, DST that utilizes captured videos from computer games along with editing and voice narration, is another good indicator of the creative potential of new narrative technologies.

This confluence of media forms is a widespread phenomenon. Books are no longer static, but they may include text, images, videos, digital narratives, and interactive elements, including games. The concept of the book, or textbook, as discussed at the beginning of the chapter, is changing, and thus the division of new narratives in the digital realm on the one hand and printed ones on the other has already begun to disappear. Traditional, text-based narratives for language learning and teaching probably will not vanish because they are part of our media culture, but they will be complemented by new forms of stories that will lead to more learner-centered and constructivist language teaching and learning.

As we are moving "from a work-centered to a play-centered society," Friedlander (2008) argues, "so do digital narratives become play" (p. 189).

Trends like game-based and game-informing learning and gamification have gained more and more interest in recent years not only in the business world but also in education. Laurillard (2002) asserts that "teaching must not simply impart decontextualized knowledge, but must emulate the success of everyday learning by situating knowledge in real-world activity" (p. 23). Media creation and sharing as well as gaming are familiar domains for today's learners. Thus, if these authentic practices are part of the learner's everyday experiences, it makes sense to utilize their potential for educational purposes. In addition to more traditional narratives, these new and emergent forms can and should be represented in language learning curricula.

REFERENCES

Aarseth, E. (2004). Quest games as post-narrative discourse. In M.-L. Ryan (Ed.), *Narrative across media: The languages of storytelling* (pp. 361–375). Lincoln, NE: University of Nebraska Press.

Alexander, B. (2011). *The new digital storytelling: Creating narratives with new media*. Santa Barbara, CA: Praeger.

Begg, M., Dewhurst, D., & Macleod, H. (2005). Game-informed learning: Applying computer game processes to higher education. *Innovate: Journal of Online Education, 1*(6). Retrieved from http://www.innovateonline.info/pdf/vol1_issue6/Game-Informed_Learning-__Applying_Computer_Game_Processes_to_Higher_Education.pdf

Bogost, I. (2011). *How to do things with videogames*. Minneapolis, MN: University of Minnesota Press.

Center for Digital Storytelling. (n.d.). Retrieved February 20, 2012, from http://www.story center.org/

Chatham, R. E. (2011). After the revolution: Game-informed training in the U.S. military. In S. Tobias & J. D. Fletcher (Eds.), *Computer games and instruction* (pp. 73–99). Charlotte, NC: Information Age Publishing.

Cook, G. (2000). *Language play, language learning*. New York, NY: Oxford University Press.

Couldry, N. (2008). Digital storytelling, media research and democracy: Conceptual choices and alternative futures. In K. Lundby (Ed.), *Digital storytelling, mediatized stories: Self-representations in new media* (pp. 41–60). New York, NY: Peter Lang.

Crawford, C. (2005). *Chris Crawford on interactive storytelling*. Berkeley, CA: New Riders Games.

Csikszentmihalyi, M. (1990). *Flow: The psychology of optimal experience*. New York, NY: Harper & Row.

Darley, A. (2000). *Visual digital culture: Surface play and spectacle in new media genres*. New York, NY: Routledge.

deHaan, J., Reed, M. W., & Kuwada, K. (2010). The effect of interactivity with a music video game on second language vocabulary recall. *Language Learning & Technology, 14*(2), 74–94.

DeMarle, M. (2007). Nonlinear game narrative. In C. M. Bateman (Ed.), *Game writing: narrative skills for videogames* (1st ed., pp. 71–84). Boston, MA: Charles River Media.

Dörnyei, Z. (2005). *The psychology of the language learner: Individual differences in second language acquisition.* Mahwah, NJ: Lawrence Erlbaum Associates.

Dörnyei, Z., & Ushioda, E. (2010). *Teaching and researching: Motivation* (2nd ed.). Harlow, UK: Longman/Pearson.

Drotner, K. (2008). Boundaries and bridges: Digital storytelling in education studies and media studies. In K. Lundby (Ed.), *Digital storytelling, mediatized stories: Self-representations in new media* (pp. 61–81). New York, NY: Peter Lang.

Egbert, J. (2003). A study of flow theory in the foreign language classroom. *Modern Language Journal, 87*(4), 499–518.

Ensslin, A. (2011). *The language of gaming.* Basingstoke, UK: Palgrave Macmillan.

Erstad, O., & Wertsch, J. V. (2008). Tales of mediation: Narrative and digital media as cultural tools. In K. Lundby (Ed.), *Digital storytelling, mediatized stories: Self-representations in new media* (pp. 21–39). New York, NY: Peter Lang.

Friedlander, L. (2008). Narrative strategies in a digital age: Authorship and authority. In K. Lundby (Ed.), *Digital storytelling, mediatized stories: Self-representations in new media* (pp. 177–194). New York, NY: Peter Lang.

Gee, J. (2003). *What video games have to teach us about learning and literacy.* New York, NY: Palgrave Macmillan.

Gee, J. P. (2004). *Situated language and learning: A critique of traditional schooling.* New York, NY: Routledge.

Gee, J. P. (2011). Reflections on empirical evidence on games and learning. In S. Tobias & J. D. Fletcher (Eds.), *Computer games and instruction* (pp. 223–232). Charlotte, NC: Information Age Publishing.

Hull, G. A., & Katz, M.-L. (2006). Crafting an agentive self: Case studies of digital storytelling. *Research in the Teaching of English, 41*(1), 43–81.

Hull, G. A., & Nelson, M. E. (2005). Locating the semiotic power of multimodality. *Written Communication, 22*(2), 224–261.

Jenkins, H. (2004). Game design as narrative architecture. In N. Wardrip-Fruin & P. Harrigan (Eds.), *First person: New media as story, performance, and game* (pp. 118–130). Cambridge: MIT Press.

Juul, J. (2005). Games telling stories? In J. Raessens & J. Goldstein (Eds.), *Handbook of computer game studies* (pp. 220–245). Cambridge: MIT Press.

Krashen, S. (1989). Language teaching technology: A low-tech view. In J. E. Alatis (Ed.), *Georgetown University round table on languages and linguistics* (pp. 393–407). Washington, DC: Georgetown University Press.

Krawczyk, M. (2006). *Game development essentials: Game story and character development.* Clifton Park, NY: Thompson Delmar Learning.

Kress, G. R. (2003). *Literacy in the new media age.* London: Routledge.

Kronenberg, F. A. (Ed.). (2011). *Language center design.* Moorhead, MN: International Association for Language Learning and Technology.

Laurillard, D. (2002). *Rethinking university teaching: A conversational framework for the effective use of learning technologies* (2nd ed.). New York, NY: RoutledgeFalmer.

MacIntyre, P. D. (2002). Motivation, anxiety, and emotion in second language acquisition. In P. Robinson (Ed.), *Individual differences and instructed language learning* (pp. 45–68). Philadelphia, PA: J. Benjamins Publishing.

Mateas, M., & Stern, A. (2006). Interaction and narrative. In K. Salen & E. Zimmerman (Eds.), *The game design reader: A rules of play anthology* (pp. 642–669). Cambridge: MIT Press.

McDaniel, R., Fiore, S. M., & Nicholson, D. (2010). Serious storytelling: Narrative considerations for serious games researchers and developers. In D. Kaufman & L. Sauvé (Eds.), *Educational gameplay and simulation environments: Case studies and lessons learned* (pp. 13–30). Hershey, PA: Information Science Reference.

Meyer, B., & Sørensen, B. H. (2009). Designing serious games for computer assisted language learning – A framework for development and analysis. In M. Kankaanranta & P. Neittaanmäki (Eds.), *Design and use of serious games* (Vol. 37, pp. 69–82). Dordrecht: Springer Netherlands.

Murray, J. (1997). *Hamlet on the holodeck: The future of narrative in cyberspace*. New York, NY: Free Press.

Nelson, M. E. (2006). Mode, meaning, and synaesthesia in multimedia L2 writing. *Language Learning & Technology*, *10*(2), 56–76.

Neville, D. O., Shelton, B. E., & McInnis, B. (2009). Cybertext redux: Using digital game-based learning to teach L2 vocabulary, reading, and culture. *Computer Assisted Language Learning*, *22*(5), 409–424.

Nyboe, L., & Drotner, K. (2008). Identity, aesthetics, and digital narration. In K. Lundby (Ed.), *Digital storytelling, mediatized stories: Self-representations in new media* (pp. 161–176). New York, NY: Peter Lang.

Peterson, M. (2010). Computerized games and simulations in computer-assisted language learning: A meta-analysis of research. *Simulation Gaming*, *41*, 72–93.

Rankin, Y. A., & Shute, M. W. (2010). Re-purposing a recreational video game as a serious game for second language acquisition. In D. Kaufman & L. Sauvé (Eds.), *Educational gameplay and simulation environments: Case studies and lessons learned* (pp. 178–194). Hershey, PA: Information Science Reference.

Ryan, M.-L. (2004). Will new media produce new narratives? In M.-L. Ryan (Ed.), *Narrative across media: The languages of storytelling* (pp. 337–359). Lincoln, NE: University of Nebraska Press.

Tews, R. R. (2002). Archetypes on acid. In M. J. P. Wolf (Ed.), *The medium of the video game* (1st ed., pp. 169–182). Austin, TX: University of Texas Press.

Toolan, M. J. (2001). *Narrative: A critical linguistic introduction* (2nd ed.). New York, NY: Routledge.

Tschirner, E. P., Nikolai, B., & Terrell, T. D. (2012). *Kontakte: A communicative approach* (7th ed.). Boston, MA: McGraw-Hill Higher Education.

Van Eck, R. (2006). Digital game-based learning: It's not just the digital natives who are restless. *EDUCAUSE Review*, *41*(2), 16–30.

Wolf, M. J. P. (2002a). Narrative in the video game. In M. J. P. Wolf (Ed.), *The medium of the video game* (1st ed., pp. 93–111). Austin, TX: University of Texas Press.

Wolf, M. J. P. (2002b). The video game as a medium. In M. J. P. Wolf (Ed.), *The medium of the video game* (1st ed., pp. 13–33). Austin, TX: University of Texas Press.

Wolff, D. (2011). Individual learner differences and instructed language learning: An insoluble conflict? In J. Arabski & A. Wojtaszek (Eds.), *Individual learner differences in SLA* (pp. 3–16). Bristol: Multilingual Matters.

PROMOTING ENGAGEMENT THROUGH A STUDENT-BUILT DIGITAL ATLAS OF MAORI STUDIES

O. Ripeka Mercier, Sarsha-Leigh Douglas,
Bruce McFadgen, Meegan Hall, Peter Adds,
Maria Bargh and Tahu Wilson

ABSTRACT

We describe an educational intervention pioneered by Te Kawa a Māui (TKaM), the School of Māori Studies at Victoria University of Wellington (VUW), which was designed to improve the attraction and retention of (particularly) Māori students, by involving them in a school-wide research publication – in this case a digital cultural atlas of Māori Studies. We present and describe the work of 250 students from 10 different Māori Studies courses, who have trialled and submitted map-based assessment for the Te Kawa a Māui Atlas (TeKaMA). We argue that the quality and variety of student work is itself an indication of engagement. We then discuss how digital aspects of the work facilitated engagement, using data from course and assignment evaluations, interviews, informal

Increasing Student Engagement and Retention using Multimedia Technologies:
Video Annotation, Multimedia Applications, Videoconferencing and Transmedia Storytelling
Cutting-edge Technologies in Higher Education, Volume 6F, 121–158
ISSN: 2044-9968/doi:10.1108/S2044-9968(2013)000006F008

feedback and an online survey. In line with other findings in the literature, digital aspects of our project had to be carefully managed and balanced, so that they did not disengage students from learning. However, our TeKaMA exercises provided multiple ways by which students could engage, with cultural mapping engaging all students, not just Māori. Our chapter discusses how this was facilitated by digital technology.

INTRODUCTION

Māori are the Indigenous people of Aotearoa/New Zealand and, as with many other Indigenous peoples and marginalised minorities (Sonna, Bishop, & Humphries, 2000), Western education systems do not provide for widespread Māori academic success. Māori student underachievement is apparent at all levels of education, becoming particularly stark at secondary and tertiary levels:

> School data indicate a significant number of Māori boys leave school with no or very few level 1 NCEA credits [the minimum secondary school qualification]. This also shows up in 2006 census data in terms of those recording no formal qualifications. In the group aged 25–34, a group where a large proportion of people have completed tertiary education, one-third of Māori men and one-quarter of Māori women record having no formal qualifications. (Callister, 2009, p. 3)

Several commentators have offered reasons for Māori underachievement (Bishop & Glynn, 1999; Pihama, Cram, & Walker, 2002; Smith, 2000) with the strongest argument concerning the lasting impact of assimilation and integration policies from 1840 to the 1960s, which marginalised Māori language, knowledge, and culture in favour of English language and curriculum, and had severe impacts upon the ways that Māori view education. The same commentators have also voiced and practiced different strategies for change.

Māori-led activism in the 1970s and 1980s towards Māori-centred and Māori-led schools has given rise to Māori language immersion *kōhanga reo* (pre-schools), *kura kaupapa* (primary schools), *whare kura* (secondary schools), and *wānanga* (tertiary education institutions). These educational institutions present a crucial alternative to mainstream schools, which still bear evidence of colonial practices and fall short of Indigenous aspirations. Even so, the availability of Māori-medium education from pre-school to tertiary level appears not to have diminished Māori peoples' desire to access mainstream tertiary education. For one thing, universities are increasingly marketing themselves as Māori-friendly spaces. All eight of Aotearoa/New Zealand's mainstream universities have Māori-themed spaces such as *wharenui* (traditional meeting houses) and Māori academic and general staff who are well-respected and high-profile individuals, providing accredited programmes with strong community networks. In addition, formal mentoring programmes fulfil a need from Māori and Pasifika students for additional support in mainstream tertiary education (van der Meer, 2011). The flow of Māori students into university means that improving the Māori learning experience in universities remains a critical area of development, and as statistics predict that 28% of children will identify as Māori in the year 2021, it is essential that education meet the needs of the next generation's demographic.

Just under 2000 Māori students enrolled at Victoria University of Wellington (VUW) in each of the years 2009, 2010, and 2011, hovering around 8% of the total enrolment for each of those years, with a slight increase each year (Victoria University of Wellington, 2012). While this is lower than the Māori population in Aotearoa/New Zealand (16%) and in Wellington (12%), it is one of the highest enrolment figures the university has ever enjoyed, and the trend needs to continue if enrolment is to keep pace with the projected increase of young Māori (Statistics New Zealand, 2012).

The key statistic for education is not enrolment, however, but completion, so graduation rates of Māori are of most concern here and, unfortunately, only 57% of Māori graduated from VUW in 2011 (Victoria University of Wellington, 2012). Te Kawa a Māui (TKaM), the School of Māori Studies, attracts about 400 Māori students per year, which means that our department of six permanent full-time staff and five contract teaching staff taught about 20% of the Māori students enrolled at the university. TKaM is thus a good place to trial a teaching and learning intervention designed to enhance retention.

The academic staff at TKaM have backgrounds in a diverse range of disciplines. In 2009, one of this chapter's co-authors instigated a discussion with the academic staff about establishing a school-wide research project that could involve a range of students, as a means to engage them in 'real' research early in their academic careers. She was mindful of Kuh's (2008) research that had identified a number of high-impact strategies to encourage student learning, one of which was to involve students in research from the undergraduate level. This connects with the finding that Māori students who complete their first year at university, are much more likely to persist to completion (Radloff, 2011). The academic staff sought to find a thematic convergence for research collaboration, and settled on a focus around a particular geographical area, rather than a theme, to populate with anthropological, archaeological, political, scientific, linguistic and performing arts-based research – thus a place-based research project drawing upon all of the staff's disciplinary areas.

This idea converged with a cultural mapping proposal the lead author had developed between 2006 and 2008 with University of Alaska Fairbanks faculty, which sought to involve secondary school students in mapping *wānanga* (camps), following the example of work in Alaska Native communities. Place-based education (PBE) is a successful approach being taken up by Alaskan schools, with studies suggesting that Indigenous students particularly thrive in culturally relevant or place-based scholastic settings (Barnhardt, 2007; Brayboy & Castagno, 2009; Penetito, 2006). PBE emphasises land-based, local and community knowledge, increasing the relevance of curriculum to Indigenous students. In the work of the MapTEACH programme (2005) in Alaska, for instance, students used Geographic Information Systems (GIS) to map and record place-based narratives from elders, making active connections across time and space in a dynamic, colourful and visual medium. The Alaska Native Knowledge Network is a repository of many other cultural atlases. One that particularly challenges cultural assumptions about representation in maps is Athabaskan elder Howard Luke's non-linear map of hunting and trapping regions in the area around Fairbanks (1998). A similar approach in Aotearoa/New Zealand would combine the proven benefits of active learning (Bishop, Berryman, Cavanagh, & Teddy, 2007) with PBE.

The TeKaMA project as a way to promote student engagement grew from this confluence of ideas. It was designed to take advantage of technological advances in mapping, introduce empirical research skills with digital technologies, connect students to place through research on local names and histories and ultimately, to enhance the Māori tertiary student experience. This chapter focuses on the ways in which digital technology impacts on student achievement of these goals. First, we describe map-based student coursework, then we analyse data collected about student learning and engagement, and finally describe how the digital aspects of the TeKaMA facilitated student engagement.

THE TE KAWA A MĀUI ATLAS

This section describes the current form and content of the Te Kawa a Māui Atlas (TeKaMA) with reference to work submitted in three specific courses, chosen because they exemplify individual and group assignments on primary or secondary research sources.

Form of the Te Kawa a Māui Atlas

The TeKaMA is the body of student work submitted through assignments in various TKaM courses. Work is only kept and incorporated where consent has been given. The database includes Google Earth assignment 'kmz' files, a small amount of GIS work, and electronic versions and/or pdf scans of assignments submitted in Word or PowerPoint. In addition, some students have submitted non-digital work, such as posters and a three-dimensional map. Thus, TeKaMA's shape is currently somewhat amorphous. Contributors of individual projects are considered co-authors of the project, and when student projects are presented online, in seminars, or in other research contexts, the author's name is attached. Contributors to group projects are acknowledged by name in separate listings.

Content – Te Kawa a Māui Courses

Students have participated in a range of map activities across 10 courses, as summarised in Table 1.

Projects can be classified as individual or group based, using research with primary or secondary sources. To give the reader a sense of the map work students do we describe and discuss work from three of the courses. Descriptions of other courses can be found in Appendix A.

Individual Research with Primary or Secondary Sources

MAOR317: Science and Indigenous Knowledge examines recent initiatives to bridge the philosophical gap between Western science and Indigenous knowledge, and explores how these knowledge systems work alongside each other. The final assignment is a Local Knowledge Project that requires students to build a database of local, personal or community knowledge using their choice of medium (see Mercier, 2011). In 2009, student Tahu Wilson geo-referenced a 1917 map of Te Whanganui a Tara (Wellington Harbour) to Google Earth, and then superimposed a record of old Māori placenames and pā (fortified settlements) sites from ethnographer Elsdon Best's work *The Land of Tara* (1917) on to the contemporary landscape (see Fig. 1). In 2011, several MAOR317 students chose Google Earth to record local knowledge. For instance, student Aneika's primary research archived

Table 1. Description of Ten TKaM Courses[a].

Course Code	Course Title	Map Years	# Students	Assignment Description	Output	Research Type	% of Grade
MAOR317	Science and IK	2009–2011	15	Individual local knowledge research project	Google Earth and GIS maps	Individual secondary and primary research	20
MAOR123	Maori Society and Culture	2010	90	Mapping biographical information of famous Māori	Google Earth map	Individual collated secondary research	5
MAOR316	Maori Politics	2010–2012	40	Mapping land protest occupations	Google Earth map	Group collated secondary research	5
MAOR122	Peopling of Polynesia	2010–2012	70	Description of assigned archaeological sites	Essay	Individual secondary research	10
MAOR112	Elementary Maori II	2011	40	Maori language critique of place-naming and mapping	Essay	Individual secondary research	10
MAOR210	Cultural Mapping	2011–2012	20	Archaeological site survey Individual research project	Reports Google Earth and GIS maps	Individual and group secondary and primary research	100

MAOR124	Maori Science	2011–2012	40	Locating and mapping a heritage tree species	Google Earth map	Individual and group collated primary research	15
MAOR489	Research Essay	2010	1	Mapping places of historical relevance to greenstone trade	Google Earth map	Individual secondary research	0
MAOR111	Elementary Maori I	2010	50	Learning Maori language place names	N/A	N/A	0
MAOR216	Treaty of Waitangi	2011–2012	60	History of a student-chosen confiscated land block	Google Earth map and essay	Individual secondary research	15

[a]Ten TKaM courses have incorporated map-based assessment since 2009, each demanding a different type of research and different output. For each course, the table describes the assessment, in which years it was set, average number of students enrolled, and value of the assessment by percentage of course grade.

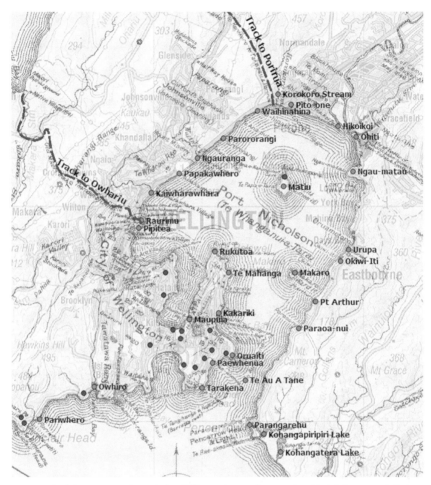

Fig. 1. MAOR317 Student Tahu Wilson Geo-referenced a 1917 Map to a Modern Topographical Map (*Source*: NZTM Topo250-16, Land Information New Zeland, Crown Copyright Reserved.), Thereby Linking Old Placenames to Contemporary Regions, An Example of Individual Research with Secondary Sources. The Map Here is a Modified Version of Tahu's Work, Produced by Bruce McFadgen.

photographs and narratives regarding food gathering areas in her *papakāinga* (traditional homeland) in Google Earth – recording previously undocumented knowledge that had hitherto been kept active through practice and intergenerational transmission.

Collated Individual Research with Secondary Sources

MAOR316: Tōrangapū Māori/Māori Politics examines a range of Māori political structures, movements, ideologies and visions. The 'Years of Occupation' tutorial assignment saw groups of students asked to locate and research Māori land protest occupations in a given year. Students described Crown actions in assuming ownership, confiscating or selling land, and discussed the motivations of local Māori to occupy their ancestral lands in protest. A research assistant collated their findings using Google Earth, superimposed a tribal boundaries map and showed it back to the class (Fig. 2). The juxtaposition of the contemporary and traditional maps highlights the on-going physical connection of Māori with the land, visually highlighting the temporal context for the occupations. The media, which portrayed the occupying locals as disruptive, radical and disturbers of peace (Morrah, 2010), ignored the longer historical context, favouring what Abel describes as a disequilibrating story that can be quickly resolved (2010). In the case of the 2010 Taipa Bay occupation, the story resolution time for media consumers was the summer it took for occupiers to be removed, and beach access for holidaymakers restored. For locals, their grievances related

Fig. 2. Sites of Land Protest Occupations; the Collated Work of 10 MAOR316 Students' Research into Secondary Sources.

to historic alienation of land are less quickly resolved, and they suffer the backlash of being vilified as 'haters and wreckers' (Harris, 2004) in the process.

Group and Individual Research Using Primary Observations
MAOR210 Cultural Mapping was introduced in 2011 to teach students to read and navigate with maps, think critically about map-based representation, gain technical skills in GPS, Google Earth and GIS, and explore and create cultural maps of their own. It explored cultural landscapes produced from various perspectives: Māori, Indigenous, Western, modern, historic, Cartesian and 'artographic'. All assessments were map based, with one major assignment requiring group work. Students were asked to update the archaeological data for pre-European Māori settlements at Te Ika a Maru Bay, a remote site near Wellington, from field observations. Discrete tasks in workshops prepared students for this assignment, such as locating existing archaeological sites using archsite coordinates. The locations of the sites were updated by archaeologist Bruce McFadgen (the assignment's architect) and students as necessary, and reports were written to both the New Zealand Archaeological Association and the land owner at Te Ika a Maru Bay; the former to update their archaeological database and the latter to suggest land management strategies that would preserve the heritage sites on the land. A second, creative/critical, assessment required students to map a topic of their choosing. The parameters were broad, and while guidelines encouraged students to draw on knowledge and skills gained during the course, students' own interpretation of what a 'cultural map' could be was encouraged. As a result, some students chose to draw upon primary sources such as local history, *waiata* (Māori songs), *whakapapa* (genealogy and relationships), autobiography, community events and walking tracks with an example found in Fig. 6. One student even built a three-dimensional wireframe 'map' to represent the levels of decision-making inherent in choosing his assignment topic.

Digital Mapping with Google Earth
There were several reasons for choosing Google Earth for our mapping projects, in spite of its copyright landscape images and mapping limitations. Google Earth is free, and our university's Information Technology staff were easily able to download and install it in all computers in two nearby student computer suites. We note that some GIS software is also free, and MAOR210 made use of QuantumGIS – again, downloaded and installed by

Information Technology staff. Google Earth, however, is user friendly, and students generally required no more than a two-hour tutorial to get conversant with the key functionality. We aim for our students to become familiar enough with mapping technologies to appreciate its challenges, limitations and possibilities in representing Māori knowledge, society, culture and history.

Other Digital Aspects and Dissemination of TeKaMA
Students engaged with other digital technologies, such as GPS devices, digital images and iPads, and original undergraduate student contributions drive us towards publishing and disseminating the best of the student work online. Appendix B discusses these aspects.

DATA COLLECTION

Our findings emerge from multiple data sources and collection methods used since 2010, in what can be described as reflective practitioner project analysis. We have data that could be collectively considered *in-class feedback* (discussed in Appendix C) or evaluations of engagement and learning connected to specific assignments and courses. This takes the form of participant observation and informal feedback, the evidence of the student work itself, course evaluations by students and student evaluations of specific assignments. This data has been collected from four Māori Studies courses over the last three years and submitted work in two of those classes. Students gave explicit consent, in retrospect via email, or in advance on assignment coversheets, for their work to contribute to the Atlas. We also solicited *overall feedback* for the Atlas project through an online survey and commentary interviews, both performed in early 2012. The VUW Human Ethics Committee gave approval (#19056) for our interviews, and for the online qualtrics survey. We discuss the *overall feedback* here.

Qualitative Analysis: Commentary Interviews

An interview schedule was designed to collect qualitative data from staff-selected students who completed map-based assessment to a high standard in TKaM courses. Questions were designed and structured to aid comparisons with the Australasian University Survey of Student Engagement (AUSSE) findings (Australian Council for Educational Research, 2010), and to assess broader student engagement patterns with those found within our own research. Interviews were semi-structured, participant-centred and project-centred, giving interviewees the latitude to describe their projects. Thus, student participants effectively gave commentary on their project(s) while a student research assistant asked a series of questions. This assistant had contributed several projects to the atlas, and her duality as researcher/ interviewer and student participant required careful consideration. Her insider perspective enhanced her ability to empathise with other students' comments regarding the TeKaMA, adding another layer of understanding to that provided by staff involved. Her knowledge of project details, for instance, the specific language, utility, scope and pitfalls of Google Earth, was a compelling reason to have her undertake and transcribe the interviews. As a peer to the participants, she set an informal and open tone during the interviews. This relationship facilitated a candidness unlikely to be present in interviews conducted by a lecturer, senior figure or designer of the TeKaMA-based activity. In this way she operated as a commissioned insider researcher, outweighing any concerns about academic integrity. In addition, she received regular supervision and mentoring, advice on survey design and interview technique, supervision on aggregating data for field reports, and feedback on written work from her co-authors.

Student interviewees were given refreshments and a $25 book voucher for their time (although they did not know this in advance). The student researcher emailed eight students, inviting them to participate, and then conducted two commentary interviews during January and February 2012. The low response rate may have been because the time of year coincided with Aotearoa/New Zealand's summer break. As a student contributor, the researcher also provided data by writing down a commentary 'interview' of her thoughts on the cultural atlas. This was later analysed with the other two interviews by the first author. Due to the low number of interviews, comments should be read as biased in favour of the project, as the three respondents all represent an invested, engaged subgroup of those students involved.

Quantitative Analysis: Online Survey

A link to an online qualtrics survey with 35 questions was emailed to 1,116 students who had enrolled in a TKaM course during 2009–2011. The survey was open to participants between 9 February and 9 March 2012. As an incentive, $50 grocery vouchers were offered to each of five respondents picked at random. We also gave three consolation prizes of $25 book vouchers. Our response rate was 9.9%. The qualtrics survey was designed to quantitatively assess what students considered by 'being engaged' in learning, to compare student engagement in the topic, spatial/map-based and technological aspects of assignments, and asked students to rate and compare their learning and engagement in projects they MOST engaged with (both mapping and non-mapping) to ones they LEAST engaged with. Forty-eight per cent of the 110 initial respondents stated that they were 'aware of the TeKaMA', and 40 of that 53 had personally completed map-based assessment. About 30 of those participants persisted to answer most questions, hence the fluctuation in the number of respondents included in the findings.

FINDINGS

Overall, students appear to have engaged in the TeKaMa project in multiple ways: assignments gave flexibility in topic and medium; students could see their work contributing to something beyond the assignment; it connected to their local communities; it embraced diverse learning methods – such as field work, group activity, research presentations; and students were able to engage in new learning through digital media not generally seen in Cultural Studies. In what follows, we consider specifically what the digital allows, and how the digital may contribute (or not) to these forms of learning and engagement.

What the Digital Allows

The digital facilitated many goals in our project, each of which will now be discussed.

Publication
Publication and dissemination was an early aim of the TeKaMA, constituting a research output for staff and students. To mediate access to work that students do not want made widely available, we envisaged multiple levels of access (Harmsworth, 1998): a deep level that managers of the site (i.e. we) would have access to; an insider level that students enrolled in our programme would see; and a public level. Our current TeKaMA

website limits access to data by showing still images of student work. A Google search of the search string 'Māori atlas' (without quotation marks) brings up the link to our site (http://www.victoria.ac.nz/maori/atlas) as its top hit, despite the term 'Māori atlas' not appearing anywhere on our website. While the TeKaMA is not regarded as an academic publication, it clearly has a public profile.

Sharing

Being able to share projects with the wider community is an advantage of the digital, and enhances student engagement through allowing friends, peers and *whānau* (family) to see student work. MAOR210 student Michael suggests that student engagement is heightened, 'if it ties into something beyond the assignment'. Completing a piece of work that contributes beyond passing a course ignites a context-based learning that other work may not achieve, especially when the digital speaks more loudly and widely than traditional forms of academic literature. The multi-media – visual and text-based – nature of maps broadens its appeal, and the digital is crucial in enabling this. Some points can be made more immediate, concise and accessible on a map rather than an essay, drawing in non-academic members of the community. Speaking of her PowerPoint-based work in MAOR317, which she shared with her mother and 'a few other people', Aneika comments:

> Yeah, I've showed my family. And they were pretty stoked about it. Mum was like 'woooo' because it means something to them too, so they could immediately relate to it. And for me it's a document that I'd keep for my family because it's so personal … I was pretty chuffed about it, so I was like 'check this out'. It's an easy way to actually show people.

The involvement of students' *whānau* (families) in their projects is a potential indicator of success – studies assert the positive effect on student engagement of family investment in (Māori) education (Bishop et al., 2007; Chinlund & Hall, 2010). We had to take care of Aneika's project, as the personal nature of the topic meant it was not appropriate for her work to be added to the TeKaMA. As this was submitted digitally, it meant erasing the file she emailed as well as any duplicates on TeKaMA hard drive and backup drives.

Our website aims, ultimately, to provide students with a showpiece for their communities, and we hope it promotes the sense of contributing to something bigger, something public and something 'real'.

Peer-to-Peer Feedback
Students have had access, through iPads and Blackboard, to interactive kmz files of the TeKaMA. Through this they have been able to see the different work going on across courses, and as one student in our online survey commented, 'I really enjoy that the project links together work from across the School, different students, levels, staff, papers, topics, etc.' Students can also quickly see and evaluate their work in the context of their peers – the digital thus enabling a review of one's own work at a formative, rather than summative, stage of the assessment. In the case of the MAOR124 *karaka* assignment (see Appendix A), the iPad feedback exercise was done at stage two of the three-part assessment, and gave students ideas about the colour choice and size of placemarks and labels, as well as giving an insight into the volume, style and content in other students' writing. The iPad and Blackboard sharing of kmz files has thus presented, crucially, a *peer feedback* rather than lecturer feedback step in producing the final assignment.

MAOR210 also used this peer feedback loop by having students present their final mapping project proposals to the class in a short oral presentation. Most students came prepared with some digital work already completed to show the class, along with their description of their project. Exchanges between students included sharing advice on digital aspects of some projects.

Collaboration and Comparison
Another aim of our project was to foster a sense of collaboration and shared ownership through group work (such as in the MAOR210 archaeological field trip), individual research on a class-wide project (such as the MAOR316 protest occupation map), individual research shared (such as in MAOR210 project proposal presentations) and the incorporation of work into a single database. This is guided by specific findings that state Māori engagement is enhanced through good relationships with other students and teachers (Bishop et al., 2007; van der Meer, 2011). The digital both facilitates and complicates this goal. Amalgamation of individual work on a class-wide project was managed by creating a standardised digital output only *after* all the student research was submitted. Direct overlaid comparisons of Google Earth work from individuals met with standardisation challenges – such as irregular use of placemark and label size, students inadvertently including other non-relevant placemarks, leading to large file sizes and cluttered outputs. This will be an on-going challenge, as we seek to encourage student creativity and freedom, while still aiming for standardisable outputs that can be collated and then disseminated easily.

ENGAGEMENT IN THE DIGITAL

Researchers have argued that it is not the mapping and digital technologies themselves that engage Indigenous students, but the way in which technological tools are incorporated and deployed within a course curriculum (Gearheard, Aporta, Aipellee, & O'Keefe, 2011; Sadik, 2008; Wallace, 2008). This is illustrated in our project by the varying degrees of student engagement, with student feedback revealing that some TKaM courses are currently more successful at this than others. Though aspects of the technology contributed to student learning, technology was rarely the driving factor. Because a variety of technologies were used throughout cultural mapping assessments, it is difficult to distinguish which technologies aided student engagement the most. Feedback suggests that though students were excited to use new forms of various technologies, this did not automatically equate with engagement or success. This is illustrated vividly in the evaluation of the MAOR124 *karaka* mapping project, which measured how 10 given aspects of the assignment contributed to student learning and engagement. Twenty-two students responded, ranking each aspect using a Likert scale, with 1 corresponding to 'very beneficial' and 5 corresponding to 'not at all beneficial'. Plotted in the graph in Fig. 3 is the average Likert scale rating for each aspect. With a score of 1.5, the most beneficial aspect to student engagement was learning to recognise *karaka* – good news, as this was an important aim of the assignment. However, the

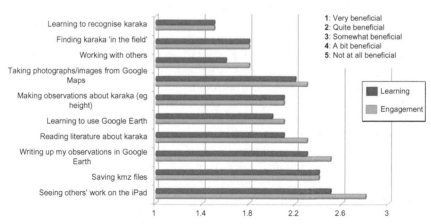

Fig. 3. Twenty-two MAOR124 Students Evaluated the Karaka Assignment, Rating How Beneficial Aspects of the Task were to Learning and to Engagement.

least beneficial to engagement were technical applications such as Google Earth (2.5) and work on the iPad (2.8). That seeing others' work on the iPad ranked as least important, to both learning (2.5) AND engagement, was a surprise. Students visibly enjoyed the activity (some more than others), but they clearly did not see the link between technology and their engagement or learning. As we asserted in the *Formative Feedback* section, to enable peer review is one advantage of using iPads, but students did not consider this as valuable to their learning as other aspects of the assignment. The most beneficial activity for learning, interestingly, was working with others (1.6), and as about 80% of the class were Māori, this corroborates evidence cited by Bishop et al. (2007) and van der Meer (2011). Not all of the class worked with someone else (though there was some sharing of information in the iPad tutorial) but their discussions about the *karaka* and other trees they had found were beneficial for this particular exercise. This section will look at what else our data says about how the digital facilitated student engagement.

Meaningful Integration

Students clearly like cutting-edge technologies (e.g. iPads), as evidenced by the enthusiasm with which some students used them in tutorials, but they have to be meaningfully integrated into an assignment, and make a transparent contribution to course learning objectives. The field trip to Te Ika a Maru Bay by MAOR210 suggests that place-based learning can engage students, but that a clear set of objectives and meaningful integration of GPS, GIS and Google Earth were just as valuable. Student feedback was solicited on what aspects of the MAOR210 course most stimulated/helped them to learn (see Fig. 4), with 9 of 13 students citing the field trip. Technology was also popular, with 5 students of the 13 surveyed citing it as a factor in stimulating or helping them to learn.

The ability to visit archaeological sites not just as passive observers, but to comment upon sites and contribute observations to an established body of work, gave students a sense of achievement and realisation that, even at the undergraduate level, their research can be published. As well as writing reports to the landowner and the New Zealand Archaeological Association (NZAA), each student produced their own unique geo-journal of the field trip. Students selected four photographs their group had taken in the field, used them as a placemark icon in Google Earth and commented on the significance of each photograph in the dialogue box (see, for example,

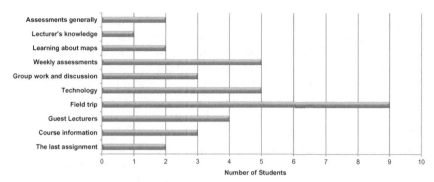

Fig. 4. Thirteen MAOR210 Students Commented on What Most Stimulated/ Helped Them to Learn in the Class. The Field Trip was Most Popular, with Technology and Weekly Assessments Coming as a Second Equal.

Fig. 5. A Screen Capture from Ataria Sharman's Google Earth Geo-journal for the MAOR210 Field Trip.

student Ataria Sharman's in Fig. 5). Geo-journals and geo-biographies can digitally embed a person in the landscape. In the case of MAOR210 geo-journals, they provided an opportunity for students to capture their experience of being, and learning, in and from the landscape.

Technology, Mapping and Topic

Our online survey asked students to nominate a mapping project in which they were MOST engaged. They were asked to rank their response on a Likert scale from 1 (strongly agree) to 5 (strongly disagree) to the question 'I was interested in the *kaupapa* (purpose, method, structure) of the project.' Twenty-six of 30 agreed or strongly agreed, for an average of 1.63. They were then asked the question 'I enjoyed the ... component of the project' and were given two options. Nineteen of 29 agreed or strongly agreed that they enjoyed the *spatial mapping* component of the project, for an overall average of 2.07. By contrast fifteen of 28 agreed or strongly agreed that they enjoyed the *technical aspects* of the project, for an overall average of 2.32. The data suggests that students most enjoyed the kaupapa or topic, then mapping aspects and least enjoyed the technical aspects. We make the comparison with care, noting that the students were generally favourably disposed to all aspects of the project in which they MOST engaged (Table 2).

As a comparison we asked students to consider the same questions for a mapping project with which they LEAST engaged. Only five students volunteered responses to this. This is possibly because no fewer than five respondents and possibly not many more than five did two or more mapping projects. Twenty respondents did 1-2, but we are unable to distinguish how many of the 20 did more than one project. On the other hand, the low response rate could have been due to students not equating LEAST engaged with one of their mapping projects. When compared with data on the project in which students most engaged, we found that students rated being interested in the *kaupapa* at 1.4 (a higher score than the 1.63 for the project students MOST engaged in), but 'enjoyed the mapping aspects' at 2.4, and

Table 2. Summary of Responses from an Online Survey of Student Experience in Three Self-nominated Mapping and Non-mapping Projects.

Project Type	I Was Interested in the Kaupapa	I Enjoyed the Spatial Mapping Component	I Enjoyed the Technological Aspects
Map – MOST engaged ($N = 30$)	1.63	2.07	2.32
Map – LEAST engaged ($N = 5$)	1.4	2.4	3.2
Non-map – MOST engaged ($N = 12$)	1.33	N/A	N/A

Note: A Likert scale was used with 1 meaning strongly agree and 5 meaning strongly disagree.

'enjoyed technological aspects' at only 3.2, with 40% disagreeing. It appears that the technological aspects were at least part of the reason why these students engaged least in the digital mapping projects in question, particularly given the students were evenly split over the question of whether technological aspects were important to the project (3.0) and the higher rating here for interest in the *kaupapa*. These results suggest that students generally rated their engagement with mapping higher than their engagement with technology, but both were far less important than the *kaupapa* (topic).

We also asked students to compare their experiences of the map-based projects with any other project they strongly engaged with at VUW. Although we asked this question AFTER the probe about the project they least engaged with, 12 students responded, with five of the projects originating from MAOR coded courses, four from Humanities courses, two from Biological Sciences courses and one course from Commerce and Administration. Eleven of 12 agreed or strongly agreed that they were interested in the kaupapa, for an average of 1.33, which is better than the 1.63 and 1.4 scores from map-based projects. An overwhelming majority, 11/12, cited 'Research' as one of the things they most enjoyed about the non-mapping project they most engaged with. This was followed by 'relevance of topic to me' (7/12), with 'topic', 'increased my knowledge' and 'good lecturer/tutor' mentioned by 6/12. 'Technologies/resources used' was mentioned by just 25%, supporting the message that the digital facilitates enjoyment only inasmuch as it supports other aspects such as topic and research.

Persistence in Spite of Difficulties

Taking a lead from the AUSSE survey on engagement (2010), we probed for student persistence in spite of challenges with the digital technology. In our online survey, students were asked to consider a mapping project with which they most engaged, and to rank their response to the question 'I found the logistics of the technical components easy' on a Likert scale from 1 (strongly agree) to 5 (strongly disagree). Twenty-eight respondents were divided, and their rankings averaged out to 2.93, with most disagreeing that the logistics were easy. However, to the statement 'I persisted, even when challenged by technical difficulties,' 19/28 respondents agreed or strongly agreed, for an average of 2.11. Although only 5/37 students chose 'persisting in spite of challenges' as evidence of engagement (they were asked to choose 8 of

24 options), we think this is a clear indication of engagement in spite of difficulty with the technology. In addition, most felt that technical aspects were important to the project (2.31) and most enjoyed the technical aspects (2.32). Crucially, 17/28 students agreed or strongly agreed that they were proud of the work they had accomplished in relation to the technical aspects of the project. This reveals persistence in spite of difficulties, and an overall sense of pride in accomplishment and working through technological hurdles. In such situations, students can find greater fulfilment in the task at hand than if they had progressed unhindered. Addressing and overcoming these challenges encourages deep learning and creates dynamic and informed work.

The Cry of 'More'

Students encountered various technological aspects in MAOR210 Cultural Mapping, and group work may have helped to facilitate uptake of digital skills across the class. However our in-class evaluation showed that five students (of 13 surveyed) would have liked to spend more time on technological aspects, particularly GPS and GIS. This sentiment is echoed anecdotally in other classes. The character of their individual comments indicates that some of those students had enjoyed their taste of the technology and wanted more, and some wanted more support with the technology, supporting literature that suggests with greater training, projects with technical components can blossom (Gearheard et al., 2011).

Time constraints and prior knowledge (or lack thereof) of technologies could hamper those students who were not comfortable with technologies in comparison to their more technically literate peers. For others, such as Sarsha, the prospect of the technology is the real barrier to overcome.

> I was also stoked that I picked it up with relative ease, as me and technology don't often get along too well. I think the course eradicated some of my technophobias and I managed to have some fun with it … I think Google Earth was a really good method of mapping this particular topic. I was really happy with how it looked and it has potential for improvement (more from my side – gaining more knowledge of the program, and generally sprucing it up a bit).

In this case, it is perhaps the unfamiliarity with the technique, and perhaps prior poor experiences with technology, that have contributed to Sarsha's 'technophobias'. With good and managed tuition, clear instructions and objectives, difficulties with technologies can be overcome.

Above and Beyond – the Evidence of Student Work

We have several examples of students going further than the assignment called for, and doing more than what was taught in tutorials. The quality and variety of work received is then an indicative measure of engagement.

For instance, students were told how to import images as placemark icons, but then others discovered the effect of matching the image to the three-dimensional contours in Google Earth. For instance, Sarsha has been involved in community punk events since 2003, and has helped design and distribute event flyers for almost 10 years. To capture her work, she represented this by overlaying digital scans of the posters and flyers on the Wellington contours in Google Earth, mimicking their distribution, plastered over the urban landscape of Pōneke (Wellington). Her visually arresting work replaces the geography and topography of central Wellington as rendered by Google Earth with an undulating mosaic of 10 years of flyers made by and for the local punk scene. Ironically, we could not secure permission to allow the reproduction of her work here, but it can however be viewed on our website.

Art student Aiko drew upon the paths in Google Earth for her MAOR210 Cultural Mapping project (pictured in Fig. 6). Her work is a geo-autobiographical relational web, providing a geographical representation of her social network in Europe, developed during her three years living there. She documents where she met people by using pictures of the people as placemark icons. She also connects people who know each other, revealing surprising coincidences among the people whom she met and who know each other. She also colour coded parts of the web by the types of relationship she has with the people there. As she describes her project, the digital iconography comes to represent spatial connections: 'I can call this map my cultural diary. Each icon and line have special meaning for me and remind me of the time and history that I had between these people.' She reported getting frustrated with Google Earth which would become 'heavy' and 'quite slow' with the addition of too many picture files, but her work is evidence of engaging in the digital to its maximum potential.

Another student in MAOR210 who pushed Google Earth to its limits was Mariana, who used a Taranaki *pātere* (rhythmic chant) 'Ka Huri Taku Aro' as the basis of her cultural map. She used the Google flyover function to move across the landscape in time, and with a specific type of flight path, to match the timing and story of the *waiata*, sung by locals in an mp3 recording. She recorded a tour of her flyover to be played simultaneously with the audio file. Her map is thus an audio-visual engagement with a

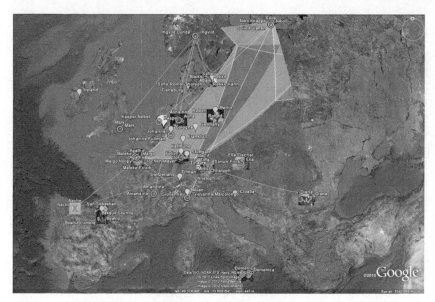

Fig. 6.   Aiko's 'Geo-Cultural Diary' for MAOR210 Maps Her Friendships with
People from Europe.

digital landscape. Google Earth was somewhat limiting for her project, as
she was not able to embed the sound file within Google Earth, and to
incorporate the two files would have required literacy in a compatible movie
editing programme. Of the technical challenges in her project she writes that
'they ranged from relatively small issues of misplaced points to bigger, more
challenging barriers such as manipulating the 'camera' angle and shots to
portray certain movements and scenes.' Nonetheless, she concluded, 'one
can only gain a deeper understanding of the place from the two
[perspectives] and thus these two ways of "seeing", or more particularly
"mapping", can only complement each other.' In this case, the digital was
commandeered to render the oral history in an ambitious and exciting way
for the revitalisation of local, Māori and Indigenous narratives.

CHALLENGES OF DIGITAL MAPPING

The logistics of designing and setting up assignments for the digital realm
fell on a couple of staff with the help of research assistants. While every

effort was made to spare students from teething problems – for example, by testing tutorial instructions on slower student laboratory computers well ahead of class – at times instructions were unclear, or were misread, leading to wastage of time, impacting negatively on students' engagement in the assignment. Student feedback relays that some needed more time to familiarise themselves with the technology used in courses. Though teacher capabilities with technologies were not suggested as issues, difficulty with technologies and software were offered as barriers experienced by students in all TKaM courses reviewed. Commentary interviews endorsed this sentiment also, with one student stating 'I would have liked to have done something a bit more interactive, like a video or movie … but there were time constraints and stuff like that.' The fact that students can see the potential of such technology, given the right conditions and enough time, shows students are developing interest in the diverse ways that digital projects can render their work.

Academic Concerns

An issue emerging from our work and seen in other studies of digital learning relates to the lowering of academic standards of writing. Due to the multi-faceted nature of map-based assessment in TKaM courses, students tended to focus on digital and visual aspects of projects, while writing styles suffered. This is particularly the case where text is written directly into an online forum, such as a Google Earth description box or a blog, but it has also crept into traditional academic writing arena such as Microsoft Word documents. Sadik discusses academic degradation in his study of digital storytelling in Egyptian schools (2008). Most projects showed that few sources were used across classroom groups, the main source being the internet, while writing styles were informal, lacking academic substance. We see all these hallmarks in our students' projects, and we have written guidelines for citing and referencing in Google Earth to update our school Academic Writing Guide. However, what we battle with is really the association of the digital with unpolished written language, such as seen in emails, online posts and text messages.

Conversely, the informal nature of the digital can aid student engagement – for instance, students who wrote the most engaging (and thus engaged) geo-journal entries for MAOR210 were ones who were able to write freely, without pressure to conform to academic conventions (see Fig. 5).

Access to Technology

Access to technology was a concern expressed by Wallace (2008), in an Australian study of Indigenous student engagement with digital technologies. But the same can be said for Indigenous access to academic outputs generally. In discussing academic literature, Aneika stated: 'It's just lost in books and that restricts who can use it, who can access it ... to have something that's interactive you know, it's awesome.' The visual side of map-based assessment is germane to Cultural Studies. Though interactive mapping of information is not traditionally academic in style, it effectively conveys information and contributes to student learning and engagement. As Aneika reiterates, 'you can use other forms of technology to assist in the way that you present things. And it's not wrong to do that.'

Eady and Woodcock's (2010) study of collaborative education illustrated that Indigenous community members expressed concern over the lack of power afforded by Indigenous peoples worldwide, and related to this, was the lack of ability of their peoples with digital technologies. They saw digital literacy as a means to strengthen the Indigenous voice, and a way to become equal partners in society. Though lack of access to digital technologies was not apparent to our students – largely due to access to university computer laboratories for student use – limited ability with digital formats was a concern for some. Due to limited funding, access to facilitative digital technologies for the TeKaMA as a whole is a project-wide issue.

Compatibility of Mātauranga Māori (Māori Knowledge) and Digital Technology

Course content was as important to the success of the project as the technology, the digital simply opened a different way to explore topics. Students thus engaged in a multi-level, multi-sensory experience with Māori knowledge. This holistic approach mimics that practiced in *mātauranga Māori* (Adds, Hall, Higgins, & Higgins, 2011). Yet as seen in the online survey, it was the subject matter or content of assessments which most stimulated student enjoyment. The challenge of conveying traditional Māori knowledge via the digital, foreshadowed by Mariana's comment in a previous section, is in how to make technology an appropriate vessel for conveying cultural content.

TKaM students were asked in commentary interviews if they felt comfortable with relaying matauranga Māori in digital mapping forums used in TKaM courses. Students expressed that though technologies provided a wealth of possibilities, care was needed in conveying sensitive information. As Aneika commented, 'I'm trusting that people are respecting that it is local knowledge in this case.' Indeed, many students intentionally did not consent to their projects contributing to the Te Kawa a Maui Atlas, because of the sensitive and personal nature of material contained within.

For many students, these map-based projects provided an important opportunity to connect with and disseminate whānau or tribal knowledge. Aneika expressed the necessity to reinvigorate local Māori knowledge for future generations:

> If there was no way of collating all that kind of knowledge then it's just going to get put aside somewhere. So it's a good way to inform people ... to save that knowledge, and make sure that it is passed on.

In doing so she echoed the sentiments of Yolngu Aboriginal tribal elder Mangay Guyula (Verran & Christie, 2007), who negotiated a way to use DVD digital technology to record his knowledge and to fulfil political and emancipative aims. Students see their work contributing to the greater goal of recovery and survival of Indigenous knowledge. While the project seeks to enhance Māori student engagement, not all students who enrol in Māori Studies courses are of Māori descent. A significant amount of student work contributed to the TeKaMA was produced by international students (Fig. 6) and non-Māori New Zealanders. Mapping assessments contributing to the TeKaMA both inform and challenge historical approaches to recording history, whose history it is, and how it is presented. That the project can meet multiple objectives and support all, not just Māori, in contributing to building an inclusive society, is a testament to the utility of place-based work.

CONCLUDING REMARKS AND FUTURE STUDIES

Both existing research and our own demonstrate that 'high-impact' digital research projects such as the TeKaMA have significant potential for student engagement on several levels. This descriptive chapter has detailed our preliminary findings concerning student engagement with the TeKaMA in its first three years in our Te Kawa a Māui/Māori Studies programme. Our findings add to the sparse repository on student engagement with digital learning tools within tertiary-level Cultural Studies, particularly within Aotearoa/New Zealand, as well as acting to inform and improve our future use of map-based assessment at TKaM, Victoria University of Wellington.

So what have our findings told us and how will we carry those lessons into the future?

Feedback has indicated that the cultural mapping ecosystem at TKaM fosters student engagement on several levels: it encourages self-directed learning, uses a culturally relevant pedagogy, takes for granted the validity of Indigenous knowledge, teaches transferable skills in digital technologies and communication, provides the option of relating scholastic projects to communities and areas familiar to students, gives an outlet for primary resource material and gives students agency in their research while providing inclusive learner-to-learner experiences. The quality and diversity of map-based projects is itself an indication of how cultural mapping can engage students.

However, spatial mapping needs to be integral and meaningful to the assignment's purpose and alongside that the technology needs to support the aim of cultural mapping. While our students demonstrated readiness to overcome technical challenges and pride in their accomplishments when they do, they and our staff need to see the relevance of the digital to the assignment and be given adequate training. Also, if spatial and technological aspects do not support wider efforts in the recovery and maintenance of Māori and Indigenous knowledge, they can disengage students.

The development of this project has been exciting for both students and staff, with students exploring with genuine interest how Māori studies can be represented using map-based projects. In this respect, technological learning tools that support wider publication and dissemination of student research, if interwoven with solid course management, meaningful integration, group work and enough tuition, can support increased student engagement in learning. Students can use digital cultural mapping to contribute something meaningful beyond the course, to other communities, both of which engage and enhance their learning experience.

ACKNOWLEDGEMENTS

First and foremost, we acknowledge the many hours that staff and students have contributed to the TeKaMA through setting and completing assignment work. We are grateful to Fraesar Williams for checking the data herein. This chapter was financially supported by the Ngā Pae o te Māramatanga Summer Scholar scheme and the VUW Faculty of Humanities and Social Sciences' Research Leave fund. The project has received financial support from VUW's Teaching and Learning Fund 2010, and the Summer Scholars' Research Fund 2009/10 and 2010/11. This chapter grew out of presentations

to the Higher Education Research and Development Society of Australasia
and the World Indigenous Peoples' Conference on Education conferences in
2011, which were supported by MANU-Ao, the VUW Office of the Pro-Vice
Chancellor Māori, the VUW Faculty of Humanities and Social Sciences
Conference Fund and a Ngā Pae o te Māramatanga Conference Attendance
Grant 2011.

REFERENCES

Abel, S. (2010). A question of balance. *New Zealand Herald*, 3 August. Retrieved from http://
www.nzherald.co.nz/opinion/news/article.cfm?c_id = 466&objectid = 10663343

Adds, P., Hall, M., Higgins, R., & Higgins, T. R. (2011). Ask the posts of our house: Using
cultural spaces to encourage quality learning in higher education. *Teaching in Higher
Education*, *16*(5), 541–551.

Australian Council for Educational Research. (2010). *Doing more for learning: Enhancing
engagement and outcomes*. Camberwell: Australian Council for Educational Research.

Barnhardt, R. (2007). Creating a place for Indigenous knowledge in education: The Alaska
Native Knowledge Network. In G. Smith & D. Gruenewald (Eds.), *Place-based
education in the global age: Local diversity*. Hillsdale, NJ: Lawrence Erlbaum Associates.

Best, E. (1917). The land of Tara. *Journal of the Polynesian Society of New Zealand*, *26*(104),
143–169.

Bishop, R., Berryman, M., Cavanagh, T., & Teddy, L. (2007). *Te Kōtahitanga phase 3.
Whanaungatanga: Establishing a culturally responsive pedagogy of relations in mainstream
secondary school classrooms*. Wellington: Ministry of Education.

Bishop, R., & Glynn, T. (1999). *Culture counts: Changing power relationships in education*.
Palmerston North: Dunmore Press.

Brayboy, B. M. J., & Castagno, A. E. (2009). Self-determination through self-education:
Culturally responsive schooling for Indigenous students in the USA. *Teaching
Education*, *20*(1), 31–53.

Callister, P. (2009). *Which tertiary institutions are educating young, low-skill Māori men? A
research note*. Wellington: Institute of Policy Studies.

Chinlund, E., & Hall, M. (2010). Views from Last Resort: Experiences of Māori undergraduate
students who transitioned from tertiary bridging programmes. Paper presented at the
New Zealand Association of Bridging Educators Conference, Wellington.

Eady, M., & Woodcock, S. (2010). Understanding the need: Using collaboratively created draft
guiding principles to direct online synchronous learning in Indigenous communities.
International Journal for Educational Integrity, *6*(2), 24–40.

Gearheard, S., Aporta, C., Aipellee, G., & O'Keefe, K. (2011). The Igliniit project: Inuit hunters
document life on the trail to map and monitor arctic change. *Canadian Geographer*,
55(1), 42–55.

Harmsworth, G. (1998). Indigenous values and GIS: A method and a framework. *Indigenous
Knowledge and Development Monitor*, *6*(3), 3–7.

Harris, A. (2004). *Hīkoi: Forty years of Māori protest*. Wellington: Huia.

Kuh, G. D. (2008). *High-impact educational practices: What they are, who has access to them, and why they matter.* Washington, DC: Association of American Colleges and Universities.

Luke, H. (Ed.). (1998). *My own trail.* Fairbanks, AK: Alaska Native Knowledge Network.

MapTEACH. (2005). *Mapping technology experiences with Alaska's cultural heritage.* Retrieved from http://www.mapteach.org

Mercier, O. R. (2011). Globalising Indigenous knowledge for the classroom. In G. J. S. Dei (Ed.), *Indigenous philosophies and critical education: A reader* (pp. 299–311). New York, NY: Peter Lang Publishing.

Morrah, M. (2010). Tensions flare over 'sacred' land at Taipa Bay. *3 News,* 22 November. Retrieved from http://www.3news.co.nz/Tensions-flare-over-sacred-land-at-Taipa-Bay/tabid/423/articleID/187431/Default.aspx

Penetito, W. (2006). Place-based education: Catering for curriculum, culture and community. *New Zealand Annual Review of Education, 18,* 5–29.

Pihama, L., Cram, F., & Walker, S. (2002). Creating methodological space: A literature review of Kaupapa Māori research. *Canadian Journal of Native Education, 26*(1), 30–42.

Radloff, A. (2011). *Student engagement in New Zealand's universities.* Melbourne: Australian Council for Education Research.

Sadik, A. (2008). Digital storytelling: A meaningful technology-integrated approach for engaged student learning. *Educational Technology Research and Development, 56,* 487–506.

Smith, G. H. (2000). Māori education: Revolution and transformative action. *Canadian Journal of Native Education, 24*(1), 57–72.

Sonna, C., Bishop, B., & Humphries, R. (2000). Encounters with the dominant culture: Voices of indigenous students in mainstream higher education. *Australian Psychologist, 35*(2), 128–135.

Statistics New Zealand. (2012). *Māori population estimates.* Retrieved from http://www.stats.govt.nz/browse_for_stats/population/estimates_and_projections/maori-population-estimates.aspx

Van der Meer, J. (2011). Māori and Pasifika students' academic engagement: What can institutions learn from the AUSSE data? In A. Radloff (Ed.), *Student engagement in New Zealand's universities* (pp. 1–10). Melbourne: Australian Council for Educational Research.

Verran, H., & Christie, M. (2007). Using/designing digital technologies of representation in Aboriginal Australian knowledge practices. *Human Technology, 3*(2), 214–227.

Victoria University of Wellington. (2012). *Victoria University of Wellington Annual Report 2011.* Wellington: Victoria University of Wellington.

Wallace, M. (2008). *Effects of the learning federation's curriculum content on Indigenous students' motivation to learn and their engagement in learning.* Melbourne: The Learning Federation.

APPENDIX A: OTHER COURSE ASSIGNMENTS

MAOR123 Te Iwi Māori me āna Tikanga/Māori Society and Culture

MAOR123 students selected one of the 120 *poupou* (carved figures) from within the carved meeting house, *Te Tumu Herenga Waka*, at VUW to research, in an assignment designed to use the *wharenui* as a pedagogical tool (Adds et al., 2011). The collection of *poupou* represent Māori characters mythical, legendary and historic – male and female – from as early as the beginning of time (demi-gods Hinenuitepō and Māui) to as recently as 1950 (for instance, Māori leaders Apirana Ngata and Te Rangi Hiroa). In a place-based modification to the assignment, each student researched three significant events in the life of that ancestor and located the events on paper maps of Aotearoa/New Zealand and the Pacific Ocean during tutorials, and electronically on Blackboard, using the test hotspot function. By uploading an image file to which students can digitally pin a marker, instructors can test student recall of spatial information with the Blackboard hotspot function. A research assistant compiled students' map-based 'geo-biographies' in Google Earth. The best 18 student projects from 2010 combined to form the *poupou* map, and part of student Tania Gaffey's research on her ancestor Tawapata is shown in Fig. A1.

MAOR122 Te Pūwhenuatanga o te Moana-Nui-ā-Kiwa/The Peopling of Polynesia

This course includes a field trip to a *pā* (fortified village) site in the Wairarapa, for which students draw an archaeological site map, thus testing their recognition and description of archaeological features. In 2010, students were also asked to choose a pre-European archaeological site recorded in the archsite database, and research its history. The assessment required students to unearth new information to add to what was provided in the online archsite database.

MAOR112 Wanawana te Tū/Māori Language 1B

This course focuses upon elementary listening, speaking, reading and writing skills in the Māori language. In 2010/2011 students were set two place-based essay topics. The first asked them to write an essay, in the Māori

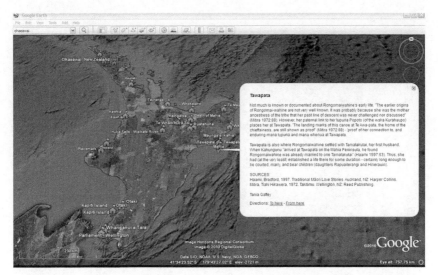

Fig. A1. Screen Capture of Collated Geo-biographies for MAOR123, Consisting of 18 Student Projects Compiled into One Google Earth kmz File.

language, about placenames in the region the student was from. The other posed the statement that 'Maps are not a productive tool for Māori, but rather alienate Māori from their land', and looked for arguments for and against.

MAOR124 *Te Pūtaiao Māori/Māori Science*

This course examines Māori knowledge and science in both traditional and contemporary contexts. It examines the differences and similarities between Western and Māori ways of knowing, for instance, how the perspectives can be combined in the context of learning about a native species of historic significance, such as the *karaka* tree. These trees are a living reminder of the Māori tradition of eating *karaka* berries and their empirically developed methods of harvesting and preparing them, as well as their use for staking out settlements. In a three-stage assignment, students were first given some training on how to recognise resource-rich trees (including *karaka*) and plants, then used a large-scale orienteering map to locate native flora on campus. Students then used City Council heritage maps to locate ancestral

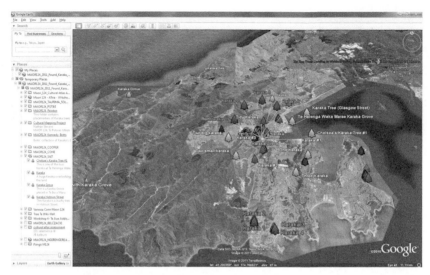

Fig. A2. Twenty-eight MAOR124 Students Located and Mapped Karaka Trees Growing Around Wellington. This Google Earth Map is a Collation of Their Individual Primary Research.

groves of *karaka* trees and mapped them using Google Earth. In the third stage, students worked individually or in pairs to go out and find 10-20 *karaka* trees within the Wellington area. These field observations of *karaka* were then mapped and described using Google Earth. Students' work was compiled into a class map (see Fig. A2) showing a rough distribution of *karaka* in Wellington, connecting to work done by the Department of Conservation and Bruce McFadgen. The cultural value of the assignment was in students reconnecting with the arboreal descendants of an ancestral food source occupying their local urban landscape.

APPENDIX B: DIGITAL TOOLS

Staff and the Digital Aspects

Most participating staff were familiar with Google Maps, but had not used Google Earth before, so to minimise the training and additional workload for staff and students, assignments were designed to be integrated as seamlessly as possible into class work – oftentimes requiring that research assistants collate student work in Google Earth. We turned this work back to students quickly, enabling them to see their work in the context of others' work, thus making timely feedback a part of their learning. For example, for MAOR316, which was taught in four blocks over the summer, student work done during their second class was collected and compiled in time to show back to them during their third class.

Where students needed to use Google Earth for projects, we tailored instructions for each course, so as to train students as quickly as possible to the required level of skill, through purpose-written guides for Google Earth and Quantum GIS for MAOR123, MAOR216, MAOR317, MAOR210 and MAOR124.

GPS and GIS

As mentioned, MAOR210 students were trained to use GPS Garmin E-Trex units to find and also mark points on the landscape during their field trip to Te Ika a Maru Bay. As part of this, they had to convert New Zealand Transverse Mercator coordinates into World Geodetic System 1984 Longitudes and Latitudes, compatible with what GPS units calculate from satellite-determined positions. MAOR122 instructors used GPS units during their *pā* (fortified village) visit, and there is more scope for student activity there. MAOR210 students were given a handrail tutorial through Quantum GIS, which enabled them to produce a map with all 15 sites at Te Ika a Maru Bay marked and labelled. Their use of both Google Earth and Quantum GIS gave students a sense of how the programmes operated differently, and the kinds of additional work that a GIS programme can do.

Other Digital Aspects

Students were required to take digital photos during field trips in MAOR210 and orienteering exercises in MAOR124 and MAOR210, and were provided digital cameras for this purpose. Other students used their own cameras and their own initiative in taking, or using existing, photographs to embellish their projects. Many students made use of the Google Earth function that allows photographs to be used as placemark icons, using all the various options for display.

For MAOR123, students were presented with maps and asked to pinpoint places on the map that were significant in the life of their chosen *poupou* character. We chose a clunky solution to the problem of putting digital pins on a map, by adapting the Blackboard 'hotspot' test function to capture student-defined positions. We uploaded medium-high resolution jpeg maps of the North Island, South Island, Pacific Ocean and Conceptual Spaces to Blackboard 'tests' in a dedicated 'Map Spaces' folder for students to work with. We defined the whole map as within hotspot range, Blackboard recorded the grid reference where students placed their marker, and we correlated that to a geographical position on a Google Earth map. In the case of students who could not physically locate their chosen character on Earth, they were asked to conceptually 'place them on the map', with a series of images offered, and the option given for students to upload their own images. In practice, the hotspot proved a frustration for users, some of whom reported that they put their mark on a point on the map only to have it move somewhere else, or disappear altogether, possibly due to an internet browser or Javascript incompatibility. Also, as the map was a jpeg still image, there was no facility to zoom in on areas, a function people are attuned to through its ubiquity in Google Maps and other mapping applications online. For future iterations of the project we would like to develop a map wiki that allows multiple users to place digital pins and labels on a centrally available zoomable map or image.

Students in MAOR123 and MAOR210 blogged assignments on Black-board. Some students, without direction or tuition, were able to upload their own images and links into their posts to embellish these. Two or three MAOR317 and MAOR210 students used PowerPoint to develop story books, with the user navigating their way through different stories through student-defined networks of links, managing this with little to no direction from staff.

Organising placemarks from completed Google Earth projects into a folder to be saved as a kmz file proved a challenge for students and their course coordinator. Clear and specific instructions, guidance given during tutorials and warnings about the pitfalls were only partially effective in getting students to bundle their digital work correctly. While this kind of specificity is a literacy of the sciences, where hardware and software gives little margin for error, it is perhaps somewhat alien to Arts and Humanities students, perhaps explaining the difficulties some students had with the saving kmz task. By contrast, GIS kml files were somewhat less complicated.

Te Kawa a Māui Atlas Database

Students in courses doing work that may contribute to the Atlas were given a short presentation in class about the aims of the project, and a PowerPoint displaying other students' work. These presentations generally created a 'buzz', but while students had to do the mapping assignment assigned in their course, they were not compelled to contribute their work to the wider project. TKaM assignment cover sheets were updated to include a consent box option for students wanting their work considered for the TeKaMA. Student projects consented for use were organised into a cohesive set of work. Quality control of student writing and digital mapping was done by research assistants, overseen by the first author. We have shared the compiled collection of Google Earth-based projects with students in MAOR124 and in MAOR210, who used the kmz to explore the TeKaMA. It has also been uploaded to a set of iPads used by School staff, running Google Earth and Kmz Loader as Applications. The iPads were used in tutorials as a way for students to physically interact with the Atlas via the touchscreen, literally putting their finger on the map of student work. The Kmz Loader Application has limitations – for instance, it sometimes fails to load additional files by syncing and it will not display the data underneath custom-made icons. This means that students who took photographs at a site, and uploaded their jpg file as a placemark icon rather than using standard icons provided by Google Earth, would not have had their data displayed using this method. Ultimately, our aim is to produce a database that is widely accessible and fully interactive. The iPads are useful for small group tutorials. Our website is a step in the direction of wider dissemination.

Te Kawa a Māui Atlas Website

A single, non-interactive page about the TeKaMA was initially developed, and has been available since 2010. It included a description of the project and three images of the first student projects. With our collation of the best student work between 2010 and 2011, the website was extended in 2011/2012 by VUW Web Services to display digital images of the work from

10 individually named students, as well as group work from dozens more. Work is currently organised by seven courses, with a description on each page and sample images in five courses. One student in our online survey noted: 'I would also like to see the project being integrated into more courses. An introductory website explaining the project and with clear guidelines and instructions for use would help attract students.' As anticipation of the public-facing TeKaMA grows amongst students, this showcase of selected work is one step towards a more widely useable, interactive TeKaMA website, under development for making available online in the future. Currently, links to still images and descriptions of student work can be accessed via the url http://www.victoria.ac.nz/maori/atlas.

Archaeological Sites at Te Ika a Maru Bay

As mentioned, the 2011 MAOR210 Cultural Mapping class field trip visited Te Ika a Maru Bay to find and comment on the condition of archaeological sites in the area. Students worked in four groups, each locating and commenting on 4-5 sites, of a total of 15 in the area. The best of their observations were collated into two reports by a research assistant and an archaeologist. Students involved in the site survey have thus been involved in 'real' research at undergraduate level, and the reach of the TeKaMA extends to the New Zealand Archaeological Association (NZAA), who will publish the report in their forthcoming newsletter. Recommendations for land development have been sent to the owner upon whose land these ancient reminders of Māori occupation lie. This field trip may constitute the first Māori Studies group to conduct such work for the NZAA database – usually done by students in archaeology or geography courses. They bring a different disciplinary perspective to the task, as well as an unjaded enthusiasm for field work. The land-based socio-cultural research trip also fulfils Kuh's definition of a high-impact practice, Bishop and Glynn's concept of active learning and the notion of PBE.

APPENDIX C: DATA COLLECTION

Informal Observations

The first author had the greatest investment in establishing project map-based assessment in courses, and took particular note of informal, solicited and unsolicited student feedback on the work in her own classes and others, and tended to automatically and immediately re-integrate this feedback into assignments, also designing and redesigning tutorial instructions in direct response to student experience with this material.

Student Work Itself

Some of the evidence of engagement that we present is from student work in class assignments, and takes the form of reflections on the resources made available to the student, the task at hand, or the wider implications of the students' work and likely impact on their communities. We argue that the diversity, creativity and quality in student projects is itself evidence of engagement. Some students go beyond what is expected of them. Others have provided written commentary on their own learning that we reproduce here, correlating that evidence with the surveys we conducted.

Student Formative Evaluations

The Centre for Academic Development (until late 2011, the University Teaching Development Centre, or UTDC) conducts standardised evaluation of VUW courses at the request of the course coordinator or tutor. Student formative feedback from TKaM courses that included map-based assessment sometimes contained data related to their work on the Atlas project. Courses for which this is the case are MAOR122, MAOR123, MAOR124 and MAOR210. The evaluations for MAOR210 are directly relevant, as this Special Topic course is completely devoted to generating student skills, knowledge and work to contribute to the TeKaMA.

Assignment-Specific Student Evaluations

With one or two exceptions (e.g. MAOR122), most of the map-based activity we introduced to courses was newly designed to create a pathway for student course work to contribute to the TeKaMA. As some assignments constituted up to 20% of the total course assessment, it was important to evaluate the activity. For instance, in 2010, MAOR123 students were asked to evaluate the *poupou* mapping assignment, and they used a variation of the standardised UTDC student formative evaluation to do so. The survey was distributed during class, and the 63 responses (95 enrolled) were analysed once final grades were entered. MAOR122 students were offered a tailored anonymous Blackboard survey of their 2010 cultural mapping activity. This was voluntarily completed by 8 students of 70 enrolled. Twenty-two MAOR124 students (out of 35 enrolled) evaluated the *karaka* assignment in 2011 using a specially designed in-class survey form, again only analysed once the course final grades were entered.

LEARNER ENGAGEMENT IN AN INTERCULTURAL VIRTUAL EXPERIENCE

Müberra Yüksel

ABSTRACT

Lately, multimedia information and communication technologies are acting as catalyzing media that open up increasing opportunities for all with access to such technologies. Digital technology also offers potential to increase access to interactive as well as intercultural experience that develops cross-cultural competencies, while learning content may be further enhanced through collaborative learning in various areas. Kadir Has University in Istanbul undertook a challenging project with the initiative of the College of Staten Island (CSI) – CUNY (City University of New York) and became the international partner of a distant learning course through video conference between 2004 and 2009. The conceptual model behind this project is called the Global Experience Through Technology Project (GETT) initiated by CSI with the goal of using internet technology to bring university students of different cultures together in a virtual classroom.

Increasing Student Engagement and Retention using Multimedia Technologies:
Video Annotation, Multimedia Applications, Videoconferencing and Transmedia Storytelling
Cutting-edge Technologies in Higher Education, Volume 6F, 159–179
ISSN: 2044-9968/doi:10.1108/S2044-9968(2013)000006F009

INTRODUCTION

With globalization, digital technology is acting as a catalyzing medium, opening up increasing opportunities for all with access to multimedia information and communication technologies. Such technology also offers potential to increase access to education, and to intercultural experience that develops global competencies and supports students to get ready to become "global citizens." In the 1960s McLuhan had coined the term "global village" and highlighted the ways in which the medium and the message act synergistically. Indeed "the global embrace" predicted by McLuhan has abolished the linear conception of time and space for the internet has transformed our way of communicating along with our way of thinking and learning.

With the significant role played by communication technologies in education and training, it is now critical to improve the training of the trainers to include intercultural perspectives and to develop interculturally aware and sensitive practices in teaching. Lately, surviving in a complex and virtual world depends largely on affirmative attitudes toward diverse cultures and uncertainty along with cross-cultural adaptation and flexibility rather than control. Application of educational technology serves as a bridge to introduce new perspectives and cultural issues.

Nowadays, with the rapid development of information and communication technology, web-based instructional programs through video conferencing over "blackboard" have been diffusing in higher education. In order to meet students' rising expectations, the universities that are adopting new technologies and offering different alternatives are regarded as innovative. In cross-cultural learning, such technology has the potential to dissolve cultural barriers and taboos. Can experiencing "other culture" by being exposed to various perspectives through formation of work teams or pairs with diverse backgrounds in a virtual classroom develop such awareness is the major research question of this chapter. The chapter will summarize the lessons learned from the use of technology and multi-perspectives in a virtual learner-centered education through SWOT analysis (i.e., strengths, weaknesses, threats and opportunities as internal and external dimensions of environment), pre and posttests among students and the consequent reflections observed during this innovative class of international students in five years.

Overall, learner engagement in an intercultural virtual class project depends on the extent to which students are able to build a shared learning culture that facilitates the discussion of alternative views and multiple perspectives from different angles. The prerequisite to create such a climate is faculty's own development of a collaborative learning and sharing knowledge through new media.

What are the key learning competencies that are necessary for cross-cultural communication and learning and how do we develop our inter-cultural competence based on experiential learning for today's "global village"? This chapter also aims at presenting a learning style model for continuous improvement in a virtual program. The model is derived from David Kolb's (1984) Experiential Learning approach using his learning style inventory (LSI) and learning skills profile (LSP) (Boyatzis & Kolb, 1991, 1995) at the beginning and at the end of the classes.

"Kadir Has University (KHU) in Istanbul undertook a challenging project with the initiative of the College of Staten Island (CSI/CUNY) and became the international partner of a distant learning course through video conference in 2004. Then, CSI and KHU were connected with two other partners, Shanghai Television University and the University of Port Elizabeth, in China and South Africa using internet-based videoconferen-cing. Nowadays, American College of Thessalonica from Greece has joined our discussion board of our joint virtual learning project. The conceptual model behind this project is called the Global Experience Through Technology Project (GETT) initiated by CSI focused on the goal of harnessing internet technology to bring university students of different cultures together in a virtual classroom" (Lewenthal & Kress, 2005, p. 184). Due to different time zones, technical complexities and coordination difficulties, the three other partners have not continued collaboration. Besides, paired student work and teaming up by dyads in assignments (one student from Turkey and the other from the United States) worked more effectively than larger teams in four or five different countries.

This chapter summarizes the lessons learned from the use of technology and multi-perspectives in teaching and the consequent reflections and empathy observed during this innovative class of international students in four years. Discussing critical success factors about distance learning and the challenges involved in internet-based learning are the main objectives of this chapter. In cross-cultural learning, technology has the potential to dissolve cultural barriers and taboos. The rising awareness of the need to develop intercultural communication, global competencies and perspectives may be explained by the trends below:

1. a technology push and an economic imperative that reduces spatial and temporal separation,

2. a demand for peace and global justice,
3. a demographic trend of diversity, and
4. ethical concerns and issues.

These factors will bring collaborative usage of new educational technologies to enhance the development of the next generation of leaders. If such a cross-cultural experience enhances moving from one set of values to another through a process of cultural transition that enables better interaction with others in the "global village," then one may state that it is essential to develop intercultural competence or at least the language and learning competencies (Yamazaki & Kayes, 2004).

THE GOAL OF A VIRTUAL CLASS PROJECT

Digital technology is acting as a catalyst for intercultural learning and communication, accelerating change and opening up ever increasing opportunities for those with access to multimedia information and communication technologies. Central to such systemic development is the preparation of tomorrow's leaders of educational technology, such that they may adopt multilevel and intercultural perspectives on the complex educational systems within which they work (Davis, 2002). In particular, I will focus on a transatlantic project that is working to establish cross-institutional and cross-cultural communities using strategies that utilize digital technology in blending for online collaborative work with limited face-to-face interaction of students, faculty, and technical staff. Consideration of this project may help us to provide the basis for presentation of directions for further research.

By and large, there is growing awareness of the need to develop intercultural communication and global perspectives. Martin and Nakayama (2000) identify six motivating factors to improve intercultural communication such as:

1. A *technology push* that links diverse groups of people for collaboration.
2. Access to variety of cultures by minimizing the effects of distance.
3. An *economic imperative* as trade and commerce become increasingly global in scale and yet must continue to meet local needs and concerns.
4. The *personal motivation* that comes with our inquisitive and exploratory nature as human beings developing self-awareness.
5. An *imperative of peace* and its maintenance in the long term.
6. A *demographic imperative,* as our societies become increasingly diverse.

7. *Ethical imperatives* that arise from challenging ethical issues that arise with variations in norms and perceptions.

With the increasingly complex part played by communication technologies in education and training, we believe that it is now critical to improve the education of educators and the training of the trainers to include intercultural perspectives or global competencies and to actively develop interculturally aware and sensitive practices in facilitating/teaching (Davis & Cho, 2005; Davis, Cho, & Hagenson, 2005).

The use of computer-mediated communication and other digital technologies in bringing together new communities of learners can also provide an experience that is akin to immersion in an unfamiliar and culturally different environment. Distance education today includes strategies to encourage the formation of collaborative study groups and learning communities. Students commonly find this way of learning very stimulating and engaging by the end of the course and it is not unusual to find that some students wish to continue their virtual community beyond the end of the class schedule (Davis, 2002).

Theoreticians mainly drawing on Hofstede's (1980) work on cultural differences identify the other cultures (of emergent economies) as being often characterized by higher degrees of collectivism, higher power distance, lower uncertainty avoidance, and associative/contextual thinking. By and large, Turkey is found to be mostly a country with a high power distance with strong authority relationships, a high uncertainty avoidance and low risk taking with a low long-term orientation, a high social identity (or in-group) based collectivism. Status rather than performance is crucial in giving feedback or setting incentives and rewards; while achievement orientation is also significant (Javidan, Dorfman, De Luque, & House, 2006). All these differences in cultural dimensions as compared to the United States with low power distance, high individualism, and uncertainty avoidance make this project an interesting case of inquiry.

Similar to the above theoretical grounds with respect to university students, in our prior study on "global" competencies among employees in Istanbul (2001), our findings showed that the development trend in global and intercultural competencies are in the right direction; however the pace of change would accelerate if generally accepted top priority competencies are to be put into practice at work. There are relative development needs particularly in leadership, learning from failures, mistakes, or through team work as well as facilitating and coaching others to succeed. The power distance between management and other employees, controlling micro-management, and "zero-sum game" understanding disable leadership and teamwork competencies and limit leadership styles to "telling and selling" that is directing and supporting rather than coaching and delegating styles of situational leadership (Hersey & Blanchard, 1969).

However, when strategic leadership and leading roles (e.g., coaching, facilitating, mentoring, and delegating) are practiced rather than tactical micro-management, a trustful organizational climate, participatory and collaborative understanding may flourish. On the whole, inventions and innovations are no longer made by occupation into new territories, it is accomplished by viewing and grasping the world from an entirely different perspective and organizing accordingly (Yüksel, 2001).

Not falling into know-how gap or not becoming solely copy-cats may be attained by becoming a self-learning person as well as a learning organization both of which starts by facing a mirror to assess and appraise from within through self-reflection. The question to be posed is do we want to look good in form and tangibles or to be good in essence and intangibles? Do we prefer acting as if we are adapting to the changing demands or have we paved the way for transforming ourselves and our organizations for the imperatives of the near future? Are we prepared for the knowledge economy with due respect to the global intra and intercultural competencies? Are we getting close to the new high-skilled student (future or candidate employee) profile demanded by this internetizing evolution or digital revolution? These questions addressed in this prior research on employees have also shed light on our inquiry of virtual classmates' competencies (Yüksel, 2007).

Our discussion thus far has identified a need to incorporate intercultural perspectives in education, and to model good practice in the preparation of future leaders/faculty in educational technology. It has also identified a broad challenge for educators today. How do we develop our intercultural competencies for today's "global village." In research by Yamazaki and Kayes (2004), the main cross-cultural learning competency clusters are found to be positively related to Kolb's corresponding dimensions of experiential learning theory such as interpersonal, information, analytical, and action learning skill sets (1984).

Our assumption is that one may use cultural differences to enhance learning, because the shock of a different culture or perspective often stimulates cognitive and emotional dissonance, which in turn brings us to a better understanding of others and ourselves. When managed appropriately, the individual can be enabled to reflect on personal behavior and perceptions that had become routine and thus invisible from an early age (Davis & Cho, 2005). Discussing critical success factors about learning at a distance through a situational (SWOT) analysis and summarizing lessons learned from the use of technology that enhances information sharing and learning some of the global competencies that are at the crux of cross-cultural competence are critical.

"The need to create attitudes that go beyond tolerance toward embracing difference and living constructively and compassionately in a multicultural world is critical to the survival of humankind and the planet. We cannot act fast enough to encourage the development of the necessary skills by those motivated to live in the dynamic of inbetweenness." Moving from ethnocentrism to ethnorelativism requires a significant "other culture" experience — be it real or virtual ... Keeping attitudes of "openness and caring" for others alive, growing, and present as students and in the future employees they become require continuous learning (Pusch, 2005).

METHODOLOGY FOR OVERALL ASSESSMENT OF THE PROJECT

SWOT analysis (as a method which includes strengths, weaknesses as the internal observed aspects of the context and opportunities and threats as the external possible variables of the environment) is reported to be a useful planning tool for situational analysis, for program evaluation, and for quality improvement. SWOT analysis allows one to collect and analyze a great quantity of information about the SWOT of a program. SWOT analysis is one of the ways to evaluate the current situation as it is; therefore, we decided to analyze the online classroom project in Kadir Has University with SWOT. In order to make a SWOT analysis, we (lecturers and assistants) interviewed with the two technical administrators and three lecturer/coordinators, and five students in a structural way limiting our questions on advantages and disadvantages. The four open-ended questions in a four quadrant model including both internal/recent and external/ prospective dimensions are summed up as pros and cons.

A: Strengths

What are the currently existing strengths of the virtual experience?

(a) It provides time and place flexibility.
(b) Both the faculty members and the students can be online synchronously.

(c) It is an interactive education type; students can ask questions while having the lectures.
(d) System offers lots of class materials. Refined lecture notes are enriched by the content design team.
(e) From the beginning of the 14 weeks scheduled class program, faculty members prepare comprehensive lecture notes. This would help them become more structured and disciplined.
(f) It helps faculty members and students to adapt to technology more easily.
(g) It helps faculty members and students to improve their foreign language (English).
(h) It increases competition between universities. Therefore it encourages quality improvement in higher education.

B: Weaknesses

What are the present weaknesses?

(a) This system may cause education costs to decrease in the long run; however the initial investment is expensive.
(b) It is a new system and demands fluent English; so our students are not as interested as their counterparts in the United States.
(c) Some of the faculty members are against this kind of education programs or courses, so it is difficult to sustain such courses or programs (ended in 2009).
(d) Students cannot be checked whether they listen or not, since they chat with their pair at CUNY during the lecture.
(e) System expands responsibility and course loads of faculty members, increases their administrative burden since there is considerable preparation for the virtual blackboard and cross-checking of slides, handouts, etc.

C: Opportunities

What are the potential opportunities for the model of such a project?

(a) Increases the professional satisfaction of faculty members.
(b) Creates opportunity for students to meet with foreign students and enhance their English.

true comparison to the other side, seeing as how I lived in the
l I was seven."[2]
ior and a Political Science major. I was born in New York but
s are from Guatemala. I'm excited about getting your points
concerning issues facing Turkey, the US and the world."
ch a pleasure being surrounded by intelligent people who are
have a free flow of ideas and opinions on any range of topics.
ticularly interesting that half of those people were miles away
ed similar viewpoints as ours. It seemed as if we were seeing the
of globalization firsthand."
al classroom project is the best educational experience I've had
ough my partner and I did not have an ideal working relation-
s still beneficial. My (Turkish) partner and I had interesting
ons regarding the US actions in Iraq, music, literature, globali-
. Through our chat sessions, the differences between my partner
ned. Our conflict was not based on cultural differences; rather,
ilar to the types of conflicts I experience with classmates here
vork together as a group." (Lewenthal & Kress, 2005)

the faculty at CUNY stated: "This experience helped highlight
. I have learned from years of working with international
tural differences don't make much of a difference if you're just
en to each other" (*ibid*, 2005, p. 188). Indeed, listening actively
found to be one of the most significant competencies needed to
ntercultural communication and learning.

l Erasmus students from Poland. We came to KHU in Istanbul,
wanted to live abroad and learn another culture. We look
both this course and our one semester experience in Istanbul."
ing students from preparing to study abroad, they were
prepared and familiar; one of them even was able speak and
l Turkish.)
little worried about the language & technology, still we are
out the course and meeting with foreign students."

nts from CUNY were mostly honor students from different
elds; while Turkish students were mainly from the Faculty of
ion with a few students from Business Administration.
dents participated in the course voluntarily, while Turkish
ame hesitant to choose this elected course on "Globalization and
ues" since such a virtual class experience required a good
English and a different learning style. That is why we wanted to

(c) Creates opportunity for students to meet with foreign students and enhance their intercultural competencies.
(d) By teaming up in either two or more; students learn more through interaction.
(e) Faculty members also learn a lot about course content and about the new technology.

D: Threats

What are the possible threat items about this type of learning?

(a) Common internet threats or breakdowns due to overload can be a problem in this area as dissemination of each transaction is provided through the general computer networks.
(b) It may be a threat to formal education if this model of education is widely employed.
(c) Blended learning overcomes some of the threats since face-to-face interaction and/or real community work in the field develops competencies further so at least real encounters between pairs each year might be made possible.

The above list may be longer; for the sake of brevity one can say it was worth the experience; however, the qualitative and quantitative findings on what students said and did will demonstrate the larger picture of this experience since the project was both student-focused and action-oriented. For future projects, the staff and scholars should be trained consistently and the success of this type of education should be measured after each course with pre and posttests so that evaluation and development may go on.

THE ONLINE CLASSROOM EXPERIENCE

The virtual classroom as a distance education/learning project has been a challenging experience from the beginning, since the participating students were coming from diverse backgrounds; however, they had one thing in common. They were all more familiar with the new media than the lecturers like me since they are all used to chatting, SMS and MMS messages, e-mailing or using other social media and messengers to express themselves and to interact with each other. Hence, the video conferencing along with chatting, e-mailing, and virtual blackboard as techniques also revealed different pedagogical goals such as:

(a) Allowing students to interact with each other as much as possible to the extent of letting them chat even during the presentations and lectures to make them become active learners.

(b) Encouraging them to ask questions and comment upon lectures as well as all relevant issues so that instead of posing questions the answers of which are already known and conveying the students a coherent body of knowledge, we made them organize the information discussed in class.

(c) Supporting students to sort out their own conflicts and disagreements between and among themselves through a series of weekly and monthly assignments, some of which as part of a semester term paper or project, in an interactive set-up (they were working in pairs, e.g., US and Turkish students were preparing their monthly assignments together) so that they can develop their own perspective or question their frames.

(d) Acting more as a facilitator/moderator or as a coach rather than teaching them or leading them in a telling or selling style in the conventional way so that the students may work as a team or create their own leaders and through their personal or digital network (e.g., virtual discussion board, chat sessions, etc.) they can also get peer support.

(e) Motivating the students for further research based on key words and research questions and giving them latitude for using their personal experience within the context of the course which is globalization and culture will enhance their creativity and make them challenge their own limits.

Even though there are many advantages with online learning as summarized above, there are also disadvantages. Not having face-to-face contact with classmates or the instructor can lead to feelings of isolation or lack of connectedness. Thus, our in-between model of a virtual classroom experience that incorporates human touch and personal interaction (at least among faculty) and conventional methods with new ones combines the best of both worlds particularly within the framework of enhancing intercultural competencies. These competencies comprise of cross-cultural competency clusters such as building relations, working together, valuing other cultures, listening and observation, coping with ambiguity, and adaptability and flexibility at least help students attain major interpersonal and adaptive and information gathering skills. Hence, blended learning seems to be more appropriate for enhancing such crucial soft skills.

While discussing critical success fact distance learning are the main objectiv behind the enthusiasm of learners/stude with respect to different activities such assignments — which have been emplo For instance, online games or chattin specific features that encourage state interactive learning. Simulative games p and the ability to induce higher levels o feeling of control. By designing courses flow through balancing competencies a groups, the struggle between frustratio so that higher levels of engagement ma

Research suggests that "the construct for the online environment. Education that an effective way to integrate techn process is to follow a constructivist m learners to use their knowledge to solve realistically complex. The issues provide apply their knowledge and to take owne The teacher's job becomes one of facilita of telling students the answer, the tea discover the answer themselves. For thi teachers need to give students time to meaning from their research and experi guest lecturers, visual aids posted on virt taries, readings shared on the topic of gl globalization, global and local cultures,

EXPECTATIONS AND FE
AND KHU S1

Selected quotes from interviews or fee enthusiasm of all students. However, decreased in number over time for they mostly because it was both in English a

- "I myself am an immigrant so I feel for me, I can really relish in this glob

and have USSR u

- "I'm a se my paren and view
- "It was willing to It was pa yet expre workings
- "The virt so far. T ship, it conversa zation, e and I less it was si when we

As one o a point th students: c willing to and deeply initiate any

- "We are since we forward (As out culturall understa
- "We are excited a

The stu levels and Communic Erasmus students be Relevant command administer pre and posttests to compare if there was any difference between learning styles in KHU and in CUNY; and before and after having taken the course regarding the virtual course as a transformational experience.

LEARNING ASSESSMENT BASED ON KOLB'S EXPERIENTIAL MODEL

Knowledge results from the combination of different phases of grasping and transforming experience according to David Kolb (1984, p. 41). Kolb drives the process of learning as a four-stage cycle of (1) concrete experience, followed by (2) observation and reflection, which leads to (3) the formation of abstract concepts and generalizations, which leads to (4) hypothesis to be tested in future action, which in turn leads to new experiences (1984, p. 21). He regards different learning modes or styles themselves as the fundamental competency of all communication. His model of experiential learning portrays two dialectically related modes of *grasping experience*: Concrete Experience (CE) is learning from *feelings* or reactions and Abstract Conceptualization (AC) which is learning from *thinking* or analyzing problems in a systematic method. Two dialectically related modes of *transforming experience*: Reflective Observation (RO) is learning from *watching* and listening and Active Experimentation (AE) learning by *doing* (Kolb & Kolb, 2005, p. 2).

The effective learner relies on all four learning modes designated in the Learning Styles Type Grid. That is, (s)he should be able to involve himself/herself fully, openly, and without bias in new experiences (CE), he must be able to reflect on and observe these experiences from many perspectives (RO), he must be able to create concepts that integrate his observations into logically sound theories (AC), and he must be able to use these theories to make decisions and solve problems (AE).

CHARACTERISTICS OF DIFFERENT LEARNER MODES ACCORDING TO THE LEARNER SKILLS PROFILE (LSP)

The profile developed by Kolb aims at assessing the level of competency development in four major skill areas which are interpersonal skills, perceptual/information skills, analytical skills, and behavioral skills, all corresponding to the four learning styles, that is, assimilator, converger, accommodator, and diverger. The inventory is based on 72 items, while the simplified model focuses on four learning styles (Kolb & Kolb, 2005, pp. 202–205). His model highlights an individual's preference on four learning modes: CE, RO, AC, and AE. Further, the AC with CE as the *y* axis indicates the level of abstractness versus concreteness, whereas AE with RO emphasizes the degree of active experimentation as opposed to reflective observation (Kolb, Osland, & Rubin, 1995).

Concrete Experience (CE):

- Represents a receptive, experience-based approach to learning, relying heavily on feeling-based judgement.
- High CE individuals are empathetic and people-oriented. They find theoretical approaches unhelpful and prefer treating each situation as a unique case. They learn best from specific examples in which they can become involved. They tend to be oriented more toward peers and less toward authority in their learning, and benefit most from feedback and discussion with fellow learners.

Reflective Observation (RO):

- Tentative, impartial, and reflective approach to learning.
- High RO individuals rely on careful observation in making judgements, and prefer learning situations such as lectures, allowing them to take the role of impartial observers.

Active Experimentation (AE):

- Active doing orientation to learning, relying on experimentation.
- High AE individuals learn best by engaging in projects, homework, small group discussions. They dislike passive learning situations like lectures.

Abstract Conceptualization (AC):

- Analytical, conceptual approach to learning, relying heavily on logical thinking and rational evaluation.
- High AC individuals are oriented toward things and symbols, less toward other people. They learn best in authority directed, impersonal learning situations emphasizing theory and systematic analysis. They are frustrated by and benefit little from unstructured discovery learning approaches like exercises and simulations.

Based upon these above four modes of learning, Kolb has constructed his grid model on the next section.

LEARNING STYLES TYPE GRID

Accommodator

Best at CE and AE. Greatest strength lies in doing things, carrying out plans, experiments, and involving in new experiences. Tends to be more of a risk taker than the other learning styles. Tends to excel in situations where one must adapt to specific immediate circumstances. In situations where the theory and plans do not fit the facts, s/he will most likely discard either the plan or the theory. Solves problems in an intuitive, trial and error manner. Tends to be at ease with people but is sometimes seen as impatient and pushy. Educational background is often in technical or practical fields such as business. In organizations accommodators are found in action-oriented jobs, often in marketing and sales.

Diverger

Best at CE and RO. Greatest strength lies in imaginative ability. Excels in the ability to view concrete situations from many perspectives. Performs better in situations that call for generation of ideas such as in brainstorming sessions. They are interested in people and tend to be imaginative and emotional. They are aware of meanings and values, have broad cultural interests and tend to specialize in arts. They adapt by observation, rather than action. Mostly seen in managers from humanities and liberal arts background. Human Resource managers, counselors, organization development specialists in organizations tend to have this style.

Converger

Best at AC and AE. Greatest strength lies in the practical application of ideas. Good at problem solving, decision making. People with this style do best in situations such as conventional intelligence tests where there is a single correct answer or solution to a question or a problem. Knowledge is organized in such a way that through hypothetical deductive reasoning can foster it on specific problems. They are unemotional, preferring to deal with things rather than people. They tend to have narrow technical interests and choose to specialize in physical sciences. Usually seen among engineers.

Assimilator

Best at AC and RO. Greatest strength lies in the ability to create theoretical
models. Excels in inductive reasoning in assimilating disparate observations
into integrated explanation. Less interested in people, and more concerned
for abstract concepts, but also less concerned with the practical use of
theories. It is more important that the theory be logically sound and precise.
It is a characteristic of the basic sciences rather than applied sciences. In
organizations assimilators are found in research and planning departments
(Kolb et al., 1995, p. 54).

FINDINGS ON KOLB'S LEARNING STYLES

We focused on understanding particularly the dominant learning styles of
Kadir Has University students who are voluntarily choosing this challenging course since technology and language is more difficult for the Turkish
students than their counterparts. Interestingly, most of the students at KHU
were found to be diverger and/or assimilators through the inventory (a total
of 82%) meaning that they learn mostly by abstract conceptualization and
reflective observation and are more imaginative; whereas students at CUNY
acted more like converger and/or accommodators (approximately 75% in
total) meaning that CUNY students learn by combining abstract conceptualization with active experimentation and they were more at ease with
taking risks and linking analysis with practice.

Although a shorter version of inventory was used and the sample size of
KHU was about half of CUNY during the last two semesters (24–54), we
were able conduct the survey thoroughly for all KHU students for this one
year at the end of the project. Yet, even with a small sample, these findings
were in line with our anticipation that students in CUNY were more risk
takers, problem solvers as well as being issue and action oriented. Students
in KHU were found to be more creative and perceptive as well as more
theory oriented, since they were all from the Faculty of Communication
in 2009. Since this fact holds true for prior years as well, the sample is
representative of all KHU students.

Our primary goal of using this inventory along with pre and posttests of
students on their learning expectations was to see if there was any difference
particularly in learning competencies so that we may make some last
refinements in both the course material and the assignments. We have also
tried to check if there was some change in the learning styles after the course;

our expectation was that the complementarity of learning styles might be transformed as a consequence of assignments with pairs. Apparently, one semester course was not sufficient to make such a transformation. Besides, a few self-assessed open-ended questions were not sufficient.

However, using Kolb's inventory aided our understanding of both the cluster of students' dominant learning styles and patterns of participant or observant behavior. Our priority (with respect to the application of LSI only) was on the KHU students since they faced higher stakes. They were afraid of being misunderstood by their peers at CUNY since they were not comfortable with their English. However, chatting during and after courses helped them to overcome their panic so they gradually improved both their communication and their language.

As a consequence of the findings of the inventory, we have redesigned our course outline and syllabus of the final semester to include theoretical and practical issues in a balanced manner and invited a number of guest speakers who are experts of these particular issues to be able to encourage students for more participation at the questions and answers section at KHU. Moreover, we had additional discussion sessions with KHU students while CUNY students were having a break (since our video conferencing was not synchronous we were able to help the students at all times anyway) just before the QA session so that all students would be able to ask questions and make comments.

CONCLUDING REMARKS

A real voyage of discovery consists not of seeking new landscapes but of seeing through new eyes.

– Marcel Proust

Finally, let us summarize the lessons one might draw from the virtual classroom experience for four years and benefits as well as drawbacks as reflections, since we were neither prepared nor organized for such an experience when we started the project. First, pessimism ought to give way to positive thinking and faculty need to be more involved in continually shaping virtual distance education programs and web-based learning processes along with the technical experts as was the case in KHU and CSI collaboration. Further, distance learning systems based on video conferencing can be complementary to conventional face-to-face lectures rather than replacing classroom education.

We were able to have face-to-face communication in Turkey only with the full time faculty members of CUNY; even that made a big difference. The

KHU students were able to get in touch with their pairs in CUNY through different new media and for one semester course project and that much of medium richness was sufficient; however, for a complete virtual program that would not be enough. Likewise, distance learning might be a cheaper replacement for campuses for the foreseeable future. Third, we as faculty need to go beyond defense mechanisms against this technological innovation and regard it as an opportunity not a threat with pedagogical objectives in the back of our minds. Fourth, such educational innovations need to develop on needs assessment of faculty and students to be able to fulfill real needs instead of being either fads or cost-reduction mechanisms.

On the whole, changing our educational models and blending new modes with conventional methods empowers students/learners and encourages critical thinking and active experiential learning derived from how each student creates meaning from his or her experiences. In a nutshell: such a change fosters meaning-making particularly in cross-cultural communication; provides for interactive learning at multiple levels; is learner-centered and focuses on problem-solving. Moreover, it encourages active participation and learning; and allows group collaboration, cooperative learning, and maybe at a later stage crowd-sourcing.

The degree of student and faculty satisfaction in online virtual courses depends, however, to a large extent, on how well the courses are planned and taught. The quality of the course content and course instruction styles are more important than computer technical skills which we were all rather intimidated by at first. After all, if the educational goal is accomplished and the student is satisfied with the experience along with the university, the faculty and the student also benefit.

Online education is a growing trend and many universities are offering some type of distance education or an example of a virtual classroom. This is a paradigm shift in the mode of teaching and learning, if not of the institutions as a whole. There are no boundaries anymore. Students have the freedom to experiment and develop unique creative ideas while conforming to the parameters and system developed by the class through collaborative dialogue. The primary distance education platform for delivery used by the two universities is virtual blackboard. Generally, those who had prior experience with such a blackboard were also more favorable toward its continued use as a primary medium of instruction. We are still using it; at the time of initiation of this project, we were not aware of such a tool.

Although the students were generally more optimistic than faculty members and administrators about the continuation of exploring additional and hybrid or blended models for expanded distance education opportunities in international settings, still the number of voluntary students were fewer at KHU. The language barrier, new technology along with high expectations (e.g., a lot of written assignments and readings) all together meant too much risk for the students (particularly for getting good grades with less effort), even if they were aware of the high returns of learning and communicating with peers in another country. Most of the students who have taken this course responded favorably in pursuing at least part of their experiences by one or more distance education mediums, especially in international settings.

Student enthusiasm in an intercultural virtual class project depends on the extent to which students are able to build a shared learning culture that facilitates the discussion of alternative informal views and/or multiple perspectives. The prerequisite to create such a climate is faculty's own development of a shared teaching and information culture. Future research as to how students' experiential distributed learning experience might have an affirmative indirect impact on work experience in a distributed workplace or e-learning or similar virtual experiences on social media as well.

Drawing from what we have learnt so far, there are six major principles that need to be taken into consideration:

(a) The learning experience must have a clear purpose with tightly focused outcomes and objectives.
(b) The learning environment makes appropriate use of a variety of media; for instance using films, documentaries, and newspapers on internet etc.
(c) However, selection of media may also depend on nature of content, learning goals, access to technology, and the local learning environment.
(d) The learner/student is actively engaged and the faculty is acting as a facilitator and (s)he is also a learner/student particularly of the digital process and real-life experiences.
(e) Problem-based as well as knowledge-based learning is emphasized since the first highlights analysis, synthesis, and evaluation while the latter involves recall, comprehension, and application.
(f) State-of-the-art technology has to be continuously updated and supported by technical administrators (particularly if there is imbalance in the level of technology there is more need for such support).
(g) Learning experiences should support interaction, participation, cooperation, collaboration, and teamwork.

The practice of distance learning contributes to the larger social mission of education and training such as changing mental models and constructing new knowledge empowers learners and encourages critical thinking. "Knowledge becomes a function of how the individual creates meaning from his or her experiences; it is not a function of what someone else says is true" (Jonassen, Davidson, Collins, Campbell & Hagg, 1995).

In general, Turkish distance education provides learner–content interaction through mass communication technologies such as TV for open university. The need for two-way technologies is clear for more effective learning environments. By applying instructional strategies and interactive technologies that are inspired by cultural context, distance education can also enhance learner–instructor, and learner–learner interaction. For bridging this gap, video conferencing is an important feature in distance education as we have demonstrated in one course project at KHU.

In the near future, online conferencing will be more common in universities and it will be much easier and cheaper. Synchronous conferencing systems of the future will consist of a basic platform from which users can choose to conference using a variety of tools: video, audio, text-based chat, and virtual blackboard. Additionally, such systems support file transfer, remote launching and control of applications, and more. The key to effective distance education is focusing on the needs of the learners, the requirements of the content, and the constraints faced by the teacher, before selecting a delivery system. Because of these reasons, distance education programs must be carefully planned by understanding the virtual course requirements and student needs.

NOTES

1. Although we have not used simulative online games for this project, I included them since I have observed their value in collaborative learning in other undergraduate classes.
2. To protect the privacy of students, I am only giving basic information stated by some of them without their names.

REFERENCES

Boyatzis, R. E., & Kolb, D. A. (1995). From learning styles to learning skills: The executive skills profile. *Journal of Management Psychology, 10*(5), 3–17.
Davis, N. E. (2002). Leadership of information technology for teacher education: A discussion of complex systems with dynamic models to inform shared leadership. *Journal of Information Technology for Teacher Education, 11*, 253–271.

Davis, N., & Cho, M. O. (2005). Intercultural competence for future leaders of educational technology and its evaluation. *Interactive Educational Multimedia, 10,* 1–22.

Davis, N, Cho, M. O., & Hagenson, L. (2005). Intercultural competence and the role of technology in teacher education. *Contemporary Issues in Technology and Teacher Education, 4*(4), 384–394.

Hersey, P., & Blanchard, K. H. (1969). Life cycle theory of leadership. *Training and Development Journal, 23*(5), 26–34.

Javidan, M., Dorfman, P. W., De Luque, M. S., & House, R. J. (2006). In the eye of the beholder: Cross cultural lessons in leadership from Project GLOBE. *Academy of Management Perspectives, 20*(1), 67–90.

Jonassen, D., Davidson, M., Collins, M., Campbell, J., & Hagg, B. B. (1995). Constructivism and computer-mediated communication. *American Journal of Distance Education, 9*(2), 7–26.

Kolb, A. Y., & Kolb, D. A. (2005). The Kolb learning style inventory. Experience based learning system, Hay Group.

Kolb, D. A. (1984). *Experiential learning: Experience as the source of learning and development.* Upper Saddle River, NJ: Prentice Hall.

Kolb, D. A., Osland, J., & Rubin, I. M. (1995). *Organizational behavior: An experiential approach.* Upper Saddle River, NJ: Prentice Hall.

Lewenthal, M., & Kress, M. E. (2005). Making global connections: The virtual classroom project. *Proceedings of the 2005 ASCUE conference,* Myrtle Beach, South Caroline (pp. 184–189).

Martin, J. N., & Nakayama, T. K. (2000). *Intercultural communication in contexts* (2nd ed.). Mountain View, CA: Mayfield Publishing Company.

McLuhan, M. (1964). *Understanding media.* London: Routledge and Kegan Paul.

McLuhan, M. (1967). *The medium is the message.* New York, NY: Bantam.

Pusch, M. D. (2005). The interculturally competent leader. The 7th Global Leadership Forum, Bahçeşehir University, Istanbul.

Tam, M. (2000). Constructivism, instructional design, and technology: Implications for transforming distance learning. *Educational Technology and Society, 3*(2), 50–60.

Yamazaki, Y., & Kayes, D. C. (2004). An experiential approach to cross-cultural learning. *Academy of Management Learning & Education, 3*(4), 362–379.

Yüksel, M. (2001). Are we ready for the global competencies of "the new economy"? *Investor, 15,* 39–48.

Yüksel, M. (2007). Leadership and global competencies in a virtual context. Paper presented at the E-leader Conference, Hong-Kong.

VIDEO ANNOTATION FOR COLLABORATIVE CONNECTIONS TO LEARNING: CASE STUDIES FROM AN AUSTRALIAN HIGHER EDUCATION CONTEXT

Narelle Lemon, Meg Colasante, Karen Corneille and Kathy Douglas

ABSTRACT

This chapter introduces an emerging innovative technology known as MAT (Media Annotation Tool). MAT is an online tool that allows students to annotate video, thus improving student engagement and reflection. This chapter outlines the history of the development of this tool and provides analysis of data provided from a range of course integrations. From idea inception the goal was to render video active and collaborative for learning rather than traditional passive learning. In the multiple-case study it was found that students reported higher engagement/satisfaction with MAT in cases where there was learner-to-learner collaboration, teacher feedback and assessment linkage. This chapter focuses on the undergraduate cases of the study, from the

Increasing Student Engagement and Retention using Multimedia Technologies:
Video Annotation, Multimedia Applications, Videoconferencing and Transmedia Storytelling
Cutting-edge Technologies in Higher Education, Volume 6F, 181–214
ISSN: 2044-9968/doi:10.1108/S2044-9968(2013)000006F010

disciplines of teacher education, medical radiation and chiropractic, and also references a postgraduate case from the discipline of law. The data from these cases points to the success of MAT as dependent on two key factors: learning design and the technical effectiveness of the MAT technology.

INTRODUCTION

The growth in the use of e-learning initiatives in Australian universities provides programs and teachers with the choice of a variety of online tools that facilitate student learning (Herrington, Reeves, & Oliver, 2010). In this chapter we present a case study on the evolution of a new online tool, the media annotation tool (MAT). This new online tool provides a web-based interface that allows opportunity for uploading video that then can be annotated. The design, development and implementation of this tool may be interesting to other institutions, as the 'lessons learnt' with this new technology are transferrable across other learning tools of a similar nature, particularly artefact-centred collaborative learning technology. This tool was developed at RMIT University (Royal Melbourne Institute of Technology) in Victoria, Australia.

This chapter traces the development of MAT and its application to a variety of learning contexts, from idea inception in 2005, to design and trial stages, a pilot in 2009, and finally multiple disciplinary use in 2011. At each of these stages – from design through to cross-discipline implementation – student feedback has been integral to guide the next steps. MAT requires teachers in higher education learning contexts to adapt new modes of technology-supported collaboration with and for students in a higher education environment. Issues addressed in this chapter include technology deployment contexts, and examination of the outcomes of uptake in a variety of discipline learning environments across one Australian university.

While media annotation tools are relatively new in higher education and training (e.g. Glover, Xu, & Hardaker, 2007), MAT is differentiated by a structured annotatable learning cycle that allows for discussion to be directly anchored to segments of media, keeping analysis activities focussed but collaborative. While found to be innovative in both media design (Colasante & Fenn, 2009) and learning application in a 2009 pilot study (Colasante, 2010, 2011a), it is the application into multi-contextual settings across academic disciplines, sectors and student cohorts during 2011 that has allowed for comparison of innovative learning and teaching designs. The use of MAT across this multidisciplinary research project involved examining these designs in their efforts to engage higher education students at various levels, allowing them to transfer theory and practical application associated to their specific disciplines. This chapter discusses the MAT learning design, pedagogy and data, gathered from both teachers and students, that demonstrate the educational benefits of MAT. All participants in this project were seen as active learners in how MAT was being used for alternative and appropriate models of learning and assessment. Strong connections are made to work-relevant learning, supported in most cases by industry partnerships via input into the learning process.

THE DEVELOPMENT OF ANNOTATABLE VIDEO AS A LEARNING TOOL

In learning and teaching design in tertiary education, it is becoming more important to engage students with innovative pedagogy, using such tools as MAT. Increasingly, there is student engagement with digital interfaces, and many higher educational policies and practices support new technologies. While digital natives are reported to thrive in technologically mediated environments and interfaces (Starkey, 2011; Tapscott, 1998), this chapter acknowledges varying levels of learner capabilities as digital natives (Bennett, Maton, & Kervin, 2008; Berger, 2007; Corrin, Bennett, & Lockyer, 2010; Helsper & Eynon, 2009; Herrington & Herrington, 2006; Howe & Strauss, 2003; Keengwe, 2007; Lemon, 2013; Oliver & Goerke, 2007). MAT is an interface that has been inspired by popular social networking features such as that seen with Facebook and Twitter to engage students to explore alternative ways to view video on learning, work-related practices, and unpacking of theory associated to specific disciplines and thus annotate to connect to reflective and metacognitive thinking. It, therefore, is vital in the evolving design and pedagogy of MAT to acknowledge the features of twenty-first century learners who are increasingly challenging the learning and teaching strategies implemented in higher education based on teacher-centred delivery or top-down hierarchical command and control structures of the past.

Video plays a significant role in today's education (Dong, Li, & Wang, 2010; Kaufman, 2009). Video (or television) can provide a passive learning medium; however, if enhanced it can become effective in assisting student learning. The key is to incorporate student engagement through 'interactive, viewer-paced watching combined with compositional power ... [to] lead to high levels of reflective thought, particularly if the interaction is constructed by a creative author' (John & Wheeler, 2007, p. 4). To enable media to move from 'narrative' or 'linear presentational media' (Laurillard, 2002, p. 91) such as viewing video to something more engaging for learning, Laurillard (2002) also recommended complementing with other media forms to render the resources interactive, and allow exploration, linkage across topics, and to be able to 'follow their own line of investigation' (p. 124).

With the increasing growth of video data, it is envisioned that there will be more extensive research conducted to effectively segment, annotate and access these data (Dong et al., 2010). However, due to the unstructured and linear features of videos, students may have difficulties in locating a specific piece of information in a video as well as challenges in the linkage of ideas. Media annotation software interfaces and the annotation process do support students in such situations and with some guidance can usually move forward with success. Video annotation of students' efforts or video provided by teachers can represent authentic learning when providing simulations of the 'real world' of work. Video can provide a simulation that engages students and asks them to reflect on a work-related task (Colasante, 2011b). The more explicit connections between higher education curriculum content and the video content itself, the more relevant the video interactions become for the viewer. Additionally, providing analysis categories provides some structure for students to make sense of the content (Krottmaier & Helic, 2002, in Colasante & Fenn, 2009), which in MAT is achieved by using teacher created 'Marker Types'.

Next, we describe the history of the development of MAT from idea inception to the present various discipline applications of this online tool.

THE STORY OF MAT'S EVOLUTION

MAT has journeyed through a number of iterative processes, building on input from teachers, students and both learning and technical support professionals. Fig. 1 shows a diagram of these stages – moving from design through to cross-discipline implementation.

At the initial stage of development, before the tool reached pre-production stage, three branches of thinking and literature research were undertaken and cross-pollination between these branches occurred. The first

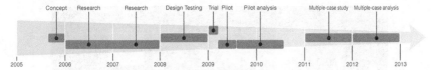

Fig. 1. Timeline of MAT's Evolution.

branch formed a pedagogical perspective, identifying possible micro-learning steps to enable building towards a cycle of learning involving meaningful engagement with media. The second branch was from a technological perspective of functional development possibilities. Both of these two branches fed into the third, interface design.

With ever increasing digital resources available to contemporary students, it was important that MAT did not simply become a passive 'transmission' type of resource or a technology that stymied learning. MAT goes beyond adding the medium of text to video to make it more interactive; it offers a flexible structure or framework for the text via multiple options so that learning has the opportunity to be guided by a light or heavy hand, or somewhere in between, as appropriate to the learning objectives. These options include:

- learner flexibility of where text is added to the video timeline (via creating Markers, see Fig. 2A);
- teacher (or learner) flexibility on categories of analysis (i.e. establishing Marker Types; Fig. 2B);
- learner 'voice' or perspective on giving each Marker a title meaningful to self and/or others (Fig. 2C);
- teacher flexibility on which discussion/annotation panels to employ in the activity cycle, and how to guide their use (i.e. uses of these regardless of their generic titles of 'Notes' and 'Comments' (Fig. 2D), plus 'Conclusion', 'Teacher Feedback' and 'Final Reflections');
- learner 'voice'/perspective for text entries into the annotation panels employed (Fig. 2E).

Additionally, MAT offers teacher and/or learner flexibility in how the learning in MAT translates back into professional practice (student placement or career), classroom activities and/or assessment. Technologically, by being web-based MAT can be opened in any of the popular browsers (Chrome, Firefox, IE, etc.), but is limited for mobile device access due to Flash™ support requirements, plus it scales better for larger screens.

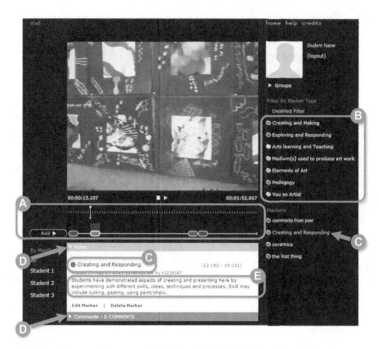

Fig. 2. Screen Capture of MAT as Used in Education (Visual Arts).

An example of MAT's use in Education (Visual Arts) is offered in Fig. 2. It shows a snapshot of a student's annotation of an uploaded video on artworks at her placement primary school. The teacher has provided the analysis categories (B) as 'Creating and Making'; 'Exploring and Responding'; 'Arts Learning and Teaching'; 'Medium(s) used to produce art work'; 'Elements of Art'; 'Pedagogy'; and 'You as an Artist'. The student has marked and annotated the video in four places, which she has categorised under the first two of these categories, evidenced as markers across the video timeline (A). The student has named her markers (C) and entered notes (E) both of which will stay anchored to the segments of video that she chose to annotate.

For the Education (Visual Arts) students, MAT involved mainly individual activity – although the students did this in class time enabling face-to-face collaboration – while some of the other cases had different learning design requirements, as can be seen in Table 1. For example, in some of these cases MAT video content actively involved respective industry representatives (Juris Doctor, Chiropractic, Medical Radiations), plus one

Table 1. MAT Case Integrations.

	Juris Doctor	Chiropractic	Medical Radiations	Teacher Education (Literacy)	Teacher Education (Visual Arts)
			Overview of Higher Education Cases Learning Uses of MAT		
Semester	S1	S2	S2	S1	S1
Objective of MAT use in higher education learning and teaching	Examine court advocacy; a key professional skill for lawyers	Apply clinical thinking to clinical encounters in the chiropractic field	Develop image evaluation skills; simulating eventual practice	Identify and critique detailed early literacy issues in draft children's storybooks	Explore visual arts teaching, including evaluating own processes and others
Video generated and uploaded by students	✓			✓	✓
Video professionally produced with industry professionals in video		✓	✓		
Collaboration with other students required	Analyse the video in small groups in class ✓	Analyse the video online in small groups to determine possible diagnoses ✓		Feedback to a paired peer on draft book ✓	
Feedback provided within MAT	Expert barrister provided each group feedback on a range of annotations ✓	Teachers provided group feedback to initial teamwork; later to individual work ✓	Teacher provided feedback to almost all individual annotations ✓	Teacher provided overall feedback in 'blog' like tool attached to MAT ✓	
Activities in MAT were assessed	Minor assessment component at semester start ✓	Semester-wide assessment requirement ✓			

application of MAT involved an industry representative providing direct student feedback in MAT (Juris Doctor).

In a study of 30 different online and blended learning environments, Bekele (2010) noted flexibility as both a factor of motivation and a factor of satisfaction. However, learning motivation is not guaranteed by providing flexibility. It is a skill for teachers to encourage students' motivation in learning before their intrinsic motivation is activated, which is not usually until a topic has progressed (Biggs & Tang, 2007). MAT does not automatically stimulate motivation, as '[w]hile the design and use of *MAT* fosters active learning, the other element of student engagement – motivation – seems to have become lost in implementation in some of the cases' (Colasante & Lang, 2012).

The boxes below provide a progressive summary of the development of MAT at RMIT University.

KEY STAKEHOLDERS TEST THE PRE-PRODUCTION MAT DESIGN

User testing of the initial MAT design was conducted using an illustrative but semi-interactive representation of MAT, via a page turning PDF file representing steps a student might take through the tool (Colasante & Fenn, 2009). Two focus groups volunteered to provide feedback on the MAT design from student cohorts where the teachers were keen to integrate MAT for specific learning purposes; they had intrinsic motivation to see a good final product. The first, undergraduate Physical Education (PE), expected to use MAT for analysis of videos of their own PE teaching practice. The second, undergraduate Applied Communication students, anticipated using MAT to analyse online audio of student-produced radio interviews. The focus groups were asked to provide feedback via two brief questionnaires; the first harnessing their initial impressions of the design, the second after they had open-group discussions with the designers. This iterative questioning provided valuable feedback on how the tool design could be improved, plus affirmed a number of design decisions. Some features were subsequently improved as a direct result of this user–tester feedback on the initial design.

THE FIRST MAT TRIAL

When the tool was near completion, a trial was organised. The first student cohort to trial MAT in learning was a class of Diploma of Medical Laboratory (vocational/college) students and their teacher. The students used MAT for two separate classroom activities to analyse videos of electrophoresis (medical science) procedures. Each set of MAT activities was to prepare the students for hands-on practical laboratory procedures, which were demonstrated in teacher-produced videos uploaded to MAT. They were asked – in pairs and in two micro-learning stages – to categorise and annotate each video, in particular to recognise equipment and solutions, and then procedural steps and hazards. The trial enabled testing of MAT functionality across two authentic user situations, under the supervision of the key web developer (MAT programmer) and the MAT designers, allowing direct assistance to the students as technical issues arose, plus enabling direct observation of the user experience and fine-tuning of the tool in response to this. Additionally, students completed feedback surveys that also contributed to improvements.

THE PILOT STUDY

The next step involved a formal pilot study of MAT as integrated into a higher education learning semester. This single-case study examined the integration of MAT into a third-year undergraduate Physical Education (PE) teaching course (subject). It explored the use and effectiveness of MAT in learning, investigating how this online learning environment might be used by students and teachers to support their intended learning outcome: to critically reflect on and evaluate their PE teaching practice. The case provided opportunities to gather baseline data before wider uptake of the tool, and to trial a research framework that was designed to scale up to a multiple-case study.

The case provided both encouraging and useful findings (Colasante, 2011a). The study illustrated that MAT was largely effective for their intended learning, to critically reflect and evaluate their teaching practice. The students achieved this by recording videos of their own teaching practice and uploading them within their small peer group area in MAT. They viewed their videos and selected and categorised sections with pre-determined teacher categories and typed in notes. A conductor-of-sorts, the teacher provided a timing structure the students were to follow, to enable individual analysis followed by collaboration within their small groups, such as a 'due date' for marking up own videos followed by peer feedback on the analysed video sections, then conclusion writing. The teacher provided feedback within MAT, deliberately targeting areas of highest impact to each student's development. The students reviewed their annotation cycles repeatedly and then transferred their findings within MAT into a reflective report for assessment submission. Overall, the results encouraged wider use of MAT across other disciplines to further test learning effectiveness (Colasante, 2010). Additionally, technical modifications were recommended for MAT as a result of the pilot study, some of which were adopted.

MULTIPLE-CASE STUDY ACROSS DISCIPLINES AND SECTORS

Employing the research framework as established and tested in the pilot case study, MAT was next examined across multiple cases. This collaborative project involved actively using MAT for work preparation/analysis activities, across a range of disciplines and tertiary sectors. These included postgraduate Juris Doctor (law); undergraduate Education (Literacy), Education (Visual Arts), Chiropractic and Medical Radiations; vocational Property Services (three cohorts) and Audio-visual Technology. In total, nine cases across six disciplines were examined, and this chapter refers to the five cases involved in the project from the higher education context.

An earlier work-in-progress report on the multiple-case study looked at four of the higher education cases with a focus on the relationship of learning design to student engagement (Colasante & Lang, 2012). It was found that students reported higher satisfaction in cases where there was learner-to-learner collaboration, teacher feedback and assessment linkage, plus – somewhat surprisingly – where teachers provided videos within MAT rather than student video generation and upload. The latter was further contextualised by reported difficulties and/or excessive time consumption in video uploading. This chapter continues the focus on student engagement with MAT, but specifically widens the data range to further explore these issues, plus includes reference to the fifth higher education case, the postgraduate Juris Doctor cohort.

METHODOLOGY: MULTIPLE-CASE STUDY APPROACH

Following the successful MAT pilot study in 2009, a larger mixed method multiple-case study was established to examine further MAT's application in learning and teaching across varied contexts. The evaluation framework was trialled in the pilot case study, and benefited from minor design adaptation for the multiple cases shared in this chapter. Multiple-case studies are commonly designed to study innovations in education, including researching the integration of new educational technology (Yin, 2009).

The multiple-case study involved using MAT for reflective practice, content-specific analysis, professional practice and work preparation analysis activities in a range of courses across the tertiary sectors. This chapter refers to the five cases involved in the project from the higher education context within one Australian university and includes courses from the Juris Doctor, Teacher Education courses of Visual Arts and Literacy, and health sciences courses from the Medical Radiations and Chiropractic programs. Table 1 displays these diverse areas involved in the study and indicates the foci for learning and teaching, and Table 2 displays class sizes, and breakdown of gender for the student participants. The 244 student participants of the higher education cases were involved in using MAT within their study and were invited to evaluate its effectiveness and how the interface addresses specific objectives. From this, 161 students across the cases volunteered to participate in the study.

Table 2. Higher Education MAT Cases – Class Size and Gender Mix.

		Juris Doctor	Chiropractic	Medical Radiations	Teacher Education (Literacy)	Teacher Education (Visual Arts)
Class size		$n = 32$	$n = 78$	$n = 57$	$\cdot\ n = 18$	$n = 59$
Student participants – survey	Number	$n = 18$	$n = 56$	$n = 49$	$n = 16$	$n = 22$
	Gender mix	Female = 7 Male = 7 Unknown = 4	Female = 16 Male = 17 Unknown = 23	Female = 24 Male = 15 Unknown = 10	Female = 12 Male = 3 Unknown = 1	Female = 16 Male = 0 Unknown = 6

Table 3. Higher Education Student Surveys Completed.

	Juris Doctor	Chiropractic	Medical Radiations	Teacher Education (Literacy)	Teacher Education (Visual Arts)	Total
Class size	32	78	57	18	59	244
Pre-surveys	18 (56%)	39 (50%)	36 (63%)	15 (83%)	18 (31%)	126 (52%)
Post-surveys	2 (6%)	37 (47%)	33 (58%)	12 (67%)	13 (22%)	97 (40%)

Note: There were a number of students in each case who completed the Post-survey without having completed the Pre-survey, with the number of Survey Participants in Table 2, reflecting the total number of students having completed either survey.

Student research participants from each case were involved in a two-part survey that allowed for collecting data pre- and post-MAT use. The survey participation levels are provided in Table 3. In particular for the focus of this discussion, pre-survey data provided basic student demographics, student ICT access and perceived skill levels, and whether they liked learning online in general. The post-survey data provided student opinions on a range of questions on whether they liked MAT in their learning, and what features of MAT they found most helpful or most unhelpful. The surveys comprised a range of quantitative (mainly Likert-styled) and qualitative or open question styles.

Additionally, a number of teachers and students and one expert/industry representative were involved in the *interactive process interviews* that were held after MAT was administered. The interviews involved the interviewee first demonstrating and explaining their use of MAT under observation, followed by a semi-structured interview. This was helpful in triangulating the data even though student participation numbers were low overall. The

Table 4. Higher Education Interviews Conducted.

	Higher Education MAT 'Interactive Process Interviews' Conducted				
	Juris Doctor	Chiropractic	Medical Radiations	Teacher Education (Literacy)	Teacher Education (Visual Arts)	Total
Teachers	3	2	1	1	1	8
Teaching assistant			1			1
Students		8	1	2	3	14
Experts	1					1

number of interviews conducted across cases is shown in Table 4, each of which was audio-recorded with participant permission.

The main limitation in preliminary MAT studies (design stage, trial and pilot implementation) involved small participation numbers due to data collection concentration in single or few cohorts, rather than low percentage of volunteer participants. While the recent study – the multiple-case study – extended across a number of student cohorts of various disciplines, the limitations still centred on participation numbers. However, this was related to uneven student participation across the cohorts, which ranged from moderately low to very high per cohort for the surveys, but very low to moderate for the student observations and interviews. The nature of voluntary participation meant that student participation would be unpredictable. However, it must be noted that the teacher participation was very high, with a 100% participation rate for teachers who were early adopters of MAT.

Ethics approval was granted to conduct this research prior to data collection. All participants were invited to participate, and were ethically respected in that their responses were harnessed during the teaching semester but not during class time, and accessed post-semester. This approach meant that there was no impact on assessment or curriculum timelines.

SELECTED FINDINGS

The following analysis draws primarily from the student survey data, supported by interview material from teachers and students. First, pre-survey material including student characteristics and familiarity with computers and online learning is discussed. Second, results from a survey administrated after student engagement with MAT are analysed, including use, student assessment of the tool and self-assessment of learning. Finally, data from students and teachers gathered via interactive interviews related to engagement in learning is discussed.

The Survey

Surveys were administered to all students prior to the introduction of MAT and following its use in their course. The pre-survey collected demographic information, activity levels, access details and attitudes to online learning. The post-survey allowed students to give feedback about the use of MAT in their course. The overall response rates were 52% for the pre-survey and 40% for the post-survey, with the Education (Literacy) group having the highest response rate across the cases. Unfortunately, due to a timing error the Juris Doctor students were not able to fully participate in the post-survey and only two responses were received. Survey participation details are shown in Table 3 (the methodology section).

Pre-survey

The demographic details for each of the cases were harnessed in the pre-survey. There were a small number of students in each case who completed the post-survey without having completed the pre-survey so their demographic information appears as unknown.

Apart from Juris Doctor (the postgraduate case), each of the cases had a mainly younger student representation with the majority of students being aged 25 and under. For gender distribution (as tabled in the methodology section), in Education and Medical Radiation there was a higher representation of females; whereas in Chiropractic and the Juris Doctor, where the information was known, the gender split was fairly even.

In each of the cases the majority of students nominated English as their first language. Of the 22 students across disciplines who stated that their first language was not English, their first language stated was Chinese ($n = 9$), Vietnamese ($n = 3$), Korean ($n = 2$), Swahili ($n = 1$), French ($n = 1$), Greek ($n = 2$), Arabic ($n = 1$), Shona ($n = 1$), Hakka ($n = 1$) and Dari ($n = 1$). Where the country of birth was known, the majority (76%) were born in Australia. Other countries listed included China (7%), Vietnam (4%), South Korea (2%), Hong Kong (2%), Malaysia (2%), Afghanistan (1%), Kenya (1%), New Zealand (1%), Mauritius (1%), Greece (1%), Iraq (1%), Singapore (1%), Zimbabwe (1%) and England (1%).

In summary, students were more often female, under 25, and born in Australia.

The second section of the pre-survey dealt with internet access, ability and attitudes to online learning. For each of the cases all students had daily access to computers and the internet, thus enabling all the opportunity to use MAT. Attitudes towards online learning in general were very favourable with over 90% in each case agreeing – in full, or some of the time – that they liked learning with resources and activities online. This positive attitude meant that students were likely to be receptive to using MAT in their course (however, some variance occurs later when the questions become more specific towards online learning in their own courses).

When asked about their computer skill level the most confident were the Juris Doctor and Medical Radiations students; the least confident were the Education (Visual Arts) students. Possible reasons for this are that the Medical Radiation students would need to have good technical skills for their course, and that Juris Doctor students tended to be of mature age and quite possibly using computers regularly in their work. The most likely place that students from all cases were going to access MAT was at home. The second most likely access venue was at university for the undergraduate students and at work for the postgraduate students (Juris Doctor).

Students were also asked about their preferred learning style and the most popular response given by Education (Literacy and Visual Arts) and Juris Doctor students was 'listening and talking', whereas for the Chiropractic case it was 'moving or manipulating', and for the Medical Radiation case 'watching or reading'. These responses, suggesting 'aural', 'kinaesthetic' and 'visual' preferred learning styles, respectively, are not surprising, given the vocational training needs of each case.

Responses to a further question on attitude towards online learning (Fig. 3) was consistent to those from an earlier question and revealed strong support for online learning in each of the five cases – especially Medical Radiation. There was however almost one-quarter of Education (Visual Arts) students who were not keen on online learning and some ambivalence amongst the Education (Literacy) students.

Post-survey

The post-survey results which follow do not include the Juris Doctor cohort due to a low number of responses ($n = 2$). Results (Fig. 4) for the usage of MAT showed that the Chiropractic students were the most regular users on a weekly basis. The other cases tended to use MAT on a more irregular basis

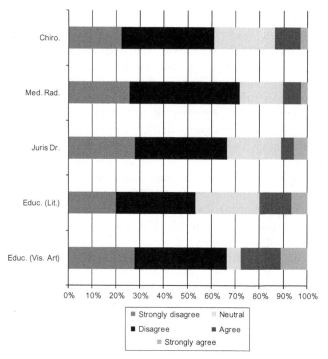

Fig. 3. I Do Not Like Using Online Learning At All in My Studies.

and the biggest group for *class time only* use were the Education (Visual Arts) students. The most common amount of time spent in one episode was 15–30 minutes across all cases (Fig. 5).

In terms of which features of MAT were accessed (e.g. watched or read), Chiropractic students were the most avid users with more than half of this group accessing all but four of the ten features listed on an Often/Very Often basis. In contrast, the other three cases tended to select 'Never' or 'Sometimes' for a range of each of the features.

A number of rating scale (Strongly Disagree to Strongly Agree) items was included in the post-survey to elicit attitudes towards using MAT in their courses. Results for items that were common for each case follow.

The group of students who enjoyed using MAT most was the Chiropractic students; conversely, Education students enjoyed it the least (Fig. 6). Perhaps not surprising, given in the pre-survey the Education students had given the lowest support to online learning.

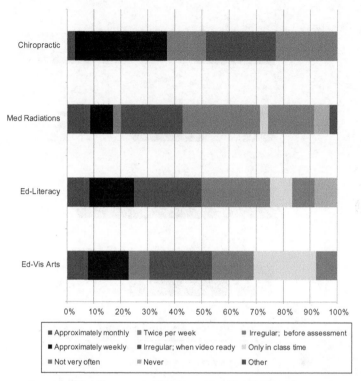

Fig. 4. How Frequently Did You Use MAT This Semester?

There was also the added requirement of the Education students to produce and upload their own videos, in contrast to the professionally produced videos for Chiropractic and Medical Radiation cases. This introduced an extra level of technical complexity, which for some was likely a cause of frustration. Another possible reason for the higher satisfaction amongst the Chiropractic and Medical Radiation cases was that the video content was highly relevant to their vocational training needs, and that there seemed to be a more systematic approach in the administration of MAT, for example, defined group activities and teacher feedback.

Responses (Fig. 7) to a similar question are consistent with these findings.

More than half of the students – except those in Education (Visual Arts) – felt comfortable in using MAT (Fig. 8); almost 40% of the Education (Visual Arts) cohort did not.

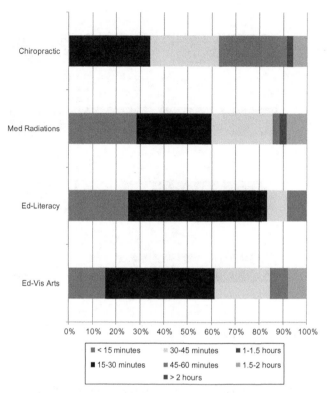

Fig. 5.   How Long, On Average, Did You Spend Using MAT in Any One Episode?

There was a strong level of agreement (Fig. 9) by the Chiropractic and Medical Radiation students in relation to the way MAT allowed for communicating and collaborating with other students. This could be due to the way that MAT was utilised in each of the cases. Indeed in Chiropractic it was a requirement that students worked in groups and nominated a leader to form conclusions for a patient diagnosis.

When asked about which issues relating to MAT were *most helpful* for learning, the responses covered: relevance to theory; collaboration; use of markers; viewing and commenting on videos; and feedback. Summaries by case follow:

• *Chiropractic*: Many of the comments related to how beneficial it was to see real life examples and how it linked back to theory. Other comments

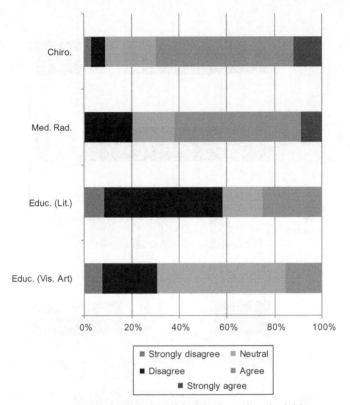

Fig. 6. I Liked Using MAT in My Learning Activities.

included favouring the online collaboration, ability to view and review, and use of markers in clinical findings.

- *Medical Radiations*: The most common response was being able to see a professional critique of images. Other comments included ability to play/ replay, annotate and reinforcing concepts.
- *Education (Visual Arts)*: The majority of comments were concerned with students appreciating viewing and commenting on the videos, and liking to use a new ICT resource.
- *Education (Literacy)*: Most of the responses related to appreciating the feedback and interaction with peers.

When asked about which issues relating to MAT were *least help-ful* for learning, the responses covered: problems associated with the

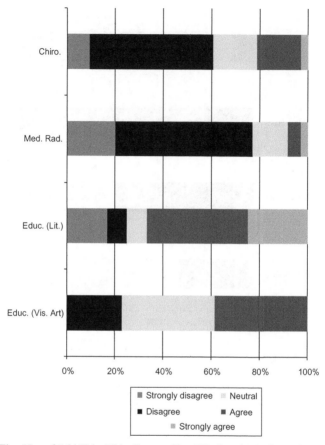

Fig. 7. The Use of MAT in This Course Has Hindered My Learning Experience
Compared to Traditional Learning.

administration of MAT; time issues; unclear purpose or relevance; and technical glitches. Summaries by case follow:

- *Chiropractic*: Some of the responses related more to the administration of MAT in the class, for example, problems with group membership, or only one clinical case to review, rather than its features. Responses more concerned with MAT functionality were lengthy time it took to use, complexities and repetitiveness.
- *Medical Radiations*: There were the lengthy a range of responses which included lack of time, poor quality of video, use confusion (which also

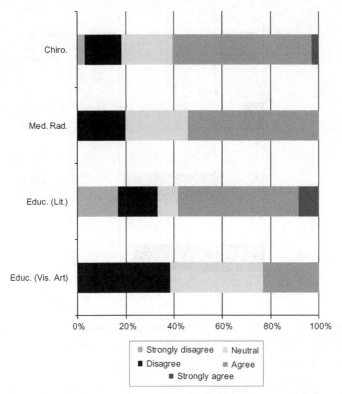

Fig. 8. I Felt Comfortable Communicating Through MAT for the Activities.

relates back to video quality in that some didn't play the video in the MAT interface), reliance on computer and internet access, and lack of opportunity to do own critiquing.

- *Education (Visual Arts)*: Many of the comments were about navigation and uploading difficulties; one student did not understand the relevance of MAT use in the Visual Arts.
- *Education (Literacy)*: Most of the responses concerned navigation and uploading difficulties.

Correlations

A bivariate correlation analysis (Spearman's rho) using rating scale items (Strongly Disagree to Strongly Agree) in the post-survey was conducted to

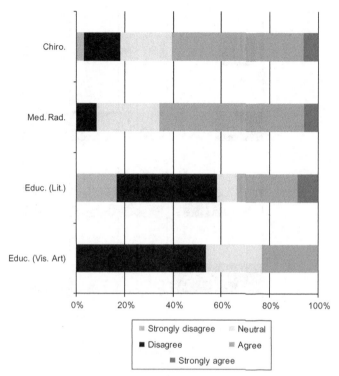

Fig. 9. Using MAT in This Course Allowed Me to Communicate and Collaborate with Other Students, and with My Teacher, in a Way that was Helpful to My Learning.

detect what drove engagement with MAT. Spearman's rho is appropriate for examining relationships between such ordinal level Likert-scale items (de Vaus, 2002), and even though the number of respondents for each case was small, the test of significance takes into account the sample size.

All rating scale items in the post-survey were included in the analysis, with the item 'I liked using MAT in my learning activities' as the *leading* item. The case disciplines were analysed separately because of the different uses of MAT and it was of interest to see if there were any significant relationships that were common across the cases (see Table A1).

Across all cases a significant relationship existed between liking MAT and 'Using MAT allowed me to communicate and collaborate with other students, and with my teacher, in a way that was helpful to my learning' indicating that the feedback and collaboration features of MAT helped engage students. Similarly, for all cases, significant correlations existed between liking MAT and recommending its use to others. Results for each case follow.

Chiropractic
Correlations between 31 post-survey items and 'I liked using MAT in my learning activities' were analysed and the significant results are shown in the appendix.

A significant *positive* relationship existed between liking MAT and 17 other items, with the strongest two correlations being:

- MAT was an excellent tool for viewing and annotating media ($r_s = .755$, $p < .01$).
- From my experiences of using MAT, I would recommend it for other students to use ($r_s = .688$, $p < .01$).

These results show that those who liked using MAT would recommend it to others and saw it as being useful as a learning tool. (The converse also holds true.)

A significant *negative* relationship existed with liking MAT and four other items with the strongest two being:

- I would have preferred not to use MAT ($r_s = -.716$, $p < .01$).
- The use of MAT in this course has hindered my learning experience compared to traditional learning methods ($r_s = -.571$, $p < .01$).

This indicates that students liking MAT also supported the use of MAT in their course.

Medical Radiations
Correlations between 31 post-survey items and 'I liked using MAT in my learning activities', an indicator of engagement, were analysed and the significant results are shown in the appendix.

A significant *positive* relationship existed between liking MAT and 13 other items, with the strongest two correlations being:

- From my experiences of using MAT, I would recommend it for other students to use ($r_s = .646$, $p < .01$).
- Having access to MAT enhanced my learning experience in this course ($r_s = .571$, $p < .01$).

Like Chiropractic, this shows a strong relationship between liking MAT and its usefulness as a learning tool.

A significant *negative* relationship existed with liking MAT and three other items with the strongest two being:

- I would have preferred not to use MAT ($r_s = -.651$, $p < .01$).
- I would have preferred to have face-to-face discussions about the learning instead of using MAT ($r_s = -.509$, $p < .01$).

This indicates that students who liked using MAT also supported the use of MAT, and preferred using an online tool rather than face-to-face delivery. (The converse also holds true.)

Education – Literacy
Correlations between 41 post-survey items and 'I liked using MAT in my learning activities' were analysed and the significant results are shown in the appendix.

A significant *positive* relationship existed between liking MAT and 12 other items, with the strongest two correlations being:

- Using MAT allowed me to receive encouraging support ($r_s = .833$, $p < .01$).
- The amount of interaction with my peers (fellow students) in MAT was appropriate ($r_s = .781$, $p < .01$).

This finding is different from the other cases, indicating that the strong relationship between liking MAT and group interaction and support was an important issue for the Education (Literacy) students. Further examination of the data revealed that there was a high level of disagreement with the support item (60%) and dislike of MAT (also close to 60%), so the lack of support was a factor in their low engagement with MAT.

A significant *negative* relationship existed with liking MAT and two other items:

- I would have preferred not to use MAT ($r_s = -.733$, $p < .01$).
- I was very unsatisfied using MAT ($r_s = -.642$, $p < .01$).

This indicates that students liking MAT also supported the use of MAT in their course, and that there was a level of consistency with responses for liking MAT and satisfaction with MAT.

Education – Visual Arts

Correlations between 35 post-survey items and 'I liked using MAT in my learning activities' were analysed and the significant results are shown in the appendix.

A significant *positive* relationship existed between liking MAT and eight other items, with the strongest two correlations being:

- From my experiences of using MAT, I would recommend it for other students to use ($r_s = .787$, $p < .01$).
- Using MAT allowed me to be involved in activities that are relevant to my eventual professional practice ($r_s = .699$, $p < .01$).

As with the previous cases, this shows a strong relationship between liking MAT and its usefulness as a learning tool; especially in this case its value in relevant professional practice.

A significant *negative* relationship existed with liking MAT and 'I was very unsatisfied using MAT' ($r_s = -.575$, $p < .01$) indicating a consistency in opinion.

Interactive Process Interviews

The interactive process interviews with students, teachers and the industry expert were analysed using NVivo and the results for a selection of items relevant to engagement follow. These include opinions of effectiveness of MAT for learning engagement, what they liked or experienced as barriers in their learning with MAT, and the role of assessment in their MAT-related activities.

Students were asked about the effectiveness of MAT for engaging in their work-relevant learning and assessment activities. The most common types of responses were that it was a relevant activity; was helpful in their learning; and that they liked how it was interactive. Suggestions such as needing a purpose, and needing to be part of the assessment, were also raised as engagement factors.

> Yeah, it's applying your knowledge, so you feel like you're actually able to do what you're learning to do.

> For my course I found watching the video and identifying the marker types for the first video was really, that was probably my favourite and most interesting.

When teachers were asked a similar question the answers were not that dissimilar, with relevant activity, and helpful for learning, as being the most common responses. They also saw the Marker features, giving feedback and the interactive nature of MAT as being useful for engaging the students. Concerns were raised by a couple of teachers about the amount of time involved, and about some of the technical glitches.

Answers given by students about what they liked most about MAT included how they found it helpful in their learning especially the ability to watch/re-watch videos; the use of markers; and reading the comments and feedback of others.

> But the most useful part of it for me was giving feedback, because the entire time, I was thinking about my own book as well and I was thinking about what makes a good book...
>
> ... getting feedback is the most motivating thing...

Barriers for engagement with MAT were also raised in the interviews and the responses could be categorised into three areas:

- *Technical*: upload problems; functionality (including broken links); not user friendly; and navigation.
- *Implementing MAT*: training and support; time constraints; instruction not clear; group work; lack of continuous use; wanting more videos; privacy issues; not assessed; and purpose not clear.
- *Features of MAT*: marker problems (in particular not being able to make them less than 30 seconds long); lack of comments; or hard to find comments; and poor quality of peer feedback.

The interviews also allowed the issue of assessment to emerge. Across the five higher education cases featured, two cases directly assessed the student activities in MAT. Both the Juris Doctor and the Chiropractic cases used these activities as a minor assessment item for the course with marks allocated. The Juris Doctor students completed their assessable MAT activities early in the semester, while the Chiropractic students' activities continued across the academic semester. Both the Education cases, Literacy and Visual Arts, allowed students to portfolio their progress throughout the semester but neither was directly assessed. For example, the Literacy students publicly presented their completed task of a child's storybook in class, as the summation of their storybook progress and collaboration in MAT.

The Medical Radiations MAT activities, while helpful for eventual professional practice (that was still a few years away for these first year students), did offer examination preparation, which the students were informed of but didn't always find this reason enough to engage. For example, one student offered:

the reason that I didn't do much is because it didn't have a direct assessment component. ... Probably if I was a more diligent student I would've done more ...

Therefore, the Chiropractic cohort was the only case to have a semester-wide assessment component to the learning requirements in MAT, while the Juris Doctor included a start-of-semester MAT assessment component.

In the next section of this chapter, we discuss the implications of this selected data.

IMPLICATIONS

A high proportion of students across all cases was supportive of using an online learning tool, and had the requisite access and skills to use MAT in their courses. Higher satisfaction with MAT was experienced in cases where there was a requirement for collaboration with other students to achieve goals, included teacher feedback, and formed a part of the assessment. Another factor was that satisfaction was higher where teachers provided videos within MAT rather than where the students generated and uploaded the videos. This may be due to students' time, effort and vulnerability in generating their own material, and the extra level of technical complexity that for some was a cause of frustration. The cases with higher satisfaction were Chiropractic and Medical Radiation where the task designs were more structured than in the two Education cases. Drivers of engagement were explored using correlations, with the feedback and collaboration features of MAT coming across as a strong factor for all cases. For instance, there was a significant relationship between endorsement (liking) of MAT by students and the use of MAT to aid learning through collaboration with fellow students and teachers. This shows that in this study the feedback and collaboration features of MAT helped engage students.

The effectiveness of MAT for engaging in work-relevant learning and assessment activities was examined and the most common factors for this effectiveness included: it was a relevant activity, was helpful in their learning, and it was interactive. However, further factors of needing a defined learning purpose and to be part of an assessment, were also raised. This is an important finding of this study as it demonstrates that future teacher adopters of MAT need to clearly explain the reason for adoption to students prior to use. It may also be necessary to include MAT as an assessment task as from this study learner engagement (or perhaps motivation to engage) is heightened when MAT is assessed. The most successful use of MAT in this study, the Chiropractic application, included direct assessment of activities in MAT.

Clear benefits of MAT, according to student perceptions, related to the authentic nature of the use of this tool in learning. Students perceived MAT as beneficial due to the 'real life' nature of the simulations and the ability to integrate theory with practice using the tool. Another feature nominated by students was reflection on learning tasks through viewing and reviewing video. Key to this are the markers that are used in MAT that provide an organising feature for analysing and review. Video annotation tools offer the potential to support both the reflection and analysis of one's own video (Colasante, 2011b) and as Luo & Pang (2010) found in their research, video annotation can allow for the slowing down, repeated viewing and identification of key aspects of the video as a connection to specific content focus. While video has long been used to capture microteaching episodes as well as to illustrate and review classroom cases/practices and to review teaching or teachable moments (Correia & Chambel, 1999; Rich & Hannafin, 2009; Schroeter, Hunter, & Kosovic, 2003), it is the possibilities of annotation that can assist in extending reflection, connections to curriculum content and professional needs, wants and practices.

Teacher or professionally generated and student generated videos have the potential to connect higher education students to their learning content as they prepare to graduate as professionals in their fields. In this study student review of material was self-paced through to teacher-guided and included the opportunity to discuss online the video material, drawing on peer, industry and/or teacher input. However, quality and reliability of the technology was a relatively frequent complaint from student participants in the study. The positive attributes of the use of MAT in learning were undermined by technical issues, such as navigation and video uploading difficulties. Apart from technical concerns there were learning and teaching design issues identified including group work issues, lack of time to complete tasks and poor explanation of the task. In the study 'liking' MAT is linked with effective engagement. Importantly, technical issues will undermine students' experience of the tool and will impact on students liking MAT. Thus, it is imperative that technical concerns be addressed for the success of this learning innovation.

CONCLUSIONS

The multiple-case study discussed in this chapter shows that MAT provides teachers with an online tool that has the potential to engage students in an authentic learning design that assists in readying students for the world of work. It has seen some success within a number of different disciplines and thus has wide application possibilities in higher education. Student engagement with MAT was particularly dependent on students liking the tool and this in turn was dependent on the learning design and the technological ease of navigation that students experience. Teachers who adopt MAT in the future will need to be aware and pay careful attention to these two concerns. There are many ways that MAT may move forward in the future, to ensure a sustainable and dynamic online tool. The need for on-going development of this learning and teaching innovation needs to include a focus on critical areas of support for teachers (technical and pedagogical), support for students (learning and technical), and further tool refinement and development. Further data analysis is in progress in this area of sustainability of the tool including support for teachers. Other analysis activities underway include discipline specific single case analysis and artefact analysis of communication activities between students within MAT.

ACKNOWLEDGEMENT

The authors would like to acknowledge the assistance of G. Marchiori in the graphical preparation of Figs. 1 and 2.

REFERENCES

Bekele, T. A. (2010). Motivation and satisfaction in Internet-supported learning environments: A review. *Educational Technology & Society*, *13*(2), 116–127.

Bennett, S., Maton, K., & Kervin, L. (2008). The 'digital natives' debate: A critical review of the evidence. *British Journal of Educational Technology*, *39*(5), 775–786.

Berger, P. (2007, April 17). Learning in the Web 2.0 world [Web log post]. *Infosearcher*. Retrieved from http://infosearcher.typepad.com/infosearcher/2007/04/learning_in_the.html

Biggs, J., & Tang, C. (2007). *Teaching for quality learning at university: What the student does* (3rd ed.). New York, NY: Open University Press.

Colasante, M., & Lang, J. (2012). Can a media annotation tool enhance online engagement with learning? A multi-case work-in-progress report. *Proceedings of the 4th International Conference of Computer Supported Education*, 16–18 April 2012, Porto.

Colasante, M. (2011a). Using video annotation to reflect on and evaluate physical educa-
    tion pre-service teaching practice. *Australasian Journal of Educational Technology*, 27(1),
    66–88.
Colasante, M. (2011b). Using a video annotation tool for authentic learning: A case study.
    Proceedings of Global Learn Asia Pacific 2011 (pp. 981–988). Melbourne, Australia:
    AACE.
Colasante, M. (2010). Future-focused learning via online anchored discussion, connecting
    learners with digital artefacts, other learners, and teachers. In C. Steel, M. J. Keppell &
    P. Gerbic (Eds.), *Curriculum, technology & transformation for an unknown future.*
    Proceedings Ascilite, Sydney.
Colasante, M., & Fenn, J. (2009). 'MAT': A new media annotation tool with an interactive
    learning cycle for application in tertiary education. In G. Siemens & C. Fulford (Eds.),
    *Proceedings of World Conference on Educational Multimedia, Hypermedia and
    Telecommunications (ED-MEDIA) 2009*, AACE, Chesapeake, VA (pp. 3546–3551).
Correia, N., & Chambel, T. (1999). Active video watching using annotation. *Proceedings of the
    seventh ACM international conference on Multimedia (Part 2)* (pp. 151–154). Orlando,
    Florida, United States.
Corrin, L., Bennett, S., & Lockyer, L. (2010). Digital natives: Everyday life versus academic
    study. *Proceedings of the Seventh International Conference on Networked Learning 2010,*
    Lancaster University, Lancaster (pp. 643–650).
de Vaus, D. (2002). *Analysing social science data.* London: Sage Publications.
Dong, A., Li, H., & Wang, B. (2010). Ontology-driven annotation and access of educational
    video data in e-learning. In S. Soomro (Ed.), *E-learning experiences and future* (Ch. 16).
    Retrieved from http://www.intechopen.com/books/e-learning-experiences-and-future/
    ontology-driven-annotation-and-access-of-educational-video-data-in-e-learning
Glover, I., Xu, Z., & Hardaker, G. (2007). Online annotation – Research and practices.
    Computers & Education, 49, 1308–1320.
Helsper, E. J., & Eynon, R. (2009). Digital natives: Where is the evidence? *British Educational
    Research Journal*, 36(3), 503–520.
Herrington, J., Reeves, T. C., & Oliver, R. (2010). *A guide to authentic e-learning (Connecting
    with e-learning).* New York, NY: Routledge.
Herrington, A., & Herrington, J. (Eds.). (2006). *Authentic learning environments in higher
    education.* Hershey, PA: Information Science Publishing.
Howe, N., & Strauss, W. (2003). *Millennials go to college.* New York, NY: LifeCourse.
John, P. D., & Wheeler, S. (2007). *The digital classroom: Harnessing the power of technology for
    the future of learning and teaching.* London: Routledge.
Kaufman, P. B. (2009). On the utility and uses of video in higher education. Intelligent
    television video for culture & education. Retrieved from http://www.intelligent
    television.com/thinkpieces/article/on-the-utility-and-uses-of-video-in-higher-education/
Keengwe, J. (2007). Faculty integration of technology into instruction and students' perceptions
    of computer technology to improve student learning. *Journal of Information Technology
    Education*, 6, 169–180.
Laurillard, D. (2002). *Rethinking university teaching: A framework for the effective use of
    learning technologies* (2nd ed.). London: RoutledgeFalmer.
Lemon, N. (2013). @Twitter is always wondering what's happening: Learning with and through
    social networks in higher education. In B. Patrut, M. Patrut, & C. Cmeciu (Eds.), *Social*

media in higher education: Teaching in web 2.0. (Chapter 12, pp. 237–261). Hershey, PA: IGI Global.

Luo, G., & Pang, Y. (2010). Video annotation for enhancing blended learning of physical education. Paper presented at the (ICAIE), 2010 International Conference on Artificial Intelligence and Education, Hangzhou.

Oliver, B., & Goerke, V. (2007). Australian undergraduates' use and ownership of emerging technologies: Implications and opportunities for creating engaging learning experiences for the Net generation. *Australasian Journal of Educational Technology*, *23*(2), 171–186. Retrieved from http://www.ascilite.org.au/ajet/ajet23/oliver.html

Rich, P. J., & Hannafin, M. (2009). Promoting reflection in teacher preparation programs: A multilevel model. *Journal of Teacher Education*, *60*(1), 52–67.

Schroeter, R., Hunter, J., & Kosovic, D. (2003). *Vannotea – A collaborative video for indexing, annotation and discussion system for broadband networks*. K-CAP 2003 Workshop on Knowledge Markup and Semantic Annotation, Florida, 2003.

Starkey, L. (2011). Evaluating learning in the 21st century: A digital age learning matrix. *Technology, Pedagogy and Education*, *20*(1), 19–39.

Tapscott, D. (1998). *Growing up digital: The rise of the net generation*. New York, NY: McGraw-Hill.

Yin, R. (2009). *Case study research: Design and methods* (4th ed.). Thousands Oak, CA: SAGE Publications.

APPENDIX

Table A1. Significant Bivariate Correlations Across Cases.

Items from Post-survey	Medical Radiations	Chiropractic	Education (Visual Arts)	Education (Literacy)
From my experiences of using MAT, I would recommend it for other students to use.	.646**	.688**	.787**	.706*
Using MAT allowed me to communicate and collaborate with other students, and with my teacher, in a way that was helpful to my learning.	.461**	.531**	.647*	.602*
Using MAT allowed me to be involved in activities that are relevant to my eventual professional practice.	.439**	.419*	.699**	
Using MAT allowed me to be challenged in an interesting way.	.491**	.566**	.586*	
Having access to MAT enhanced my learning experience in this course.	.571**	.539**	.582*	
Using MAT allowed me to communicate and collaborate with expert(s) in a way that was helpful to my learning.	.343*	.415*		.769**
I would have preferred not to use MAT.	−.651**	−.716**		−.733**
Using MAT allowed me to receive encouraging support.		.619**	.684*	.833**
I was very unsatisfied using MAT.		−.343*	−.575*	−.642*
I felt comfortable communicating through MAT for the activities.	.371*	.499**		
The amount of interaction with my teacher in MAT &/ or about MAT activities was appropriate.	.547**			.605*

Table A1. (*Continued*)

Items from Post-survey	Medical Radiations	Chiropractic	Education (Visual Arts)	Education (Literacy)
The use of MAT in this course has hindered my learning experience compared to traditional learning methods.	−.410*	−.571**		
After using MAT, I feel I could communicate my learning in other situations.		.449**	.602*	
MAT was an excellent tool for interaction and collaboration with others.		.461**	.683*	
I was satisfied with how MAT presented (design and layout).		.496**		.671*
MAT was an excellent tool for viewing and annotating media.		.755**		.678*
The use of MAT in this course has helped me to understand key concepts related to producing better quality images.	.360*	na	na	na
MAT helped me to analyse technical image quality.	.385*	na	na	na
I was satisfied with how to navigate MAT (moving between the different features).	.413*			
Using MAT allowed me to reflect on an expert radiographer's critique of a range of upper and lower limb images.	.490**	na	na	na
Without the use of MAT, I would not have been successful in this course.	.520**			
I would have preferred to have face-to-face discussions about the learning instead of using MAT.	−.509**			
MAT was difficult to use.		−.467**		

Table A1. (*Continued*)

Items from Post-survey	Medical Radiations	Chiropractic	Education (Visual Arts)	Education (Literacy)
MAT helped me to analyse presentations of health problems.	na	.473**	na	na
The use of MAT in this course has helped me to understand presentation and assessment of health problem presentations.	na	.496**	na	na
The use of MAT in this course has helped me to understand presentation and assessment of headache conditions.	na	.535**	na	na
Using MAT allowed me to build or construct meaning from my learning experiences.		.566**		
Once I was used to MAT, the quality of learning activities in MAT was excellent.		.650**		
I liked having access to expert opinion (e.g. in video and/ or by commentary).				.580*
I fully utilised the opportunity that MAT offered.				.591*
MAT helped me to reflect on the complexity of the drafting processes involved in writing.	na	na	na	.640*
Using MAT encouraged use of diverse literacies including speaking, listening, viewing and creating.	na	na	na	.655*
The amount of interaction with my peers (fellow students) in MAT was appropriate.				.781**

* Correlation is significant at the 0.05 level (two-tailed).
** Correlation is significant at the 0.01 level (two-tailed).

INNOVATIVE TEACHING METHODS FOR USING MULTIMEDIA MAPS TO ENGAGE STUDENTS AT A DISTANCE

Audeliz Matias, Sheila M. Aird and David F. Wolf II

ABSTRACT

Advances in geospatial technology, web map interfaces, and other Web 2.0 tools provide new opportunities for educators to engage students in critical thinking, problem-solving, and collaborative skills. Although little attention has been given to learning from maps in higher education, knowledge of space is critical to attitudes and decision making as global citizens. Additionally, the ability to easily create multimedia maps offers new educational affordances for students at a distance and has the potential to link geographic and cultural understanding within the context of a variety of disciplines. We discuss the development of a mapping and blogging interactive learning environment, MapBlog, as a visual platform for representing information spatially. In this chapter, the MapBlog will be discussed as an interactive learning environment and as a visual platform for representing information spatially. We present and discuss four MapBlog categories: external content, student-created content, static content, and thematic.

Increasing Student Engagement and Retention using Multimedia Technologies:
Video Annotation, Multimedia Applications, Videoconferencing and Transmedia Storytelling
Cutting-edge Technologies in Higher Education, Volume 6F, 215–234
Copyright © 2013 by Emerald Group Publishing Limited
ISSN: 2044-9968/doi:10.1108/S2044-9968(2013)000006F011

INTRODUCTION

Globally, higher education institutions strive to advance learning by building well-rounded, global citizens through personal and professional development of their students. Although there is not a unique definition of what a global citizen is, we do agree on certain qualities that are necessary to be a well-rounded human being. As citizens, we need to engage in social and ethical responsibility and reflect on issues both locally and globally. Unfortunately, postsecondary education is mostly taught in isolation. Languages, history, and natural sciences are examples of subjects sometimes instructed as individual silos of knowledge.

We should not forget that each of us live in constant interaction with our surroundings. Knowing spatial and contextual factors contribute to a more robust understanding of content across disciplines. Geographic location is an important attribute of individual and global activities, policies, and strategies as well as short- and long-term plans (Zinser, 2012). Moreover, technology has expanded our geographic horizons. Efforts to promote geographic literacy during the last decades, although successful (Downs, Liben, & Daggs, 1988), need to catch up with technology. The increase in accessible geographic data and Web 2.0 tools provides a medium for exploring the relationship between subject matter knowledge and geographic literacy.

The ability to easily create and share web-enabled maps offers a new educational opportunity to strengthen learners' spatial and geographic knowledge both face-to-face and online. This chapter presents the implementation of Google Maps to create an interactive learning environment that integrates multimedia tools such as a blogging and other Web 2.0 tools in which students explore different subjects within the geographical context across disciplines in online courses at our institution.

Online, interactive maps are used increasingly as tools for instructions at all educational levels. Multimedia maps offer a visual platform for representing information otherwise poorly expressed with only text (Hu, 2003). Advances in Geographical Information Systems (GIS), Global Positioning System (GPS), and the availability of web-based maps allow for utilization of maps as learning objects. Likewise, blogs in tandem with an interactive provide an environment where students critically analyze, share information, and learn from each other. Technology, therefore, can foster exploration and examination to prepare critically thinking global citizens (Lucey & Grant, 2010).

More pertinent to our topic, the development of geographic and geospatial application in Web 2.0 has allowed for one computer to access information on another computer regardless of the location. This enables access to an almost unlimited amount of data. Individuals can tag web content (e.g., photos) by adding keywords and latitude/longitude coordinates, also known as geotagging. Geotags can be manually created or automatically generated by devices such as cell phones. In this chapter we present examples of how to leverage the use of multimedia maps. We developed a mapping and blogging learning object based on Google Maps, a Mapblog, to engage online students in collaborative exercises. Through this tool, students get introduced to the geography of a particular region, develop research and communication skills, and a stronger grasp of the topic. During the last four years we have used this tool for a variety of pedagogical purposes in our courses. The four MapBlog categories we explore are: external content, student-created content, static content, and thematic.

LEARNING FROM MAPS

The increase in availability of GPS tools and the advent of map interfaces and of authoring tools, such as blogs, have made the creation of multimedia maps more practical than ever. Initial challenges such as course data resolution and the lack of a mechanism to create portable versions of maps with aggregate data (MacEachren & DiBiase, 1991) have been overcome. The creation of information-rich maps enables sharing of data for community planning, agriculture, business, industry, resource conservation, culture, and education. Appropriately integrated web mapping tools furthers formal and informal education by promoting a learner-centered environment. Google Maps, for example, can provide a number of ways in which students can interact with each other, the instructor, and content in real time.

The engagement of students in online education is especially important because learning is more self-directed. Students are more likely to succeed in online courses that are highly interactive (Fulford & Zhang, 1993), allow them to be active participants (Prensky, 2005; Verneil & Berge, 2000), and promote collaborative learning (Miller & Miller, 1999). Today's learners prefer a community approach to problem solving and creativity (Dziuban, Moskal, Brophy, & Shea, 2007). In addition, computer-based simulations and graphic presentations benefit students (Mabrito, 2004). However,

Griffin, MacEachren, Hardisty, Steiner, and Bonan (2006) found viewers engage more when using animated maps instead of fixed maps displaying the same information.

Students today are determining how and when they want to be educated and are becoming more technologically savvy and multimedia literate. User-generated content has proliferated with the advent of web publishing tools and social networking sites. Researchers agree that the integration of Web 2.0 tools in online courses foster communication at multiple levels (e.g., Helvie-Manson, 2011; Ramli, 2010; Revere & Kovach, 2011; Wolf, Beckem, & Matias, 2011). Custin and Barkacs (2010), for instance, stated that blogs facilitate learner–learner and faculty–learner collaboration. Hence, blogging creates an online community where students actively participate in cooperative, collaborative, and conversational learning. Some of these media tools facilitate visual and geographical representations important to teaching and learning. We can create and share videos (e.g., YouTube), pictures (e.g., Flickr, Pinterest), text (e.g., WordPress, Blogger), and personal stories (e.g., Facebook) with a simple click. Additionally, the Geospatial Web or GeoWeb (Papadimitriou, 2010) is emerging as an opportunity to interact with available geographical data and multimedia. Students are able to create and annotate maps using tools such as Google Maps without any previous training. Multiple media, such as videos, images, and text, can be added to web maps to stimulate authentic learning experiences. These maps can then be shared and embedded as a resource (Bull, 2007).

Multimedia mapping, thus, provides a system for students to collect and share location-based information without difficulty. Consequently, learners become authors of the maps rather than solely the readers and construct their own understanding and knowledge. Most existing mobile phones and digital cameras have built-in GPS receivers. Photos taken from most cell phones and digital cameras have an associated Exchangeable Image File (EXIF) containing detail not only about the camera but also location information including latitude, longitude, and exact address (Vamiso, 2010). For the first time ever we are in a position as educators to harness the possibility for students to produce content knowledge in a geographic context anywhere and anytime.

As a result, the social-constructivist view on knowledge production is strongly relevant to the use of multimedia maps. Constructivism, derived mainly from the works of Piaget (1970) and Vygotsky (1978), states that learning takes place in context and the learners construct much of what they learn through experiences. Concepts constructed by students through the interaction with the instructor and other students define social-constructivism (Kraiger, 2008; Powell & Kalina, 2009). This focus on social context creates a spatially rich understanding of the geographic and cultural environment when engaging students through and with multimedia maps. Although the research about social-constructivism applied to geographic knowledge is sparse, by emerging learners into a unique geographical and social context, this theoretically carries with it all the advantages of online interaction as well as the benefits of a social-constructivism approach. Social constructivism is not simply the result of using the multimedia maps it is the constructing of a unique social environment in which learning can occur.

Maps enable learners to develop critical skills to observe and identify patterns, associations, and spatial perspective (Griffin et al., 2006). You can place a marker and add text, images, links, and video clips (Bull, 2007). Possible applications of powerful and relatively easy tools, such as Google Maps, to create multimedia maps are numerous. For instance, learners can tell a story from different perspectives across a geographical area (Bull, 2008), take a self-guided tour of library collections (Griggs, 2011), explore geographic areas in the context of a book (Lamb & Johnson, 2010), and engage in problem-solving activities that involve field data collection (Lwin & Murayama, 2011).

THE MAPBLOG: A MAPPING AND BLOGGING LEARNING ENVIRONMENT

We first started to explore the application of maps in online teaching and learning in 2006 with the development of the Second Voyage of the Beagle simulation (Guba & Wolf, 2007). We were interested in helping students learn about Charles Darwin's journey around the world onboard the H.M.S. Beagle and experience his scientific exploration in the context of the travels. Thus, using Google Earth, we created a world map where students could trace the path of the Beagle's second voyage and Darwin's field work. The map gives the students the ability to zoom in and explore the areas he visited (Fig. 1). A content and navigation tool bar guides the learner through the timeline of events providing information about the expedition, images of the area, links to resources, and passages and images from Darwin's journal entries. The use of this interactive learning object was scaffolded throughout the course to offer insight related to the content discussed in the modules.

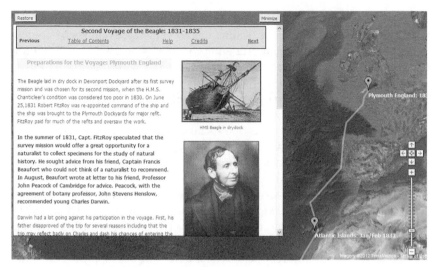

Fig. 1. The Second Voyage of the Beagle Map, Our First Attempt to Develop Interactive Maps.

With each module, students get a closer look at Darwin's findings and learn about scientific inquiry. Because the activity was interactive and fun, the students spent more time learning by engaging with it for longer periods of time. Reflections on learning revealed that the map simulation was highly regarded by many students as a way of bringing Darwin's journey to life. Although the Second Voyage of the Beagle simulation was well received by the students and it assisted them to think about spatial knowledge, we also wanted to encourage cooperation among students and faculty. Thus, we decided to explore a better way of providing information through a dynamic map interface that could allow for student collaboration.

The rapid expansion of Web 2.0 authoring tools, such as blogs, help promote social-constructivism. Hence, blogging offers an excellent addition to interactive learning maps. After several iterations, we combined the use of Google Maps with a Drupal platform to support blogging capabilities and develop a more robust learning object, the MapBlog. It is important to note that the MapBlog utilizes a collection of services using Google Maps Application Programming Interfaces (APIs). The improved interactive map has two distinct views: a blog view and a map view (Fig. 2).

First and foremost, the MapBlog is a blog. The advantage of this format is that it offers a familiar interface for students to interact with the

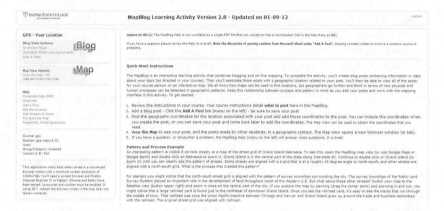

Fig. 2. A Screen Shot Showing the Main Page for the MapBlog Learning Environment. The Interactive Learning Object has Two View Options: Blog View and Map View.

MapBlog. In the blog view students can add and edit their own blog posts as well as add to- and view comments by other students. The map view, on the other hand, displays an interactive map. Posts can include text, links, images, and video. Students can control the formatting and layout of the posts using the editor tools that are similar to the ones in the learning management system. A post made to the MapBlog is a "blog post." But the MapBlog extends basic blogging by allowing users to associate the post with a geographic location so that the post can be viewed using a map-based interface. In this way, the location becomes a visible attribute associated with the post.

The primary reason for developing our own map-based interface is that it allows us to customize the maps as needed. The MapBlog affords us control of the content for both academic continuity and in terms of connecting the visual pedagogy with learning outcomes in the online courses. Importantly, it also allows us to ensure student privacy is preserved. In addition, all entries added to a MapBlog are saved into a database that we maintain. Therefore, we have a record of the student's work that can be kept for as long as it is needed.

Other location-based tools, such as Woices and the Google Lit Tours, also harness geographical and cultural context with possibilities for online learning. However, they do not offer the degree of flexibility or dynamic nature the MapBlog can provide. The Google Lit Tours, for example, present educators a set of downloadable tours based on popular literature using Google Earth. Although a great resource for teachers making literature elements visible, it involves the download and creation of students' own KMZ files, a special type of GIS files. A significant barrier for educators implementing GIS techniques in their courses is lack of time for learning the tools and how to incorporate them in content learning. On the other hand, by utilizing tools students are familiar with, such as our mapping and blogging interface, students can take ownership of their learning.

One of the major challenges of creating the MapBlogs, however, is the implementation of a scalable approach that would allow for individual customization according to learning activities. Thus, we have spent a considerable amount of time developing a system to support the deployment and management of MapBlogs. Our current management tools allow us to automatically generate all of the MapBlogs needed for a given term. We do this using a set of code templates that contain the basic functionality of the MapBlog. These templates consist of HTML pages, stylesheets, files containing Javascript code, and PHP (hypertext Preprocessor) modules hosted on a server running PHP 5 and MySQL 5. Previously students would have to discuss their experience and observations in a discussion forum outside of the MapBlog. The Drupal platform allows for student discussion to occur directly within the MapBlog as each post allows for discussion by allowing comments. This feature vastly improves the learning experience since more time is focused on the learning object rather than on the navigation.

Categories

During the last four years we have used the MapBlog in 29 courses in the areas of cultural studies, science, language, health services, philosophy, history mathematics, and social sciences (see Table 1 for a complete list of the courses). Each MapBlog supplies a platform for implicitly representing geographical relationships of content. Be it subtle or direct, the presentation assists students in understanding key relationships using visual pedagogy in an interactive environment. Our approach to the creation of this learning object shifts emphasis away from a memorizing facts and information to an inquiry-based learning. We have identified four main classes or categories of MapBlog based on the pedagogical intent: external content; student-created content; static content; and thematic MapBlogs. However, these

Table 1. Online Courses with MapBlog Activities.

Discipline	Course Title	MapBlog Type(s)
Cultural Studies	African History and Culture	Student-created content
	Asian American Experience	External content
	Caribbean History and Culture	Student-created content
	Dance Across World Cultures	Static content
Science	Contemporary Environmental Issues	Student-created content
	Global Climate Change	External content
	GPS and the New Geography	Student-created content
	Ecology, Adaptation and Sustainable Development	Student-created content
	Winter Ecology	Student-created content
	Biology of Ecosystems	Student-created content
Language	French I	Static content
	French II	Static content
	Spanish I	Static content
	Spanish II	Static content
	Introductory Spanish: Language and Culture	Static content
	Introductory Spanish for Health Care Professionals	Static content
	Advanced Spanish for Health Care Professionals	Static content
	Spanish in the World of Business	Static content
	Introductory Chinese: Language and Culture	Static content
	Introductory Italian: Language and Culture	Static content
Health Services	Community Health	Student-created content
Philosophy	Introduction to Critical Thinking	Student-created content
History	The Middle East	External content (originally); Student-created (currently)
	The West in American Culture	Student-created content; Thematic
	Global History from the 15th Century	Student-created content; Thematic
	U.S. History to 1865: What Does it Mean to be a Free Nation?	Student-created content
Math	Voter Math[a]	Student-created content
Literature	Literary Interpretation as a Method of Inquiry	Student-created content
Social Sciences	Contemporary Global Issues	Student-created content

[a]MapBlog is not currently active in this course.

categories are not mutually exclusive and combinations are possible. As with any inquiry approach, each MapBlog category focuses on using and learning content as a means to develop information-processing and problem-solving skills.

External Content

During its inception, the main goal of the MapBlog learning environment was to provide a space for students to geotag resources available online. At the time, however, we did not have the ability to directly add and publish content created by students within the MapBlog. Thus, we were not able to take full advantage of its pedagogical capabilities. For example, in the course Global Climate Change, students have to identify an environmental issue potentially caused by climate change, find an online resource describing the issue, and add a marker near an identified site on the MapBlog platform. The same basic application of the MapBlog is used for the Asian American Experience course where students' geotag references with demographic information about a country of their choice. Because of the limitations of this first type of MapBlog, all discussions related to the activity took place outside of the learning object. It is important to know that every time these MapBlogs are used, students start with a blank map as we do not keep a database of links added every term. Some advantages of this approach are that we do not have to worry about privacy issues or maintenance problems due to broken links. However, to be more effective at encouraging deeper and more relevant constructions of knowledge by our students, we decided to expand the MapBlog capabilities and abandon the idea of the external-only content approach.

Student-Created Content

The types of relationships that students develop in an online course are central to their success. Communication with other students and the instructor is essential to the learning experience (Chickering & Gamson, 1987; Roper, 2007). The challenge, as educators, is to create a context in which course participants become both independent and interdependent inquirers. Moreover, according to the National Research Council (2000), the online learning experience should strengthen science education by providing students with digital content that has the potential to enable them to gather, analyze, and display data. From the perspective of social-constructivism, student-created MapBlogs facilitate socially shaped knowledge production. For example, when using the MapBlog to share data gathered though fieldwork activities, students have the opportunity to examine and recognize problems by exploring their communities.

Science education is based on practice and interpretation, thus MapBlogs are appropriate tools for problem-based learning in the sciences. We have used student-created content MapBlogs as a digital journal in several of our science courses. In the GPS and the New Geography course, students utilize the MapBlog twice as a learning tool, using scaffolding during the length of the course. First, they collect data about their location using a handheld GPS and each of their posts should at least include the exact latitude and longitude as calculated using the handheld GPS. Thus, they also learn about accuracy and precision as viewed by the difference in coordinates from their equipment and the Google-based map used on the MapBlog. Later, students calculate the geographic center relative to the location of everyone taking the course. For both assignments they are encouraged to use links and images as well as to write a small description of their findings in their MapBlog's posts. They also have to engage in reflecting writing. To our surprise, by sharing with each other their locations through the MapBlog, students expressed a "sense of belonging," "being part of a community" that they have not experienced in other online courses at our institution.

The same scaffolding strategy is used in several science courses. Students are required to make at least three posts during the semester about local environmental issues in the Contemporary Environmental Issues course. They have also collected data of flora and fauna during the winter months to learn about Winter Ecology. In another instance, in Biology of Ecosystems, students documented Aldo Leopold's observation of the natural world as described in his book, *A Sand County Almanac*. They also role play in the Ecology, Adaptation and Sustainable Development course as a Peace Corps volunteer to a developing nation experiencing hunger and design a strategy to help the selected community.

With each post students add to the MapBlog they need to include: a subject heading; a brief description of the topic/issue (e.g., historical notes, scientific names of plants, the main problem, etc.); a photograph/image; and a link to a resource. Thus, students are not only engaging in an interactive online environment via maps and blogging, they are also discovering and practicing science inquiry. This approach is also useful when having students working on the field collecting data for independent research projects where they are encouraged to pursue ideas themselves. Fig. 3 shows a student-created content MapBlog developed as part of an undergraduate research project. The students identified trees, collected geospatial data using a handheld GPS receiver, and took digital photos. Using a MapBlog

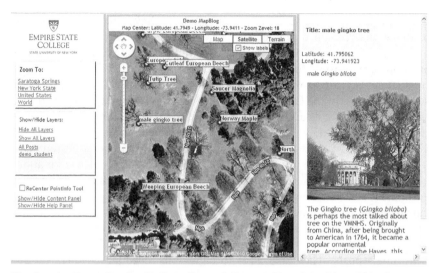

Fig. 3. An Example of a Student-Created Content Type MapBlog. This Category of MapBlog Is Ideal for Activities Involving Data Collection as it Serves as a Digital Repository where Students can Add Photos, Text and Links Related to a Geographic Area.

to organize the collected data helps with data organization and serves as a repository that can be accessed and shared by the student, instructor, and others. It also makes inquiry-based learning and social collaboration easier. Thus, helping students gain skills they need to become lifelong learners that can access, analyze, and synthesize information and apply it to different situations.

Static-Content Map
While our mapping and blogging learning object offers an excellent method for students to share information that illustrates geographical relationships, it can also act as a presentation tool for academic content. A static content MapBlog is one where the students can view posts of material created and vetted by the course developers without having access to edit and/or add any material to the map. Thus, the material is stable which allows for a robust reference tool that can include: hyperlinks, text, images, and video. Students then engage in discussions about the material presented on forums threaded throughout the course in the learning management system rather than in the

MapBlog. This could be seen as an advantage or a disadvantage in terms of pedagogical value and resources. Although students are unable to research and add their findings to the map portion of the MapBlog, the content is still interactive and encourages engagement. For us, an advantage of this approach is that the information presented is tailored to meet specific course objectives and remains unchanged. As a result, static MapBlogs presents an opportunity to share resources between different online courses as well as on the web as open educational resources.

Static MapBlogs provide the perfect learning environment to explore culturally defined areas or regions that bear similarities. For example, we developed a multimedia map that shows countries where Spanish is the official national language, the Spanish Map (Fig. 4). A blog post was created for each Spanish-speaking country. A brief description about the history, economic, and demographic information of each country as well as linguistic variances is included in every post. The posts also include hyperlinks to websites (in both Spanish and English), embedded videos, images, and portals to immersive panoramic interactive tours. The Spanish Map is shared by students taking several lower-level Spanish courses as a

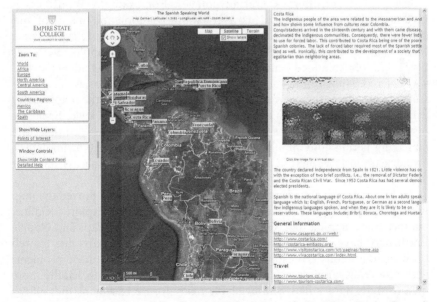

Fig. 4. A Screen Shot of the Spanish Map, One of the First Static Content MapBlog.

resource tool that they can use for their assignments. By using a common MapBlog, multiple course offerings can share resources and maximize the development process.

Although these MapBlogs have been well-received by faculty and students alike, we have encountered several intrinsic challenges. First, links and embedded resources used to present content need constant updating. Unless, we create our own content, we run the risk of losing content created by third parties. Second, providing instructors editor access to the maps is a difficult and risky task. All of our MapBlogs are located in one central, secured server administered by the Office of Integrated Technologies. Third, we also experienced instability with complex Web 2.0 applications across browsers that increased calls to the help desk from both instructors and students. Lastly, due to its architecture, embedding static MapBlogs directly into web pages, although not impossible, is not stable and creates problems displaying content.

At the beginning of 2012, in order to minimize these challenges, we decided to change the platform holding the content and the mapping API of this category of MapBlogs. The content was moved from Drupal to a WordPress platform hosted on the Empire State College servers. This new blogging platform offers several advantages. For example, WordPress is used in other online courses as a collaborative tool and many of our students use this platform for personal purposes. Thus, the learning curve for navigating the blog is less steep as they are already familiar with this blogging tool. An added benefit is that the platform affords students several ways of reorganizing the content, such as by tags or categories. This gives students an alternative view to the visual representation of the map so they can choose the presentation that best matches their learning style. From the instructional designer perspective, WordPress also makes editing and managing permissions simpler, accommodates more Web 2.0 technologies, broadcasts posts with RSS feeds, and functions properly across different internet browsers.

Additionally, we abandoned the use of Google Maps and moved the map view of static content MapBlogs to ESRI's ArcGIS Explorer Online, another free mapping tool. Geo-browsers such as Google Maps and Google Earth may have problems rendering large vector-based maps due to web browser limitations (Hudson-Smith et al., 2007). They also have problems with rendering large data files. ArcGIS Explorer Online can handle more data formats, larger files, and available ready-to-use basemaps that allows for greater instructional design flexibility. It also has an interface compatible with mobile devices as well as a dedicated mobile application. Furthermore, this mapping software lets us create and embed code to seamlessly insert the maps within a course or web page as an open resource. The affordances of the new static content format give us an opportunity to expand the types of features incorporated. For example, both the Italian and the Canary Islands maps contain embedded virtual tours besides text, images, and other multimedia. This change of format, however, only applies to static content MapBlogs.

Thematic Map
Generally, cartographers divide maps in two categories: general-reference maps and thematic maps. Topographic maps, for example, are considered general-reference maps that provide land information (Robinson, Morrison, Muehrcke, Kimerling, & Guptill, 1995). On the other hand, thematic maps display spatial patterns of physical, social, historical, or other phenomena. They tend to be single purpose, displaying a "theme." Common examples of patterns illustrated with thematic maps include: population density (Coutant & Westheimer, 1993), life expectancy, and voting patterns (Slocum, McMaster, Kessler, & Howard, 2009). The choice of symbolization is critical to the usefulness of thematic maps. Robinson et al. (1995) describe four different types of symbols used in the design of these maps: point symbols, area symbols, volume symbols, and line symbols. Instead of simply offering a map illustrating particular spatial relationships, thematic mapping uses the symbols to tell a story about the place (Thrower, 2007). Indeed, Peterson (2000) described the benefits of the use of thematic mapping to teach economics. Using thematic maps as visual portrayals of economic data, he concluded, enhance students' understanding of the relationships presented by the data. Map colors, symbol sizes and densities help students visualize the information presented and place the values in a spatial context. Thematic mapping, therefore, fosters an active learning environment beneficial to teaching economics (Peterson, 2000).

Many elements of thematic mapping are present in the MapBlog learning environment and we can argue that all of our MapBlogs utilize thematic mapping principles in some way. Notably, static content and student-created MapBlogs are thematic maps. The Caribbean Map (Fig. 5), developed for our Caribbean History and Culture course, illustrates this situation. The intent of the static portion of the MapBlog is to offer interactive layers for students to easily access information about geopolitical, historical, and cultural relationships. We created a quick navigation toolbar, left of the map, for students to have immediate access to areas according to themes. Using thematic layers, we created sets of area symbols

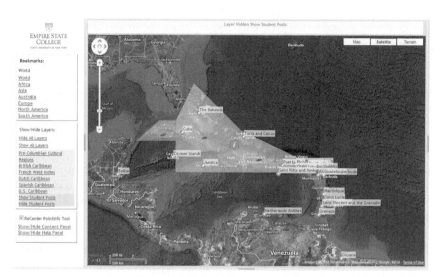

Fig. 5. A Screen Shot of the Caribbean Map, a Thematic MapBlog. The Quick Navigation Toolbar Allows for Students to Have Immediate Access to Areas According to Themes or Layers.

(symbols that assign value or characteristics to an area) representing: Pre-Columbian cultural regions, British Caribbean, French West Indies, Dutch Caribbean, Spanish Caribbean, and U.S. Caribbean. These layers can be displayed or hidden using the navigation toolbar. Basically, students can interact with the thematic MapBlog and select how they wish to view specific groupings of data or geographical relationships of content.

Soon we realized the potential of applying the use of thematic mapping to engage students in collaborative learning by creating their own thematic layers within the Caribbean MapBlog. Students then individually research relevant to a particular Caribbean nation of their choice throughout the length of the course and are required to contribute to the map in different occasions. In addition, if the MapBlog is utilized twice for different content within the course it can be structured to continue as a separate layer with students able to view original blogs and interaction. Once the student determines the location they wish to investigate, the longitude and latitude input is linked to their blog. The blog allows for the conversation to unfold and the inquiry to be taken a step further utilizing peer-review of each others' findings and reflect on their own learning. Both the peer-review comments and reflection utilize the blog part of the learning environment.

With this level of data complexity, the ability to select and de-activate layers with the navigation toolbar is a valuable design strategy that does not compromise students' ability to interact with the material.

FINAL REMARKS

Interactive maps, particularly those utilizing Web 2.0 tools, are suitable for learning activities in almost any subject area in higher education. They link people and places locally and globally. The ability to easily create multimedia maps offers new educational affordances for students at a distance. It is easier than ever to engage our students in geographic and spatial skills that moves away from traditional emphases in factual knowledge. In terms of promoting the development of good citizens, employing multimedia maps creates a sense of holism and collaboration that encourages learning in a global setting.

Our mapping and blogging tool, the MapBlog, offers a myriad of opportunities to create an interactive learning environment for distance learners. Based on informal course feedback, MapBlogs are particularly useful to engage students in research, problem-solving activities, critical thinking, and scientific inquiry through student-created content. Thematic MapBlogs also foster active learning. On the other hand, external and static content MapBlogs present some technical and pedagogical limitations. Google Maps makes possible the creation of annotated maps without much effort (Bull, 2007). However, we continue to explore the use of other web-enabled mapping tools, such as ArcGIS Explorer Online by ESRI, for the creation of interactive learning objects. In addition, we are currently developing a thematic MapBlog featuring a choropleth map based on the population densities of individuals who speak Spanish as a first language. This type of thematic map utilizes a graded color scheme to display area symbols.

As we move forward, we will continue to explore new strategies for the use of MapBlogs as well as ways to improve them. Current affordability of mobile devices and increased network reliability enable ubiquitous access to data collection tools on the go. Perhaps we need to explore ways to make uploading data to MapBlogs accessible through mobile devices. Certainly that would encourage students to actively participate anytime, anywhere. Some people, however, have expressed concerns about privacy issues and the use of blogging and other Web 2.0 tool that allow for geotagging and sharing of location information. For example, Vamosi (2010) warns about the unintended sharing of personal details through digital photos. We must, perhaps, negotiate shifts in the meaning of privacy beyond the first and second party relationships at the national and global levels (Elwood & Leszczynski, 2011). Although we advocate for the harnessing of these tools for knowledge construction, as educators, we also have to be aware that some students may dislike the idea that other people can know where there are at any given moment when collecting and sharing data. Ultimately, the goal is to produce well-rounded students who gain a fuller academic, ecological, and cultural understanding as well as foster connections across disciplines.

ACKNOWLEDGMENTS

The original development of the MapBlog was funded by The Charitable Leadership Foundation (New York) through Empire State College's Science and Math Project. We thank Kent Stanton (Informz), Nicola Allain (SUNY Empire State College), George Guba (University of North Carolina at Pembroke), Nataly Tcherepashenet (SUNY Empire State College), Phillip Ortiz (SUNY Empire State College), and Diane Shichtman (SUNY Empire State College) for their instrumental work and support. We also thank Pauline Carico (SUNY Empire State College) and the anonymous reviewers for their valuable comments and suggestions.

REFERENCES

Bull, G. (2007). Creating and sharing interactive maps. Paper presented at the International Society for Technology in Education, August, pp. 36–37.

Bull, G. (2008). Storytelling in the Web 2.0 era. *Learning and Leading with Technologies, 35,* 10–11.

Chickering, A. W., & Gamson, Z. F. (1987). Seven principles for good practice in undergraduate education. *American Association of Higher Education Bulletin, 39,* 3–7.

Coutant, B. E., & Westheimer, G. (1993). Population distribution of stereoscopic ability. *Ophthalmic & Physiological Optics, 13*(1), 3–7.

Custin, R., & Barkacs, L. (2010). Developing sustainable learning communities through blogging. *Journal of Instructional Pedagogies, 4,* 1–8.

Downs, R. M., Liben, L. S., & Daggs, D. G. (1988). On education and geographers: The role of cognative developmental theory in geographic education. *Annals of the Association of American Geographers, 78,* 680–700.

Dziuban, C., Moskal, P., Brophy, J., & Shea, P. (2007). Student satisfaction with asynchronous learning. *Journal of Asynchronous Learning Networks, 11,* 87–95.

Elwood, S., & Leszczynski, A. (2011). Privacy, reconsidered: New representations, data practices, and the geoweb. *Geoforum, 42*, 6–15.

Fulford, C. P., & Zhang, S. (1993). Perceptions of interaction: The critical predictor in distance education. *American Journal of Distance Education, 7*, 8–21.

Griffin, A. L., MacEachren, A. M., Hardisty, F., Steiner, E., & Bonan, L. (2006). A comparison of animated maps with static small-multiple maps for visual identifying space-time clusters. *Annals of the Association of American Geographers, 96*, 740–753.

Griggs, K. (2011). Geotagging digital collections: Beaver tracks mobile project. *Computers in Libraries, 31*(2), 16–20.

Guba, G., & Wolf, D. (2007). Darwin's voyage: Evolution of a learning object. In C. Montgomerie & J. Seale (Eds.), *Proceedings of World Conference on Educational Multimedia, Hypermedia and Telecommunications* (pp. 266–273). Chesapeake, VA: AACE.

Helvie-Manson, L. (2011). Facebook, "friending," and faculty-student communication. In L. A. Wankel & C. Wankel (Eds.), *Teaching arts and science with the new social media* (Vol. 3, pp. 61–87). Cutting-edge Technologies in Higher Education. Bingley, UK: Emerald Group.

Hu, S. (2003). Web-based multimedia GIS: Exploring interactive maps and associated multimedia information on the Internet. In M. P. Peterson (Ed.), *Maps and the Internet* (pp. 335–344). NewYork, NY: Elsevier Science.

Hudson-Smith, A., Milton, R., Batty, M., Gibin, M., Longley, P., & Singleton, A. (2007). *Public domain GIS, mapping and imaging using web-based services.* UCL Working Paper Series, Center for Advanced Spatial Analysis. Retrieved from http://www.casa.ucl.ac.uk/working_papers/paper120.pdf. Accessed on December 20, 2011.

Kraiger, K. (2008). Transforming our models of learning and development: Web-based instruction as enabler of third-generation instruction. *Industrial and Organizational Psychology: Perspectives on Science and Practice, 1*, 454–467.

Lamb, A., & Johnson, L. (2010). Virtual expeditions: Google Earth, GIS, and geovisualization technologies in teaching and learning. *Teacher Librarian, 37*, 81–85.

Lucey, T. A., & Grant, M. (2010). Using technology to prepare critically thinking global citizens. *Social Studies Research and Practice, 5*, 119–138.

Lwin, K. K., & Murayama, Y. (2011). Web-based GIS system for real-time field data collection using a personal mobile phone. *Journal of Geographic Information System, 3*, 382–389.

Mabrito, M. (2004). Guidelines for establishing interactivity in online courses. *Innovate, 1*. Retrieved from http://www.innovateonline.info/index.php?view=article&id=12

MacEachren, A. M., & DiBiase, D. (1991). Animated maps of aggregate data: Conceptual and practical problems. *Cartography and Geographic Information Systems, 18*, 221–229.

Miller, S. M., & Miller, K. L. (1999). Using instructional theory to facilitate communication in Web-based courses. *Educational Technology & Society, 2*. Retrieved from http://www.ifets.info/journals/2_3/miller.html. Accessed on February 10, 2012.

National Research Council. (2000). *How people learn: Brain, mind, experience, and school (Expanded edition).* Washington, DC: National Academy Press.

Papadimitriou, F. (2010). Introduction to the complex Geospatial Web in geographical education. *International Research in Geographical and Environmental Education, 19*, 53–56.

Peterson, K. D. (2000). Using a geographic information system to teach economics. *Journal of Economic Education, 31*, 169–178.

Piaget, J. (1970). Piaget's theory. In P. H. Mussen (Ed.), *Carmichael's manual of child psychology* (3rd ed., Vol. 1, pp. 703–732). New York, NY: Wiley.

Powell, K. C., & Kalina, C. J. (2009). Cognitive and social constructivism: Developing tools for an effective classroom. *Education, 130*, 241–250.

Prensky, M. (2005). Engage me or enrage me: What today's learners demand. *Educause Review, 40*, 60–65.

Ramli, R. (2010). Technology enhanced learning: Fostering cooperative learning through the integration of online communication as part of teaching. *World Academy of Science, Engineering and Technology, 69*, 611–614.

Revere, L., & Kovach, J. V. (2011). Online technologies for engaged learning: A meaningful synthesis for educators. *The Quarterly Review of Distance Education, 12*, 113–124.

Robinson, A. H., Morrison, J. L., Muehrcke, P. C., Kimerling, A. J., & Guptill, S. C. (1995). *Elements of cartography* (6th ed.). New York, NY: Wiley.

Roper, A. R. (2007). How students develop online learning skills. *Educause Quarterly, 30*, 62–65.

Slocum, T. A., McMaster, R. B., Kessler, F. C., & Howard, H. H. (2009). *Thematic cartography and geovisualization* (3rd ed.). Upper Saddle River, NJ: Person Education.

Thrower, N. (2007). *Maps and civilization: Cartography in culture and society*. Chicago, IL: University of Chicago Press.

Vamiso, R. (2010). What your digital photos reveal about you. PCWorld.com. Retrieved from http://www.pcworld.com/article/205296/what_your_digital_photos_reveal_about_you.html. Accessed on December 16, 2011.

Verneil, M., & Berge, Z. (2000). Going online: Guidelines for faculty in higher education. *Educational Technology Review, 6*, 13–18.

Vygotsky, L. S. (1978). *Mind in society: The development of higher psychological processes.* Cambridge: Harvard University Press.

Wolf, D., Beckem, J., & Matias, A. (2011). Interactive technologies: Enhancing academic learning and stimulated student engagement with social media. In T. Bastiaens & M. Ebner (Eds.), *Proceedings of World Conference on Educational Multimedia, Hypermedia and Telecommunications* (pp. 2639–2644). Chesapeake, VA: AACE.

Zinser, R. (2012). A curriculum model of a foundation for educating the global citizen of the future. *On The Horizon, 20*, 64–73.

DEVELOPING GLOBAL PERSPECTIVES, RESPONSIBILITY, AND PARTNERSHIPS THROUGH VIDEOCONFERENCING

Stephanie E. Raible and Wayne Jacoby

ABSTRACT

The chapter presents findings from five qualitative reports from educators within the compulsory education sector who have partnered with a United Nations-recognized, nongovernmental organization (NGO), Global Education Motivators (GEM), in order to either introduce or expand curricular support for their students or to engage in professional dialogue with fellow educators facilitated through international videoconferencing programs. Through a long-standing collaboration between these educators, GEM has jointly developed programming which educates students on the United Nations and global issues including sustainability, human rights, child labor, poverty, and peace and conflict studies. Using an email-based survey questionnaire, the reported cases aim to explore the educators' motivations to introduce and expand their students' global engagement through the media of videoconferencing. The chapter highlights the potential outcomes of international videoconferencing for

Increasing Student Engagement and Retention using Multimedia Technologies:
Video Annotation, Multimedia Applications, Videoconferencing and Transmedia Storytelling
Cutting-edge Technologies in Higher Education, Volume 6F, 235–266
ISSN: 2044-9968/doi:10.1108/S2044-9968(2013)000006F012

educators as a classroom tool or a professional development resource, as well as detailing a case study of an NGO–college partnership in which the NGO provides expertise, student internships, and noncredit professional development opportunities to its campus community and beyond.

INTRODUCTION

Despite the rise in the use of videoconferencing for personal and professional purposes fueled by the introduction of free, Internet-based videoconferencing services (e.g., Skype, Google Hangout, and Video), the use of the technology as a fully integrated classroom tool has been drastically slower. With videoconferencing becoming an increasingly affordable and available classroom technology to more and more educational settings across the world, the expanded possibilities of how to integrate the technology into course curricula present ample opportunity for educators in this regard. Svitak (2010) identified five ways in which educational institutions across all levels can utilize the technology: connect with area experts, conduct a virtual field trip, collaborate with others in other geographic areas, provide access to courses unavailable across sites, and offer professional training for teachers and educators. All of these modes of engaging classrooms and educators have been a key part of the operations of Global Education Motivators, or "GEM," a nongovernmental organization (NGO) housed within Chestnut Hill College in Philadelphia, Pennsylvania. GEM has served as a provider of such services to educational institutions of all levels, offering programming for students, teachers, administrators, and university faculty for over two decades, with its videoconferencing services becoming available in 1999.

In this chapter, the reported experiences of GEM and its students serve two roles: as a case study of an organization that develops and organizes globally minded educational programming for both the campus and lifelong learners, as well as to illustrate the common threads of perspectives, partnerships, and responsibility that connect the cases of five of GEM's more active participants. The five case reports were gathered through a qualitative study utilizing online, open-ended questionnaires in order to explore the modes through which partnering with GEM has impacted the practice of the educators at the compulsory level, whether serving as a teacher, educational technology specialist, or school administrator. More reports were welcomed for the study. However, in order to discuss the impact of a consistent and longer-term relationship, case participants were narrowed down to contacts that have collaborated with GEM to host educational programming for their students and to engage in activities contributing toward their own professional development over a span of at least five years.

RELEVANCE FOR HIGHER EDUCATION

There are several connections to higher education in the presented case, which broaches the concerns of both education faculty and staff across institutional departments. Such benefits to the university community can have an impact on many areas of a college or university setting, well beyond the scope of the examples provided. To better understand some potential areas of connection, a select number of examples have been highlighted as an illustration of the case's relevance and connection to higher education.

The organization's partnership with Chestnut Hill College has been a mutually beneficial relationship for both GEM and the college, developed over a period of decades. The relationship can be classified as having three main shared benefits: joint programming, technology access, and students. GEM was granted office space within the college and access to the rooms and resources at the college in exchange for the college community's access to the expertise of GEM's globally oriented programming and events. The relationship shaped the college's core curriculum across all majors through jointly securing funds to develop a Global Studies course. GEM still plays a collaborative role within the Global Studies curricula, through planning a field visit to the United Nations headquarters in New York City and through faculty support in developing videoconferencing events that are integrated within their class lesson plans. The college has also partnered with GEM on campus programming recognized through the United Nations Academic Impact (UNAI), including one of their most recent joint collaborations, the annual United Nations Teachers' Conference on Human Rights. The Conference features both prominent faculty within the college community and invited external practitioners speaking in either face-to-face or videoconference format.

In addition to collaborations and programming support, GEM and Chestnut Hill College have partnered for years through joint use of technology. When the NGO won a contract for videoconferencing equipment, they approached the college with an offer to exchange storage space within a theater-style classroom, in exchange for having access to the technology;

the college agreed to the proposed arrangement and expanded to provide more classroom space for videoconferencing as more capable technology became available to the NGO. GEM and Chestnut Hill College had the first equipment of its kind among the Greater Philadelphia colleges and universities. GEM and the college welcomed the equipment and housed the Polycom unit in a large theater room at the basement of the college's library for the ease of use of GEM and the Chestnut Hill College community. As part of this relationship, GEM also played a role in educating the college community about the technology involved, primarily through inviting collaboration with instructors.

A third area of interest to the higher education community is the unique opportunity students have to engage in experiential education through the NGO-college partnership. In the development of its relationship, Chestnut Hill College awards academic credit for internships supervised by GEM. Within the case reports, a Chestnut Hill College alumna's experience as a student intern at GEM is illustrated. Her opportunity to gain professional experience while studying to be an elementary school teacher is another shared benefit of the college–NGO relationship, with dozens of current students and alumni benefitting with customized internships right on campus, and GEM's ability to utilize the talents and enthusiasm of the campus student body. Students of the college with an interest in education or global issues have the opportunity to serve as an intern or possibly a United Nations Youth Representative for the NGO. Such a position would entitle them to a security badge granting access to the United Nations in New York City, in addition to the UN Department of Public Information's Nongovernmental Organization (UNDPI-NGO) programming and meeting space.

Lastly, beyond the Chestnut Hill College community, approximately one-third of GEM's collaborating clients, which include both individuals and institutions, are within the higher education sector, and when including those who self-identify as lifelong learners or who are seeking professional development, the proportion of GEM's programming audience reaches, if not exceeds, 50% of its total participants. Over the past three decades, GEM has both developed and collaborated on programming with, and offered its services to, numerous universities and colleges in the United States and abroad. As a facilitator of interuniversity collaborations and virtual exchanges, GEM operates as a unifying nexus of groups with mutual interests and a link to the United Nations and its agency staff for speaker events.

All of the five case participants interviewed had either initially joined GEM as a college student (as detailed above) or as a lifelong learner seeking personal or professional development. The four lifelong learners, who were the more senior education professionals interviewed, started a rapport with GEM from word-of-mouth recommendations or through meeting at a professional development and training event. Thus, despite the limited number of cases, the case reports span both traditional and nontraditional adult learners working in, or planning to work in, education. As a provider of classroom videoconferencing support and event building, and of professional workshops on a variety of global topics catered toward teachers and educators, the case of GEM highlights a unique campus partnership in teacher education. In addition, continuing education departments and alumni relations offices that are looking to expand their reach or to reconnect with their graduates would stand to gain from understanding the benefits of offering noncredit, videoconference-based programming.

ABOUT GLOBAL EDUCATION MOTIVATORS

The mission of GEM centers on working with educators and students to promote a better understanding of the world and its people. Its core philosophy to "bring the world into the classroom" teaches a global perspective facilitated through the use of technology, a pairing that has guided the organization since its foundation in 1981. Although originally founded as a private, educational nonprofit corporation, GEM was awarded a public, NGO status, in association with the UN Department of Public Information in 1986, and it has continued to maintain a close association with the United Nations in great part due to the consistency of its leadership and the recognition of its programming. As a provider of both on-site and distance learning for learners of all ages to learn more about global issues as well as to teach about the United Nations, GEM's work has drawn the interest and support of many preeminent figures including leaders at the United Nations and prominent activists.

STRIVING TO REMAIN ON THE CUTTING EDGE: TECHNOLOGY AT GEM

GEM started employing technology in its earliest days in two primary ways: the foundation of the United Nations' first online database, UNISER, and a video exchange program, Video Pals. Through first initiative, GEM helped the United Nations establish and maintain UNISER as the sole online global repository of UN documents and was the only source outside of the United Nations in New York where individuals could get up-to-date resolutions, committee reports, and other resources such as the Third World News and Amnesty International, among others. In this capacity, GEM had hundreds of clients, the majority of which were higher education institutions across the globe. However, with the digitization and development of the United Nations own open-access website and databases, GEM began to focus exclusively on student education and educator training. Moreover, it was this second initial use of technology that ended up leading the NGO to focus its attention on videoconferencing.

Founded upon the idea that youth communicating with peers across cultures was a fundamental aspect of building understanding and peace, GEM started the Video Pals program with videotape exchanges between schools in the United States and schools in foreign countries. The videotape exchange program consisted of GEM matching schools in areas of mutual interest and grade level in different countries, as well as providing the videotape conversion services to render the videos compatible. The exchanges often took several weeks between the recording, editing, converting, mailing, and viewing stages; the lengthy process between interactions caused the duration of the international classroom relationships to vary considerably, with some classrooms showing commitment to a back-and-forth dialogue through video exchange, and other pairings losing touch early on in the process due to lack of time, resources, or a waning interest in the project.

Continually moving with the times, GEM transitioned the Video Pals program model from videotape exchanges to videoconferencing by the late 1990s. Because the start-up costs of conferencing technology were prohibitive, GEM sought support for funding. GEM was able to initially secure funding for videoconferencing equipment if it was willing to house the equipment at an inner-city school for their joint usage. GEM donated the equipment to a public high school within the School District of Philadelphia, but scheduling of educational programs around the high school's events proved to be difficult, as the district's use of the unit as videoconferencing equipment was primarily used during the technology's infancy stage, in a one-to-many mode: a way to bring the teacher's expertise to remote areas and struggling urban schools through distance learning (Laurillard, 2002; Smyth, 2005). After two years of sharing equipment, the NGO reapplied and secured funding for its own unit to be housed physically within the college classrooms near the GEM office.

Videoconferencing is a real-time, two- or multiple-way video and audio stream of two or more sites that is delivered through a phone, Internet, or network connection (Knowlton, Rowland, Knowlton, & Chaffin, 2005). With its modern benefits, videoconferencing can be classified within three main categories: cost, access, and interaction (Gillies, 2008). Access refers to the ability of videoconferencing to break down financial and geographic barriers and open up educational settings to global discussions. Even remote populations once inaccessible to outsiders can connect to others through videoconferencing, as its use has become more cost-effective and user-friendly with greater access to stable video- and audio-feed connections. Interaction, the social dialogue formed between participants among the videoconferencing sites, is the most critical element for participant learning and engagement. It is particularly during these interactive portions of videoconferencing in which the most salient characteristics of engagement become palpably manifested (Gillies, 2008).

Interaction is the key building block to how individuals construct learning (Bates, 2005; Gillies, 2008; Smyth, 2005), and videoconferencing presents the unique opportunity to facilitate dialogue between individuals and groups that might not have otherwise been able to both see and hear each other without the technology. The quality of the social interaction through videoconferencing has been improved through the advances in technology. The majority of GEM videoconferencing programs can be classified as hybrid or blended-learning formats, in that the multiple virtual sites interact with peers in remote sites, but also incorporate face-to-face discussions and activities among the participants present in the room. Videoconferencing, with both in-person and virtual elements, tends to connect participants through a shared experience:

> There is the sense of togetherness and shared experience, a camaraderie which can help offset the particular danger of attrition where students study both remotely and individually. (Bates, 2005; Wheeler, 2005; Wheeler & Amiotte, 2004 in Gillies, 2008, p. 109)

An individual's learning and identity is constructed and shaped through social interactions (Berger & Luckmann, 1967), and the social components to videoconferencing help create authentic learning environments comparable to face-to-face interactions. When evaluating the technology's impact on the professional development of classroom teachers, videoconferencing can be both an authentic learning environment and a time-efficient way to connect educators with field experts, specialists, and other educators (Martin, 2005).

CHALLENGES OF VIDEOCONFERENCING

Historically, the costs of running videoconferencing programs were prohibitive. GEM's early videoconferences were carried out through high-speed telephone line connections, costing upwards of $20,000 for an all-day global videoconference exchange between multiple sites internationally. Because the videoconferencing connection was only possible through the use of high-speed telephone lines (ISDN), all partner sites were charged long distance telephone charges. Multiplied by the number of lines or channels needed for successful video and audio transmission, building partnerships with educators and students in developing countries proved difficult. When international sites did participate in videoconferencing, they often only had limited lines or channels for connections, causing frequent technical challenges to build an effective and continuous dialogue between groups.

Slow connectivity speeds, a lack of multimedia applications and high costs were the norm, but that all quickly changed. Point-to-point discussions through telephone lines moved from 1 line/2 channels to 3 lines/6 channels to ISDN lines to Internet Protocol (IP) connections, a series of key shifts that gradually, though significantly, contributed to achieving markedly improved quality in sound, picture, and overall multimedia presence during videoconferencing events. With time, affordable and stable Internet connections represented a boon that both made videoconferencing between international sites affordable and allowed educators from developing countries to participate, as there are usually no telecommunication costs associated with IP-based calls.

With the voice-over IP (VoIP) freeware market providing greater capacity and capability for hosting multi-site, large-group videoconferencing events, the international audiences who can participate are much more diverse than at the start of GEM's videoconferencing exchanges in its past. GEM's use of Voice-over IP (VoIP) freeware technology has been particularly helpful in building new partnerships with schools and educator groups in developing countries that are new to videoconferencing and have limited access to videoconferencing equipment as a matter of circumstance. Due to its dependence on strong technology with greater capabilities, GEM continues to primarily use codec units, utilizing both Tandberg and Polycom systems for the majority of its videoconferencing programs. Many limitations still riddle the overall reliability of freeware technology, including the dependence on consistent Internet connections and a difficulty in capturing the audio and video of larger groups. Additional key issues with freeware persist, such as the successful projection of images to a large screen, which relatively does not visually compare with the quality of images captured with a codec unit.

STUDENT ENGAGEMENT AND LIFELONG LEARNING ORIENTATIONS

The term "student engagement" remains at the center of most discussions of student learning and can be found in institutional mission statements to show a college's commitment to its student development and growth. Definitions tend to encompass either the psychological or behavioral engagement of a student within the classroom or activity; some more complete definitions combine the two, requiring that to show measureable engagement, a student must be psychologically present and willing, as well as behaviorally manifesting traits of someone who is engaged. Kenny, Kenny, and Dumont (1995) have even sought to venture so far as to identify categories of student engagement indicators in a college setting. However, these still mainly focus on the temporal engagement of the student, without further attention to a student's past and future orientations.

Therefore, this use of the term "student engagement" has limitations, as it does not necessarily address the complexity of learning and the breadth of its manifestations and appearances. Alternatively, the term lifelong learning orientation encompasses the behavioral and psychological features present in definitions of student engagement, while refocusing attention on the various forms of learning within formal, informal, and nonformal settings. This learning-focused term permits for an understanding of how the learners are engaged in the activities, as well as how they transformed their orientations and practice.

The term lifelong learning orientation presumes an understanding of the notion of lifelong learning. Lifelong Learning (LLL) is not a new concept, though its modern usage is popular and expanding. The concept of lifelong learning must be defined as one's cradle to grave learning trajectory through formal, informal, and nonformal education, paired with "the conscious and continuous enhancement of the quality of life, his own and that of society" (Dave, 1976 in Medel-Añonuevo, Ohsako, & Mauch, 2001, p. 2). Many institutions have utilized the term LLL to replace adult, continuing, or mature education departments and course offerings. Labeling these departments as "lifelong learning" leads many toward an assumption that lifelong learning is that which happens after one's formal education, that it is a more flexible form of learning, or that it can be defined and contained within one area of an institution; rather, lifelong learning happens before our students arrive to campus. It readily occurs while they are resident at our institutions, and it happens within and outside the classroom and campus environment. Furthermore, lifelong learning builds and grows after one's education, throughout one's entire lifetime. Having this understanding, instead of entertaining the commonly associated misconceptions, is crucial to considering the limitations of utilizing student engagement, as it shows how one's lifelong learning is continuous in nature and dependent on one's past preparation, present engagement, and future outlook and aspirations.

Lifelong learning can be understood as either a series of institutional stepping stones (e.g., transition from secondary to higher education), or it can be defined as the behavioral, cultural, and social development of an individual (Ecclestone, 2009). For our purposes, the best way to conceptualize lifelong learning is the latter in order to best understand the development of the concept of a lifelong learning orientation. In addition, it may be worth mention that lifelong learning can be understood as linear, pyramid/building block or cyclical patterns to one's growth. These varied models may help to strengthen one's understanding of learning; however, they are all as equally relevant or applicable to the proposed shift to a lifelong learning orientation.

Compared to certain metrics that primarily deal with student engagement, the proposed lifelong orientation would require a qualitative approach to understanding and measuring learning:

> Learning should be seen as a qualitative change in a person's way of seeing, experiencing understanding, [and] conceptualizing something in the real world. (Marton & Ramsden, 1988, p. 271)

Furthermore, a lifelong learning orientation is a much more individualized form of understanding the longitudinal development and growth of students:

> [Lifelong learning discourses] offer ... individualism with an emphasis on self-optimizing and self-managing practices. Individuals are enjoined to participate in learning across the life course, as a means of adapting to social and economic change. (Morgan-Klein & Osborne, 2007, p. 19)

Therefore, to summarize, the term lifelong learning orientation generally refers to an individualized, qualitative lens through which to regard one's continuous learning and development throughout their life course (inclusive of past, present, and future), compared to student engagement, which typically seeks to benchmark the present behavioral and cognitive markers of attention and involvement.

PERSPECTIVES, PARTNERSHIPS, AND RESPONSIBILITY

To develop a framework of modes of learning that can be easily identified from reported outcomes and serve as a broader scope of student learning, the discussion of the cases presented will utilize and be informed by the revised form of Bloom's three domains of learning: *cognitive*, *affective*, and *conative* (Bloom, 1956, 1964; Kolbe, 1990; Krathwohl, Bloom, & Masia, 1973). The three domains of learning (cognitive, affective, conative) can be perceived as evident in application through each of the cases' highlighted themes: *perspectives*, *responsibility*, and *partnerships*.

Perspectives

Through GEM's videoconferencing programs, participants are exposed to international *perspectives* on a common topic; the content of the sessions relate to global issues (e.g., human rights, poverty, sustainability, globalization) or the role of the United Nations as an international organization. Program participants often share the same profession, as either current students or those working as educators in school, college, or nonprofit settings. The perspective theme connects best to the cognitive domain because Bloom's taxonomy of the cognitive domain is not only inclusive of one's ability to recall or recognize facts, but encompasses deeper and more abstract applications of knowledge (Bloom, 1956); in a similar fashion, perspective is built, shaped, and reinforced through the exposure, processing, and application of information.

Responsibility

Joint projects between educators, their students, and communities result in greater interest and awareness of global perspectives and develop a sense of shared *responsibility*. The affective domain, one's feelings, or appreciation of their role within a community, relates to responsibility. Having a sense of responsibility is founded in one's beliefs and the individual's understanding of whether he or she is to play a part within a local community or global society.

Conative, defined as one's action, is best understood in the framework of the presented cases as *partnerships*. The conative domain was chosen over Bloom's better known psychomotor domain, as conative describes one's will, drive, and ambition to act, rather than simply to indicate that one has the ability to act. These partnerships are crafted between the educators and GEM as their action to engage their students in international video-conferencing, or themselves in professional development through video-conference participation. A continued partnership between GEM and these educators is formed by sustained action to develop and execute educational and training programs. This process of building and continuing a relationship also can be observed through participating as host sites for a video-conference, through which educators connect their classrooms and share a common practice with their fellow educators across the globe. These partnerships have been observed to grow organically through the personal initiatives of those connected, and have resulted in lasting bonds between educators to share practice and to connect their own classrooms through videoconferencing and forming communities of practice and learning (Eales & Bryd, 1997; Lave & Wenger, 1991).

RELATIONSHIPS BETWEEN THE THREE DOMAINS

The distinctions between the three domains may seem blurred as the three support and reinforce each other. For example, Oxfam's (1997) definition of a global citizen includes elements of three domains of learning; a global citizen "has an understanding of how the world works economically, politically, socially, culturally, technologically and environmentally" (cognitive); "has a sense of their own role as a world citizen" (affective); and "participates in and contributes to the community at a range of levels from local to global"/"is willing to act to make the world a more sustainable place" (conative). With the three domains overlapping and strengthening each other, it is important to place emphasis that "no curriculum can be complete without all three being present" (Barnett & Coate, 2005, p. 65 in Brockbank & McGill, 2007, p. 49).

The cases focus mainly on the affective and conative, as the participants did not all attend or contract with GEM for specialized programming aimed at them individually as an audience (i.e., professional development), meaning that educator cognitive development was not an explicitly identified intentional outcome of the programming. Two of the five subjects interviewed have only had a rapport with GEM as a provider of student-level programming, which means that their involvements with GEM programming have never specifically identified educators as the target audience. However, those participants initially found GEM while engaging in a professional development activity (i.e., conference). The following section presents the conducted cases and their format, data collection, and findings.

THE CASES

Both authors hold an affiliation with GEM: one as President/Co-Founder and one as a volunteer charged with United Nations Academic Impact (UNAI) events. The authors chose to conduct the study with the volunteer as the interviewer. This was determined as she had none-to-limited prior interactions with the selected participants and felt that the interaction would more likely elicit authentic responses being further removed from the primary relationship they held for the organization, and not involving the individual responsible for the oversight, organization, and running of the educational programs the participants chose to discuss. In addition, some participants did choose to transmit their survey responses to both authors, whereas some participants decided to send responses to just one author or the other. Those who did not respond to the initial request to participate were contacted by GEM's President either by phone or email to confirm their interest and availability to serve as a participant. Because of the direct organizational affiliation of the authors, access to participants was not restricted or difficult. However, several participants had missed the originally set deadline and needed a follow-up contact in order to complete the survey.

The participants were all educators who have both participated in and hosted a synchronous videoconference between other domestic and international partner sites or with officials of UN-affiliated organizations, as organized GEM. Participants were selected through non-probability convenience sampling, with all participants identified and selected for participation by GEM's President. This was done in order to effectively narrow the possible participant pool to those who have used videoconferencing through GEM for several years. The selected participant pool is not meant to be representative of the entire population of those who have been exposed to international videoconferencing sessions for educational and training purposes, and does not imply that the participant reports represent the broader range of participants that GEM reaches. The participants were selected because they are all educators within the compulsory sector, have had a relationship with GEM of at least five years, and are still currently engaging in collaborative videoconferencing events for professional development or to support classroom curriculum within the 2011–2012 academic year. The educator participants have been involved in videoconferencing programs with GEM either as a collaborator (intended for their students and not created for an educator audience) or as a professional development participant (developed for educators).

DATA COLLECTION METHODS

Participants were contacted by email and asked to respond to a 13-question survey related to their collaborative videoconferencing experiences through GEM and its perceived impact, if any, on their professional practice or outlook. Of the six surveys sent, four were returned. Informed consent was gained by explanation of the study and subsequent completion and submission of the surveys. Confidentiality was guaranteed for publication, although the participants were informed that their identity would be known solely between the researchers. All names have been replaced with pseudonyms to protect the confidentiality and privacy of the respondents.

Survey questions were drafted with the objective of understanding the participants' reported development in their attitudes toward videoconferencing and toward global education. The survey also intended to understand the motivations for connecting and continuing a collaborative relationship with GEM, and what impact, if any, their collaborations with GEM have had on their practice, outlook, and school (Table 1).

Participants tended to elaborate more on certain areas than others, depending on their individual experiences. The results presented employ a lifelong learning orientation lens through which are identified areas of perspective, responsibility, and partnerships, if present.

Limitations

Sending the questionnaire electronically was done in order to connect with the geographically disparate educators at their convenience, as many of

Table 1. Survey Questions Developed to Understand Participants'
Attitudes Toward Videoconferencing and Global Education.

Survey Questions

1. How did you first hear about GEM?
2. What were your initial impressions?
3. Why did you choose to start collaborating with GEM?
4. How have you used or collaborated with GEM over the years?
5. What, if any, impact has GEM had on your professional practice and outlook?
6. Since collaborating with GEM, how have you been using technology in the classroom?
7. Has this changed since knowing about GEM?
8. What motivates you to remain involved with GEM?
9. Have your global connections using technology shaped your practice?
10. Do you believe it affects your students?
11. Have you received any recognition regarding your collaborative efforts with GEM?
12. Have your collaborations with GEM altered your curriculum or that of your school?
    If so, how?

Have you promoted the use of videoconferencing in your school to those you supervise or to
colleagues?

them indicated that it was a busy time of year in their work roles; however, this limited the details within their responses in two ways. First, although the participants were debriefed on the nature of the report, many of them initially misinterpreted the task as a program evaluation for GEM's internal purposes. This was subsequently clarified for those who were confused in this manner. Second, participants were instructed to give detailed responses to the questions, yet many did not elaborate on the details of each of the videoconferencing events they referenced in their report. In order to supplement this information, GEM's President, one of the chapter's authors, was able to provide further detail of the structure and nature of these events. The provided details have been included in order to clarify the responses given in the case reports by the participants.

CASE 1: PRINCIPAL, PRIVATE SECONDARY SCHOOL

Maryann, then an elementary school principal, first learned about GEM through word-of-mouth, and she decided to first collaborate with GEM on a videoconferencing program for her school's students because of her first-hand observation of GEM's programming at another local high school:

> I was very impressed with the idea of learning outside the walls of the classroom without having to leave the school. ... Because of what I had experienced at [name of high school] ... I realized that global citizenry is a reality and that it should be practiced at the elementary level as well. It should be a way of life.

Even as someone new to both global education topics and the possibilities of utilizing videoconferencing, Maryann did not take much convincing to incorporate videoconferencing and hybrid learning within her school. As an example of an academic year-long theme her school engaged in, Maryann used GEM to provide activities to teach and promote a global and local approach to water issues. Her students participated in videoconferencing connections with other students internationally to learn about water issues in Mexico, Italy, and the United States for World Water Day. In follow-up videoconferencing events, the elementary school students gave presentations to representatives from the UN Food and Agricultural Organization on the school's local work to capture rainwater and use it in various ways in the community, as well as to promote its fundraising initiatives to support their work. The school science classrooms had an additional opportunity to videoconference with NASA to learn more about the use of water in space and to make suggestions, based on their lessons, for how NASA could use water in space for growing food during long space flights. Maryann's school also supported the videoconference learning with in-person projects. For example, the school's art teachers instructed students to create artwork based on what they learned about water-related issues, with their artwork being displayed publicly in Philadelphia to promote water conservation and sanitation awareness. This year-long engagement in global water issues also featured the publication of a novel based on a factual account of young students who strived to make the world better through their engagement and activism.

In other years, Maryann's initiative to work with her school's teachers to create a school-wide, environmental conservation awareness curriculum through videoconferencing was one of many globally oriented events she collaborated with GEM to organize:

> At the elementary level, we connected with many different countries using GEM. We met Jane Goodall [and] the family of Jacques Cousteau and did many videoconferences with [school in Mexico City].

Through pairing in-person and videoconferencing activities, her students were able to learn more about environmental and wildlife conservation issues through meeting Jane Goodall in person, and Jacques Cousteau's son via videoconference, and through learning about their Mexican school "peers" via videoconference exchanges.

Maryann has continued her relationship with GEM after becoming a principal at a private high school, collaborating with GEM to build, among other events, an annual UN Day, which involves a videoconferencing link to the United Nations for a keynote presentation aimed at educating students about the United Nations. When working with her high school teachers and students, Maryann has used the connection to GEM to help grow and support her school's global curricular and extracurricular offerings:

> We [now] have a Global Studies class and an after school club. We also paired a college writing class with a global studies class as a pilot program this year. The two teachers team up to research, analyze, discuss, and write about world concerns. It is really excellent!

GEM also widened Maryann's views of what technology can do within the classroom, particularly the advantages of videoconferencing. She has served as an advocate in her school for the use of videoconferencing as a tool to internationalize and support the global curriculum, as well as a strong resource for other high schools in her region. Both Maryann and several of her school's teachers have been featured in GEM staff development programs to share their GEM videoconference experiences with other teachers:

> I *always* promote [international videoconferencing]. My superintendent and Board members have seen us in action. Our UN conference hosts high schools in the tri-state area as we distance conference with the UN.

Beyond her recognition from her superiors and colleagues at other schools, Maryann has been recognized for her work as the recipient of many awards, including a prestigious national award for educational administrators.

Besides connecting with GEM as a resource in her schools, Maryann had used GEM's program offerings for educators as a way to develop both her and her school staff professionally:

> The experiences allowed me as an educator to speak with many other educators and understand various pedagogical methods. It helped me to realize the many similarities in teachers around the world – as well as get some very good ideas for activities and projects from them!

Maryann has linked her colleagues with the staff development opportunities for her school's teachers, as well as funding student leadership development opportunities for many of the students who excel in their classes and extracurricular activities. Years ago, Maryann supported GEM to work with and guide one of their new, young social studies teachers through professional development programming, and he now serves as the Chair of the school's social studies department. Maryann has collaborated with GEM to work with many of its other teachers for staff development purposes in hopes that it will help guide and encourage them to incorporate global perspectives in the classroom and to make the best use of the school's technology.

Maryann also noted that the professional benefits of using GEM as a continuing education provider stem not only from the development she hopes to see in her staff, but also is fueled by the opportunity to share her school's practices with other teachers internationally through videoconferencing events. She noted that the teachers and principals she has met through the videoconferencing events serve as an inspiration, as well as being around others, including GEM's staff, who believe in the benefits of a global education:

> I am motivated by the passion, dedication, and commitment … [of GEM] to bring the classroom to the world. I wish that every school could have the opportunity to experience GEM.

When summarizing the motivation to continue the collaboration with GEM, she also added her beliefs that a global education can facilitate introducing and fostering social consciousness and responsibility in her students and her school community:

> I believe that the study of world culture and politics through direct contact brings about social justice – and that is the way to world peace. The students here are more accepting of others, but also more inquisitive and concerned about world issues due to GEM. We do many projects … [including initiatives to] raise money for people in need.

When approaching the three themes of perspective, partnership, and responsibility, Maryann's appreciation of bringing an international perspective to her practice was supported through GEM's programming. In addition, by surrounding herself with like-minded professionals, Maryann seems to be fueled by their collective enthusiasm for the topic. In terms of the partnerships (conative), GEM encouraged and facilitated her ability to build a global education program. She was able to partner with other schools both abroad and in the tri-state area in order to develop annual student educational programming about the United Nations, and she and her school community were able to start a series of fundraisers for international causes and the poor. Likewise, her reported responsibility as an educator and citizen is centered on her statement that the "study of world culture and politics through direct contact brings about social justice – and that is the way to world peace." This demonstrates her feelings on why educating her students on global issues is so important to her and how she believes she can participate in spreading this message.

CASE 2: INCLUSION TEACHER, PUBLIC ELEMENTARY SCHOOL, AND FORMER GEM INTERN

Compared to the other participants, Lily was the only one to learn about GEM as an undergraduate education major at Chestnut Hill College (CHC). She had transferred to the college as a junior into the honors program, and she was within the traditional age group (18–24) during her college years. Before committing to attend CHC she was advised that she would be able to graduate within two years, but into her first semester she was later informed she would be one core course shy of completing the honors program, Global Studies. In order to make up for the one missed course, one of her professors arranged for her to fulfill the Global Studies requirement through an independent study. One of the requirements of the Global Studies course curriculum is to participate in a CHC–GEM collaborative event at the United Nations. Her trip to the United Nations represented a requirement to complete the Global Studies course as well as fulfill her degree requirements on time, so she agreed to attend, but without anticipating its impact:

> While on the trip, I noticed a sign at the United Nations regarding World Autism Awareness Day. As a future special education teacher, this intrigued me, so I began asking more about it to the people on the trip. It was then I was told to direct my questions to [GEM]. [...] This ... led me to e-mail Wayne Jacoby [President of GEM] for more information. Wayne promptly responded asking me to come to his office for a meeting. It was at this meeting that he offered me an internship to explore my questions of World Autism Awareness Day. I jumped on the opportunity. It was only through my own natural curiosity and Wayne's passion to empower youthful minds that I learned about GEM.

Lily opted to enroll in an internship with GEM, through which she worked on several videoconferencing and in-person education programs, and she was encouraged to take a leadership role in the creation of new programming. Through her work with GEM, Lily was able to develop her familiarity with running videoconferencing events and to improve her presentation skills, both of which proved to be helpful when proposing her idea for an international, real-time videoconference for World Autism Awareness Day to the Chief of Special Events at the United Nations. Her event proposal presentation was accepted, and she began to organize interested teachers, advocates, and organizations together to encourage their participation in the dialogue in order to educate others on what was happening related to autism education in many different parts of the world. She used GEM's network of international contacts to include four remote sites in her event, incorporating sites in Mexico, Canada, and Israel, in addition to GEM's regional contacts to attend the Philadelphia-based videoconferencing site at the college. Educators from as far away as Kenya attended the event at the Philadelphia-based site and many faculty members from the college community attended as well. In addition to these international sites, the videoconference was also remotely attended by the UN Ambassador from Qatar and the UN Chief of Special Events who both took the opportunity to welcome the participants, to speak, and to respond to questions from all of the videoconferencing sites. Her videoconference connections brought out a variety of perspectives on the cause and treatment of autistic children, and the event served as a great professional foundation for an aspiring special education teacher:

> ... this was indeed a global event in celebration of the 2nd Annual World Autism Awareness Day [WAAD]. I was excited because the event was being supported by the United Nations, it was mentioned in the Secretary General's comments on WAAD 2009.

She was also granted the opportunity to represent the GEM as one of its Youth Representatives, which includes a security pass to the United Nations facilities. This opportunity allowed Lily to also assist GEM in its in-person programming events at the United Nations with full access to its resources.

Lily credited her internship with GEM for changing and broadening her perspective both personally and professionally:

> GEM literally opened up my mind to the world. I knew I wanted to be a teacher and wanted to somehow make a difference in young people's lives, but GEM gave me the keys to open the doors. Knowing Wayne and participating in GEM events empowered me to think beyond my local community. I have always been a person to give back with charity, but seeing what I can do globally truly has changed my perspective.

Lily also expanded on how GEM influenced her professional and personal orientations by speaking about how GEM sparked and enforced her beliefs in the importance of internationalizing curricula and teaching global responsibility:

> 21st century learners have a greater responsibility than the generations before them. Leading them into the future requires them to understand [that] their world, in a way, did not exist prior to September 11, 2001. I now have seen there are no borders between nations and no limits to what can be accomplished when people care about a cause. I have become empowered to find a way to get young children empowered to make a difference in their world, all because someone took the time to observe and cultivate my passion for teaching and charity into the direction as a global educator.

When responding with regard to the impact of her time at GEM on her current practice as an elementary teacher, Lily explained that GEM was fundamental in exposing her to using videoconferencing as a classroom tool and its utility for aspiring educators and teachers:

> To me, I thought videoconferencing was something that Fortune 500 companies did with businesses across the globe ... it was not for teachers who wanted to connect with other classrooms. The technology exists, so why not allow it to be inclusive to anyone who wants to connect? It was very new to me. I knew little about video chats, but the Polycom systems and bridging multiple sites together on secure lines was very new to me.

Chestnut Hill College does not require its education majors to take instructional technology courses during their degree program. Student exposure to the use of new media and emerging technologies for use in the classroom is self-initiated; limited solely to any preparations students must receive in order to fulfill the requirements necessary for teacher certification.

Lily's drive to learn about the technology and its possible applications in the classroom has already created a powerful impact on her work. The extensive exposure to videoconferencing also made her feel empowered further to take a leadership role within her school's educational technology roles:

> My school system is just now entering the doors of the 21st century with videoconferencing equipment. Having prior knowledge of using it in the classroom has allowed me to begin conversations on how to use the equipment in productive ways. People often steer away from things they are unfamiliar with. Having the background knowledge I gained from GEM of conducting videoconferences globally will help me to be a leader in my district as technology becomes more available.

Having the ability to contribute toward a growing area of her school environment empowered her to be fully cognizant of the skills developed from her exposure to the technology.

Since graduating, Lily reported that she has done videoconferencing events both with and without the aid of GEM. Within the last academic year, she stated that she has connected her fourth grade classroom with fourth graders in Mexico City for a cultural exchange on the life of a fourth grader in their school. She also hosted a Maasai tribe member whom she had met through one of GEM's blended-learning programs to speak to her classroom and her colleagues' classrooms to teach their students about the Maasai community and to start a fundraiser for the Maasai community in Kenya. Beyond GEM's use of technology, Lily learned the importance of effectively sustaining the connections she made through the programs:

> I try to stay in touch with all the people I have met. [...] When you are working with the global community, you never know when the people you meet are going to need a project completed and when it might be useful to connect people from the past to get the project completed.

Even as a young professional in her field, Lily reports feeling like an important contributor to her school, manifesting her sense of responsibility toward her school community. Another manifestation of such a sense of responsibility relates to her shift from someone who was community-oriented to someone who viewed the extension of her responsibility as something both local and global in nature: "I have always been a person to give back with charity, but seeing what I can do globally truly has changed my perspective." Her comments credit her exposure to both the technology and global issues, as well as to her involvement in GEM, suggesting that she developed expanded cognitive skills. Her commitment to continue video-conferencing and fundraising efforts in her practice demonstrates her cognitive ability to engage in working partnerships with others, including GEM, her Maasai contact, and others within her school community in order to catalyze her constructed perspective and her sense of responsibility into action.

CASE 3: HEAD OF EDUCATIONAL TECHNOLOGY, PUBLIC SECONDARY SCHOOL

Rich serves as the Head of Educational Technology at a public high school in the Mid-Atlantic region. Of all the participants, Rich and Mark (sub-section to follow) had the most prior experience with the use of technology in the classroom. Because of his background and position centering on educational technology, Rich's relationship with GEM did not add video-conferencing into his repertoire of classroom tools as the relationship had for the other participants. Rather, the connection with GEM meant the ability to connect with the United Nations and other classrooms from around the world:

> I was doing some research on videoconferencing program offerings and came across information about GEM and their relationship with the UN. [...] Since GEM's program offerings used videoconferencing and addressed issues that I felt were important to the development of our students and support topics covered in our curriculum, I decided to begin collaborating with GEM to provide these programs.

Eight years ago, Rich was in the audience of his state's education association annual teachers' conference when GEM was leading a professional development workshop from Chestnut Hill College on videoconferencing. This workshop led Rich to create his school's most intensive and well-known videoconferencing event. Rich had shared his idea with his peers at the conference: a 24-hour "Around the World" videoconference where his students would stay in school all day and night to videoconference with other classrooms around the world. His peers seemed skeptical such a drastic form of videoconference would be allowed or even could capture the attention of the student attendees for a full 24 hours. After the conference, GEM helped him achieve his vision, and the intensive, international videoconferencing program still continues today. During the annual event, more than 15 schools in 15 countries interact with students at his school. The program has received strong recognition not only from his school's leadership, but was also awarded the #1 Innovative Use of Technology distinction across all state schools by the governing Department of Education.

Rich identified that one of the strongest benefits of collaborating with GEM has been the ability to use the high school's videoconferencing technology on a more consistent basis:

> We had a videoconferencing room when I came to [name of high school], but it was not being used. GEM helped me in my goal of changing that situation. Over the years our degree of collaborations has improved and remained an important part of our use of videoconferencing to support the curriculum.

One of the more consistent programming opportunities Rich has linked his school to is GEM's "UN in Your World" series. During these programs, his students have learned about the United Nations and have been exposed to global challenges through discussions with peers from India, Pakistan, Mexico, Canada, and the Dominican Republic, as well as at other schools in the United States.

Rich indicated that the joint programming had been a wonderful addition to incorporate meaningful use of videoconferencing in the classroom, although the relationship is an aspect that he highlighted as both personally and professionally rewarding. He outlined several professional advantages to his school's greater commitment to using videoconferencing and why he felt his relationship with GEM was beneficial:

> On a professional level, you cannot argue with success. GEM offers quality programs, assists us in our own programs, and helps promote collaborations between [name of high school] and schools around the world. [...] Our use of videoconferencing at [name of high school] has won numerous awards (seven and counting), recognition by the media, recognition and support from higher education around the world, and of course our own administration, board of education, students, parents, and community in general.

When reflecting on personal motivations for continuing the relationship with GEM, he explains that the passion and care of the staff play a significant role in their continued collaboration. He spoke about the staff on two occasions:

> My first impressions of GEM, and Wayne in particular, were very positive. I felt Wayne was very sincere and dedicated in his vision and mission for GEM, and therefore GEM would be a valuable resource for distance learning programs. I have never been disappointed.

When responding to a prompt inquiring about whether or not he felt GEM's global resources have had an impact on the high school's students or its curriculum, he indicated that GEM did contribute toward two important changes:

> In short, it opens the eyes of our students to other cultures and issues in the world on a personal basis. I believe this helps our students become better global citizens. [...] It has altered the curriculum in two important ways. It has increased the use of videoconferencing and collaborations with the UN and other students from other countries. Most significantly, from our increased use of content providers like GEM, we have created a whole course, *Contemporary Issues Through Video Conferencing*, that is offered to juniors and seniors at our school as part of our goal to create better global citizens.

Rich identified that the use of videoconferencing at their high school has grown exponentially among the school community:

> Since I have been at [name of high school], approximately ten years, our use of videoconferencing has gone from an average of one a year to easily more than one hundred individual videoconferences per year. As indicated above we have developed a whole new course based on the use of videoconferencing to connect with content providers like GEM, students and teachers from other parts of the US and other countries, and experts of all kinds that can provide first hand knowledge or research on specific current event topics impacting our world.

He also stated that because of the technology's popularity and the addition of the videoconferencing course offering, their technical staff have developed instructional workshops for the school's teachers across disciplines with the aim to help teachers become more comfortable with the technology and to learn about how the school's videoconferencing provider partnerships can support learning in the classroom.

To summarize, Rich's partnership with GEM led to his ability to expand his practice to include more videoconferencing programs within his school. As was also the case with Maryann and Lily, Rich's belief in the importance of global education and his role as someone who brings that to his school community patently demonstrates his sense of responsibility as an educator and someone who values a global perspective himself.

CASE 4: DISTRICT ADMINISTRATOR AND HEAD OF EDUCATIONAL TECHNOLOGY, PUBLIC TECHNICAL SCHOOL

Mark became a collaborative partner of GEM after hearing a presentation that GEM gave in the early 2000s at a distance learning conference. Mark initially contacted GEM because he reported feeling "energized about the work [GEM] was doing related to the UN and Global Education particularly using the new emerging technology of videoconferencing." Their first collaborative program centered on the situation in Kosovo and provided the UN perspective through a student videoconference with UN officials. Since their first collaboration over 10 years ago, Mark has contracted with GEM to provide programming in a variety of areas relating to current international concerns and human rights issues, as well as broader educational topics such as videoconferencing programs and student leadership training.

Mark has been very influential in his role at the school, district, and county level, as he was responsible for introducing videoconferencing to every public school in his county. When introducing the videoconferencing technology to his county's teachers, GEM was often asked to collaborate in order to generate greater interest and motivate teachers to use the equipment. Working through their training center, GEM's programs have reached many of the schools in Mark's county and beyond.

When asked what motivates him to remain involved with GEM, he responded that the ability to keep up-to-date with technology and global issues were the most important aspects of continuing the rapport:

... what motivates me is GEM's adaptation to emerging technology as well as current issues as it relates to the UN and beyond. Also, Wayne is very committed to his and

GEM's mission. He continues to drive my interest and that of my colleagues. [...] I have professionally viewed GEM in terms of their motto of "Bringing the world to the classroom." GEM and Wayne not only have provided opportunities to our students and teachers, but to myself professionally in terms of collaboration with GEM and their resources to other areas.

As was the case with Rich, Mark also reported that he has received recognition and support from his department's collaborative programming with GEM.

[GEM] has shaped how I view international issues as well as perspectives. I believe it provides a unique perspective to our students in all content areas by globalizing their understanding of issues and ideas through exposure to other cultures and views outside of their community.

Mark also reported that the collaboration with GEM has not only had its impact on him and his school's teachers and students, but the videoconferencing events with GEM have both inspired the broadening of the curricular focus of several classes at the school, as well as helped to expand the videoconferencing program across all subjects.

Mark mentioned that his relationship with GEM allows him to employ his expertise and cognitive skills. As was the case with the other respondents, Mark mentioned that the partnership and activities developed with GEM have had a personal impact on his career, "GEM and Wayne not only have provided opportunities to our students and teachers, but to myself professionally in terms of collaboration with GEM and their resources to other areas." Although he does not elaborate explicitly nor discuss directly a sense of responsibility within his profession, he does express an appreciation for the exposure to global topics as well as its impact on him and his students ("I believe it provides a unique perspective to our students in all content areas by globalizing their understanding of issues and ideas through exposure to other cultures and views outside of their community").

CASE 5: ENGLISH TEACHER, PUBLIC MIDDLE SCHOOL

About 10 years ago, Ellen was a new teacher in a public middle school in the Northeast. Curious about the videoconferences that were organized by a senior teacher in the school who had been working with GEM on school-to-school and UN videoconferences, she traveled with her senior teacher colleague to Pennsylvania to a distance learning conference where she heard

GEM's President speak and conduct several workshops. She returned to her school and convinced her teacher colleague that she should replace him as the distance learning teacher when he retired.

Since that time, she has become a leading educator in global learning, virtually taking many of her students into a world they would most likely not have experienced in their rural area. Ellen chose to collaborate with GEM because she liked the idea of extending the classroom out into the world using technology. Ellen has used videoconferencing technology on a regular basis in her classroom, as well as for her professional development, giving talks on her practice to audiences in universities and organizations across the world through videoconferencing. Ellen has been frequently recognized by her school district for her videoconferencing work and global education initiatives, and her state's legislature has even drafted a resolution regarding her work. She has had many visitors to her school to see what she does, and within her own school several of her colleagues within the science and foreign language departments have also incorporated videoconferencing into their respective class curricula.

Ellen has brought real world global awareness to her students through videoconferencing and has moved her students from awareness to action on many global and local issues. Paired with their internationally oriented curriculum, she has begun to raise substantial funds through charity walks and her personal efforts to raise funds and awareness, such as spending a weekend in a cardboard box during the winter. The money raised helped fund several collaborative projects between Ellen's classroom and GEM: planting trees; starting a microcredit project in Murutunguru, Tanzania; building a water pump project in a rural area of the state of Equitoria, South Sudan; sending two Lost Boys from South Sudan who were living in the States home to visit their family; and helping two young girls in Kampala, Uganda to attend school. They have also partnered with Maasai school students in the Ngong Hills of Kenya and raised funds to support them to stay in school. All of these accomplished projects were born out of the international videoconferences held in her classroom. Ellen expressed a strong belief that the continued engagement of her students in international topics and activism was testament to the effectiveness of integrating international videoconferencing within her curriculum.

Nurturing global connections with my students has helped my middle school students be successful in high school global classes, in job opportunities, and college selection processes. Students have gone onto political careers and service programs after high school and college graduation.

Empowered by her own experience of broadening her perspective through videoconferencing and subsequently building international relationships with other educators and classrooms, Ellen encourages her students to become world citizens through her innovative Human Rights curriculum.

IMPLICATIONS OF THE FINDINGS

Rather than investigate the educators' behavioral and cognitive engagement with participating in and facilitating international videoconferencing events, the report chose to calibrate its lens toward a broader lifelong learning orientation in order to understand the cognitive, affective, and conative domains of their learning, manifested as perspectives, responsibility, and partnerships, respectively. The report focused primarily on the participants' reports within the affective and conative domains, as those were more relevant given that the intended audiences of the majority of their video-conferences were their students.

The findings show that the partnership with GEM and the schools abroad has had a reported impact on the professional practice of the educators. All participants were supported by their superiors and school community to introduce, maintain, and grow their partnerships with GEM and its network of schools. In several of the cases, the individual received acknowledgment at the national or state level on their practice, in differing degrees of how influential GEM was in relation to the type of recognition received.

The three manifested themes of perspectives, relationships, and partnerships jointly demonstrate a lifelong learning orientation. The described cases present an interesting viewpoint of the long-term effects of those who have become believers and advocates of either global education or videoconferencing (and both in the cases of Maryann, Lily, and Ellen) after forming a collaborative relationship with GEM. Their process of leading, shaping, and continuing their engagement with international videoconferencing depicts an empowering process through which they developed a better understanding of their professional and personal roles within a global society and of how they can foment change and a sense of responsibility within their schools.

THE COGNITIVE DOMAIN: PERSPECTIVES

From each of the cases, all participants indicated that their involvement in building international videoconferencing events contributed to the development of their knowledge and perspectives on a variety of the global topics they approached in their classroom curricula and supporting in-person and videoconferencing activities. None of the participants had an extensive background with global education prior to partnering with GEM, and only two of the five had videoconferencing facilitation experience before partnering with GEM. Of the remaining three (Maryann, Lily, and Ellen), Lily especially emphasized the impact of learning how to use videoconferencing technology on her current practice as a classroom teacher:

> I knew little about video chats, but the Polycom systems and bridging multiple sites together on secure lines was very new to me ... Having prior knowledge of using it in the classroom has allowed me to begin conversations on how to use the equipment in productive ways ... I gained from GEM of conducting videoconferences globally will help me to be a leader in my district as technology becomes more available.

All participants mentioned that their experience and proficiency with videoconferencing has expanded since beginning to host international videoconferences.

THE AFFECTIVE DOMAIN: RESPONSIBILITY

The presented cases demonstrated on several occasions an overarching theme of the participants' formation of a sense of global and local responsibility. When focusing on the participants' affective learning, three of the five participants had clearly reported that their relationship with GEM, over the years, has shaped their view on their roles as educators, with two participants (Rich and Ellen) making a more indirect reference toward their affective learning. For instance, Rich does not mention the development of his sense of responsibility, yet he does mention how the introduction of the international videoconferencing events has led his students to grow into global citizens.

THE CONATIVE DOMAIN: PARTNERSHIPS

> If the purpose of higher education is to encourage the move beyond transmissional to transformative, then it should be a fundamental condition of the students' experience ... that relationship is crucial to learning. (Brockbank & McGill, 2007, p. 5)

When discussing action through international videoconferencing, nothing speaks to learning through action as much as forming and maintaining partnerships, as they show a commitment of the educators and students to each other and the issues that impact their lives. Regarding the participants' reporting on conative learning, their commitment to building and sustaining a relationship with GEM and its partners helped lead to collaborative action and projects. As indicated within her report, Maryann had collaborated with a fellow educator in Mexico; however, what was not mentioned was that this initial contact of GEM's became an independent education partner of Maryann's school, so much so that Maryann took the opportunity to join GEM on a trip to meet her counterpart in Mexico in person. Lily's mention of her relationship with the Maasai was initially formed through her work with GEM, and she now maintains those contacts through videoconferencing independent of GEM for collaborative projects, lessons, fundraisers, and awareness campaigns. Rich and Mark also both have connected with their international partner classrooms outside of formal GEM collaborations, with Rich's students using social media to keep in touch with the international videoconference classroom "peers." Finally, Ellen's introductions to international classroom teachers and educators through GEM has inspired longstanding partnerships that not only work together to fundraise and raise awareness of global issues, but to promote videoconferencing as a relationship and partnership builder.

More importantly, the cases demonstrate the interplay of the three domains through international videoconferencing. Without an understanding of global issues, the participants would not likely show a sense of responsibility, and without a sense of responsibility, it can be further assumed that the participants would not likely be compelled to spend their working and personal time and resources to act. It is with this understanding of the interconnectivity of the three domains under the lens of five personal reported cases that the development and current state of videoconferencing as a classroom technology can be appreciated as a cutting-edge, accessible, and affordable tool with the capability to engage both students and teachers in a complete and comprehensive manner.

FOR FURTHER INVESTIGATION

In order to better understand the impacts of international videoconferencing on the classrooms and personal cognitive, affective, and conative domains of the educators who use them, further qualitative studies need to be conducted. Considering the aforementioned limitations of the report – including the limited number of interviewees and the use of written questionnaire instead of in-person, videoconference or telephone interviews – further studies are recommended to build and improve upon the posed questions in order to bring an understanding of both where the educators started in their experiences with the technology, and in what ways the introduction, or expanded use, of videoconferencing technology has contributed toward the development of their perspective, sense of responsibility, and building and maintenance of partnerships.

REFERENCES

Barnett, R., & Coate, K. (2005). *Engaging the curriculum in higher education*. Maidenhead: Open University Press.

Bates, A. (2005). *Technology, e-learning and distance education*. Abingdon, UK: Routledge.

Berger, P. L., & Luckmann, T. (1967). *The social construction of reality: A treatise in the sociology of knowledge*. New York, NY: Anchor Books.

Bloom, B. S. (1956). *Taxonomy of educational objectives*. New York, NY: David McKay.

Bloom, B. S. (1964). *Stability and change in human characteristics*. New York, NY: Wiley.

Brockbank, A., & McGill, I. (2007). *Facilitating reflective learning in higher education* (2nd ed.). New York, NY: Open University Press.

Eales, R. T. J., & Bryd, L. M. (1997). Virtually deschooling society: Authentic collaborative learning via the internet. In S. Lobodzinski & I. Tomek (Eds.), *Proceedings of WebNet 97 – World Conference on the WWW, Internet & Intranet*, Toronto, Canada, November 1–5 (pp. 155–160).

Ecclestone, K. (2009). Lost and found in transition: Educational implications of concerns about "identity," "agency," and "structure." In J. Field, J. Gallacher & R. Ingram (Eds.), *Researching transitions in lifelong learning* (pp. 9–27). London: Routledge.

Gillies, D. (2008). Student perspectives on videoconferencing in teacher education at a distance. *Distance Education, 29*(1), 107–118.

Kenny, G., Kenny, D., & Dumont, R. (1995). *Mission and place: Strengthening learning and community through campus design*. Westport, CT: Praeger.

Knowlton, H. E., Rowland, A., Knowlton, D. S., & Chaffin, J. D. (2005, October). Effects of interactive video conferencing on preservice teacher education students. Paper presented at the Second annual International Keystone Conference, Indianapolis, IN.

Kolbe, K. (1990). *The conative connection: Acting on instinct*. Reading, MA: Addison-Wesley.

Krathwohl, D. R., Bloom, B. S., & Masia, B. B. (1964). *Taxonomy of educational objectives, the classification of educational goals. Handbook II: Affective domain* London: Longman Publishing Group.

Laurillard, D. (2002). *Rethinking university teaching: A conversational framework for the effective use of learning technologies*. London: RoutledgeFalmer.

Lave, J., & Wenger, R. (1991). *Situated learning: Legitimate peripheral participation*. Cambridge: Cambridge University Press.

Martin, M. (2005). Seeing is believing: The role of videoconferencing in distance learning. *British Journal of Educational Technology, 36*(3), 397–405. Blackwell Publishing Ltd., Oxford, UK.

Marton, F., & Ramsden, P. (1988). What does it take to improve learning? In P. Ramsden (Ed.), *Improving learning* (pp. 275–283). London: Kogan Page.

Medel-Añonuevo, C., Ohsako, T., & Mauch, W. (2001). *Revisiting lifelong learning for the 21st century*. Hamburg, Germany: UNESCO Institute for Education.

Morgan-Klein, B., & Osborne, M. (2007). *The concepts and practices of lifelong learning*. London: Routledge.

Oxfam. (1997). *OXFAM's cool planet, what is global citizenship?* Retrieved from www.oxfam. org.uk/coolplanet/teachers/globciti/whatis.htm

Smyth, R. (2005). Broadband videoconferencing as a tool for learner-centred distance learning in higher education. *British Journal of Educational Technology, 36*(5), 805–820.

Svitak, A. (2010, April 21). 5 ways classrooms can use video conferencing. *Mashable Tech.* Retrieved from http://mashable.com/2010/04/21/classroom-video-conferencing/

Wheeler, S. (2005). Creating social presence in digital learning environments: A presence of mind? Paper presented at the TAFE Conference, Queensland, Australia. Retrieved from http://videolinq.tafe.net/learning2005/papers/wheeler.pdf

Wheeler, S., & Amiotte, S. (2004). The death of distance: Documenting the effects of distance education in South Dakota. *Turkish Online Journal of Distance Education, 6*(1), 76–83.

ABOUT THE AUTHORS

Peter Adds is Associate Professor and the current Head of School for Te Kawa a Māui (the School of Māori Studies), Victoria University of Wellington, New Zealand. He has worked in Māori Studies at Victoria since 1984 following on from attaining a Master's degree in anthropology and archaeology, and he teaches Māori and Polynesian history and Māori customary concepts. He is on the executive committee of the Māori Association of Social Science. He is of Te Atiawa ki Taranaki descent and is in their Claim Negotiation team, having led the Waitangi Tribunal research for the Taranaki land claim. He is currently engaged in negotiations with the Crown seeking a Treaty settlement for his tribe. A former Ministerial appointment to the Board of the NZ Historic Places Trust and a member of the Maori Heritage Council, Peter has a strong background in heritage issues and was the keynote speaker at the NZ Archaeological Conference in 2010. He is an internationally recognized researcher and scholar and has extensive consultancy and training experience in areas relating to the Treaty of Waitangi.

Sheila M. Aird, Ph.D., is an Assistant Professor and Academic Coordinator of Global Studies at SUNY's Empire State College. She received her Ph.D. in Latin and Caribbean History and an M.A. in History from Howard University. Dr. Aird holds a B.A. in Anthropology and an M.A. in Anthropology with a focus on Historical Archeology from the Maxwell School of Citizenship and Public Affairs at Syracuse University. Dr. Aird teaches courses on the Caribbean, Africa, Virtual Public History, and Digital Storytelling. Her scholarly and personal interests focus on Public History, cultural and historical studies that focus on the African Diaspora, and social and media environments that can be utilized in a Public History environment.

Maria Bargh (Te Arawa, Ngāti Awa) is a Senior Lecturer in Māori Studies at Victoria University of Wellington, New Zealand. She did her Ph.D. on Neoliberalism and Indigenous people through Political Science and International Relations at Australia National University. She is editor of

Resistance: An Indigenous Response to Neoliberalism (Huia Publishers, 2007) and *Māori and Parliament* (Huia Publishers, 2010). Her recent research has focused on renewable energy projects by Indigenous peoples in Canada and Aotearoa/New Zealand, constitutional change, and Māori politics. In 2007, she received a Victoria Award for teaching from the Postgraduate Students Association at Victoria University. Maria is currently the postgraduate student coordinator for the School of Māori Studies.

Patrick Blessinger is the founder and Executive Director of the International Higher Education Teaching and Learning Association and a Research Fellow at the School of Education at St. John's University in Queens, New York, USA. He has taught over 150 college and university courses and he has served as a program chair at colleges and universities in the United States and the European Union. He consults with HE institutions in the areas of technology innovation and internationalization and he serves as an academic and accreditation advisor for HE institutions. He is the co-founder and co-director of the Institute for Meaning-Centered Education. He is the founder and editor of the *International HETL Review* and co-editor of the *Journal of Applied Research in Higher Education*. He is co-editor of several volumes within the Cutting-edge Technologies in Higher Education book series (Emerald) and co-editor of the book, *Meaning-Centered Education: International Perspectives and Explorations in Higher Education* (Routledge). He attended Auburn University, Georgia Tech, and the University of Georgia. He is a peer-recognized expert and thought leader in the field of teaching and learning and he has received several academic awards including a Fulbright Scholarship from the US Department of State and a Governor's Teaching Fellowship from the State of Georgia, USA.

Meg Colasante (M.Ed, Dip.Ed, RN) is an Educational Developer in the Academic Development Group, in the College of Science, Engineering and Health of RMIT University in Melbourne, Australia. Meg published her research in the Australasian Journal of Educational Technology, and has co-authored chapters in books on educational technology. In 2010, she received the RMIT University Teaching and Research Team Award for Programs that Enhance Learning: Innovation in Curricula, Learning and Teaching, for the creation of the Media Annotation Tool (MAT), a pedagogically based learning tool which facilitates student learning with media, through reflection, feedback, and sharing. Currently, Meg is finalizing two RMIT University Learning and Teaching Investment Fund research projects: Using a media annotation tool to enhance learning that is work-relevant and enables industry collaboration (a multiple case study evaluation across disciplines and sectors to inform models to achieve collaboration), where she is Principal researcher; and Interactive online group learning: pilot of equivalence and comparability models in Science, Engineering, and Health.

Karen Corneille has worked as a Research Assistant over a period of 17 years in the education faculties of RMIT University, the University of Melbourne, and Macquarie University in Australia. Research and evaluation project work she has been involved with include the National Quality Schooling Framework; Boys in Education Lighthouse Schools; Online learning communities in schools; State-wide numeracy and literacy testing; Middle Years schooling; Evaluation of a classroom management tool; and the School Entrant Health Questionnaire. Karen's work has been published in the *International Journal of Web Based Communities, Interaction – Journal of the Geography Teachers' Association of Victoria, Contemporary Nurse, Collegian – Journal of the Royal College of Nursing, International Journal of Nursing Practice,* and *Journal of Nursing Measurement.*

Kathy Douglas a Senior Lecturer in Law at the Graduate School of Business and Law, RMIT University in Melbourne, Australia. Her work has been published in *Journal of Learning Design, Murdoch University E Law Journal,* and *Journal of Australasian Law Teachers Association.* Recently, Kathy was involved in two RMIT University Learning and Teaching Investment Fund research projects: *Using a Media Annotation Tool to Enhance Learning that is Work-Relevant and Enables Industry Collaboration* (a multiple case study evaluation across disciplines and sectors to inform models to achieve collaboration); and *Enhancing the Practical Lawyering Skills in the Juris Doctor* (as Principal Researcher).

Sarsha-Leigh Douglas is a first year Master's degree student in Māori Studies in Victoria University Wellington, New Zealand, and is writing a thesis on the Māori environmental concept of *rangatira* (management). She has a graduate diploma in Māori Resource Management and an undergraduate degree in History. She is also a recipient of the 2012 Victoria Graduate Award. She is a key member of the Punk Pōneke community, and was a summer research assistant on the Te Kawa a Māui Atlas.

Meegan Hall is a Lecturer in academic development at Victoria University of Wellington, New Zealand, and her focus is working with Māori and

Pasifika academic staff and encouraging culturally responsive teaching and learning practices for Māori and Pasifika students. Prior to this role, she completed a law degree and a B.A. in history at Victoria University of Wellington before switching to postgraduate studies and then teaching and research positions at Te Kawa a Māui, the School of Māori Studies. As part of her current role, she is the Poukairangi Ako (Associate Dean, Learning and Teaching) for Toihuarewa, the Māori Faculty at Victoria. She also provides learning and teaching-related policy advice, and develops learning and teaching-related events, opportunities, and addresses issues for Toihuarewa members and Pasifika academic staff. She teaches on the Postgraduate Certificate in Higher Education Learning and Teaching (PHELT) programme and on undergraduate courses for the School of Māori Studies. Meegan's research specialty, Māori academic development, combines her interest in academic practice and higher education learning and teaching, with her doctoral study and ongoing research-led teaching in Māori Studies. She primarily conducts research that examines Māori academic practice, Māori pedagogies, and supports Māori student and staff achievement in higher education.

Wayne Jacoby is co-founder of Global Education Motivators (GEM) and has served as its President since its creation in 1981. Since 1989, he has developed and administered the work of GEM from Chestnut Hill College in Philadelphia, USA. As a former secondary social studies teacher of 31 years, Wayne built GEM to primarily educate students and their teachers on the importance of cross cultural communications to enhance global perspectives. This was often done in collaboration with United Nations programs and events. In 1999, he began developing international videoconferencing programs for Partners in Distance Learning, a consortium of US school districts involved in interactive videoconferencing. This set the stage for the variety of distance learning programs he does today. Through his work on the Pennsylvania State Advisory Committee for International Education, Wayne Jacoby served as invited contributor to two reports commissioned by the Pennsylvania Department of Education: *Pennsylvania's International Education Report, 2005-2008* (Pennsylvania Department of Education, 2008), and *Education for International Competence in Pennsylvania* (University Center for International Studies, University of Pittsburgh, August 1988, edited by Andrew Dinniman and Burkart Holzner).

Felix A. Kronenberg joined the Department of Modern Languages and Literatures as Assistant Professor and Director of the Language Learning

Center in the summer of 2009. Before that, Dr. Kronenberg served as an Assistant Professor of German and Manager of the Foreign Language Resource Center at Pomona College. He has taught courses such as Stereotypes in Advertising, Introduction to German Media and Film, Teaching German with Technology, and all levels of German language courses. Dr. Kronenberg also planned the new Foreign Language Resource Center at Pomona College and the Language Learning Center at Rhodes College, which opened in the fall of 2010. He was awarded the 2009 Marie Sheppard Award by the International Association for Language Learning and Technology, and has been a fellow for the National Institute for Technology in Liberal Education. He was the president of the SouthWest Association for Language Learning and Technology until 2010. He recently edited the book *Language Center Design* (International Association for Language Learning Technology, 2011), for which he also wrote a chapter on language center design at small educational institutions. Dr. Kronenberg has presented extensively on various issues involving language learning and technology at regional, national, and international conferences. He has been a consultant for various colleges and universities and has provided numerous workshops and professional development opportunities for language teachers and professors. His special interests are digital story-telling, language center design, computer simulations/games and L2 acquisition, and blended learning.

Narelle Lemon, D.Ed., is a Senior Lectuer in Teacher Education at the School of Education, RMIT University in Melbourne, Australia. Narelle has been invited to give keynote speeches, and publishes widely nationally and internationally in arts education and digital technologies contribution in learning and teaching. Dr. Narelle Lemon has experience as a chief investigator on a three-year funded Australia Arts Council grant with Musica Viva; 'Public Art Teaching Excellence: Improving teacher practice through engaging with contemporary public art in the art classroom' with Kaldor Public Art and Department of Education and Early Childhood Development (DEECD); FUSE Digital Learning Resources Program: Artroom 2.0 Virtual Mobile Studio with Art Education Victoria and DEECD; and RMIT funded investigation 'Using a media annotation tool (video) to enhance learning that is work-relevant and enables industry collaboration'. Dr Lemon has published over 40 publications as well as curriculum documentations, commissioned reports and has been invited nationally and internationally to present on image based research, early years voice and communities of practice. Her connections to industry have demonstrated substantial contributions to the fields of teacher professional development and demonstrate her capacity to work effectively with others, plan for and enact methods, and analyse data to significantly contribute to the field(s).

Audeliz Matias is Assistant Professor and mentor of science, math, and technology for the Center for Distance Learning at the SUNY-Empire State College, where she mentors and teaches a variety of courses in science and technology. She received her Ph.D. in geological sciences from Northwestern University. Prior to joining as a faculty member, Audeliz served as the coordinator of curriculum and instructional design for the science, math, and technology area for three years at the Center for Distance Learning. Dr. Matias is involved in innovation and emerging technology efforts for teaching and learning. She helped with the creation of several learning objects using multimedia maps as well as the Mobile Learning Task Force at her institution, which she chaired during 2010–2011. Her scholarly interests focus on geoscience education and effective practices in online learning including the use of virtual environments such as Second Life, social and media environments, mobile learning, multimedia maps, and the use of scientific datasets to promote active learning.

Bruce McFadgen is a registered Land Surveyor, and worked for the New Zealand Department of Lands and Survey until 1968. He then completed a B.A. and an M.A. in Anthropology at the University of Otago, followed by a Ph.D. in Geology at Victoria University in 1979 before working as a staff archaeologist for the New Zealand Historic Places Trust. He is the author of *Hostile Shores: Catastrophic Events in Prehistoric New Zealand and their Impact on Maori Coastal Communities* (Auckland University Press, 2007). McFadgen was employed as a scientist by the Department of Conservation from 1987 to 2003 when he took early retirement to take up the 2003 JD Stout Fellowship at the Stout Research Centre. He has served on the Royal Society of New Zealand's Skinner Research Fund Committee since 1987, as President of the New Zealand Archaeological Association 1986–1988, and is currently editor of the journal of the New Zealand Institute of Surveyors. He currently works as a contract archaeologist and Research Associate at Te Kawa a Māui, Victoria University of Wellington. He also teaches the use of GPS and GIS technology in a number of Māori Studies courses, as well as taking students on field trips to sites of historical significance to Māori.

O. Ripeka Mercier (Ngāti Porou) is a Lecturer in Te Kawa a Māui (Māori Studies) at Victoria University of Wellington, New Zealand. In 2002 she became the first Māori woman to gain a Ph.D. in Physics. She worked on colossal magnetoresistors, superconducting tapes, and Antarctic sea ice before migrating to Māori Studies when she enrolled in a B.A. in Māori language in 2003. Ocean's current teaching and research explores the interface between Māori and Indigenous knowledge and science in tertiary and secondary educational contexts. Her research interests are wide ranging – Indigenous geography as pedagogy, Māori perspectives on film, audio commentary as text and methodology, Māori language physics – but can be broadly categorized as methodologically bridging disciplines, fields, and knowledge systems. She is the presenter of Project Mātauranga, a 13-part science series commissioned for Māori Television. She leads the Te Kawa a Māui Atlas project, which seeks to enhance student engagement through a digital publication of map-based student research. Due partly to this work she received a Victoria University Teaching Excellence Award in 2011, and in 2012 she won an Ako Aotearoa National Tertiary Teaching Excellence Award for teaching in a Kaupapa Māori context.

Leila A. Mills works as a Secondary Math Teacher, Instructional Specialist, Test Coordinator, and Summer Programs Administrator for the Richardson Independent School District, Texas, USA. She serves as part-time Associate Professor of Business, Information, Engineering, and Technology (BIET) at Collin College. Leila is also a doctoral candidate and a research assistant within Learning Technologies in Computer Education and Cognitive Systems at the University of North Texas. She focuses her research on learning and teaching with integrated communications technology (ICT), effects of students' attitudes toward school, and students' STEM (science, technology, engineering, math) career interests. Before becoming an educator, she was employed as a computer programmer and systems analyst for government services and private firms with focus on the development of real-time management information reporting systems. She holds a B.Sc. in Technology of Management from the American University in Washington, DC, and an M.A. in Interdisciplinary Studies/Information Technology from the University of Texas, Dallas.

Stephanie E. Raible has worked in higher education across 11 institutions in 3 countries. She currently serves as a Lecturer of Global Studies at Chestnut Hill College and as an Assistant Director of Graduate Admissions at Drexel University. In addition to these roles, she acts as an NGO

Representative to the United Nations for Global Education Motivators and as the Co-Chair and Founder of the International Network of Innovators in Education (INIE), a project supported by the European Commission. She holds an M.A. in Lifelong Learning Policy and Management from the Institute of Education (University of London) and University of Deusto and an M.S.Ed. in Higher Education Management from the University of Pennsylvania.

Kyle F. Reinson joined the faculty at St. John Fisher College (USA) in 2007 where he teaches introductory and advanced courses in public relations, social media, and business communication. Prior to starting his career in higher education he was a corporate director of public relations and public affairs for two publicly held real estate companies. He remains active in professional consulting through his firm Reinson Creative Consulting and regularly attends academic and professional conferences pertaining to his interest areas. Kyle has published book chapters and reviews and is currently completing his Ph. D. in Economic Geography, International Business and World Trade in the College of Arts and Sciences at the University at Buffalo. He holds an M.A. in Communication from Florida Atlantic University and a B.A. from the University of Nevada. Kyle Reinson is on the editorial review board of the *International Journal of Mentoring and Coaching in Education* and the American Journalism Historians Association's Curriculum Committee and was a 2008 Indiana University Teaching Fellow. His research interests include pedagogy in higher education, the future of professional communication and its history, corporate social responsibility, information exchange in democratic societies, and the role of knowledge workers in society.

Sean Robinson is Associate Professor of Higher Education Leadership at Morgan State University in Baltimore, Maryland, USA. His teaching interests include leadership theory, higher education administration, organizational behavior, student development theory, and research methodology. His research centers on the identity formation and expression of underserved and underrepresented individuals within different types of institutions, including both K-12 and higher education settings. His current projects include an exploration of the mentoring experiences of minority doctoral students, the mentoring experiences of LGBTQ youth, and the shifting nature of LGBTQ identity development in a technology-mediated world.

Jenny S. Wakefield is a doctoral student in educational computing (ECMP) program and also a Teaching Fellow in the Department of Learning Technologies at University of North Texas. She holds an M.S. in Computer Education and Cognitive Systems with a focus on Instructional Design/ Learning and Teaching with Technology. Jenny's BAAS is in Applied Arts and Sciences with a major in Applied Technology and Performance Improvement, also from UNT. Jenny works as an Instructional Designer and Web Developer at the University of Texas at Dallas in the Office of Undergraduate Education. Her recent work includes supporting learning of 21st century students in higher education using virtual worlds in the Student Second Life Success Program and the online course design for the UT Dallas Freshman course UNIV1010. Jenny's research has been published in *Knowledge Management & E-Learning*, she has co-authored several book chapters on the use of social media, games, simulations, virtual worlds, and transmedia in education and has been the editor for several handbooks. Jenny aspires to become a professor of Learning Technologies in higher education upon graduation.

Laura A. Wankel, Ed.D. is the Vice President for Student Affairs at Northeastern University in Boston, Massachusetts. Prior to Northeastern she was the Vice President for Student Affairs at Seton Hall University where she served since 1995. While at Seton Hall she also held titles of Vice Chancellor for Student Affairs and Vice President for Student Affairs & Enrollment Services. During her tenure she had been responsible for a variety of services and programs including Undergraduate Admissions, Student Financial Aid, Student Accounts, Registrar, Dean of Students and Community Development, Public Safety and Security, Student Health Services, The Career Center, Disability Support Services, Student Counseling Services, Housing and Residence Life and Athletics & Recreational Programs. Before Seton Hall University, Dr. Wankel served as Assistant Vice President for Student Affairs at the State University of New York at Purchase from 1987 to 1995. From 1983 to 1987, Dr. Wankel was Assistant Dean for Campus and Residence Operations at SUNY Purchase. Prior to that, she served in student affairs positions at the University of Pittsburgh. Dr. Wankel has been an active NASPA: Student Affairs Administrators in Higher Education member at both the regional and national level. She has served as a program reviewer for several NASPA national conferences, member of the Region II Advisory Board, Pre-Conference Program Coordinator, and member of the 1994 national conference committee. She has also been on the editorial boards for the *NASPA Journal* and the *Journal of Student Affairs Research and Practice* (*JSARP*). She has been the Regional Vice President for Region II of *NASPA* and serves on the NASPA Board of Directors.

Dr. Wankel holds a Bachelor's degree in American History from SUNY Oneonta where she graduated magna cum laude. She holds an M.Ed. from the University of South Carolina and an Ed.D. in higher education administration from Teachers College, Columbia University. Dr. Wankel also received a certificate from the Institute for Educational Management (IEM) from the Harvard Institute for Higher Education. Dr. Wankel has served in a consulting capacity to a number of education-related projects, including, Learn and Serve America and the Corporation for National and Community Service (AmeriCorps).

Dr. Wankel has a chapter on crisis management in *Understanding Student Affairs in Catholic Colleges and Universities* that is based on the tragic residence hall fire at Seton Hall University. She is co-editor of *Reading the Signs: Using Case Studies to Discuss Student Life Issues at Catholic Colleges and Universities in the United States*. She is co-editor of *Higher Education Administration with Social Media* and *Misbehavior Online in Higher Education* with Emerald Group Publishing Limited. She has also served on the Board of Directors of the Association of Student Affairs at Catholic Colleges and Universities (ASACCU), and has presented on issues in higher education nationally as well as in Lithuania and Japan.

Scott J. Warren, Ph.D., works as an Associate Professor of Learning Technologies at the University of North Texas, USA. His research examines the use of emerging online technologies such as immersive digital learning environments and educational games and simulations in K-20 settings. Prior to working in higher education, he taught both social studies and English in public schools. His early work included creating the Anytown virtual world to support writing, reading, and problem solving. His current work includes *The 2015 Project* (http://start2015.thinktanktwo.info) and *Refuge* alternate reality courses. Scott has a Ph.D. from Indiana University-Bloomington in Instructional Systems Technology.

Tahu Wilson is a Master's degree student at Victoria University of Wellington, New Zealand. His thesis research entitled *White Privilege and the Invisibility of Whiteness* explores institutionalized racism in Aotearoa/ New Zealand, and his methodological approach draws from Māori Studies,

Politics and International Relations. He was a research assistant on the Te Kawa a Māui Atlas.

David F. Wolf II is the coordinator of advanced learning design for the Center for Distance Learning at the SUNY-Empire State College. He oversees the coordination of complex learning objects under development for the online curriculum. David received Master's degree at Binghamton University in the multidisciplinary program: Philosophy and Computer System Science. He has pioneered the development of interactive learning tools, simulations, thematic mapping, visual mashups, and mobile learning tools. His scholarly interests focus on: exploring multimodal learning objects, interactive tools, presenting content to display temporal or geographic relationships, simulations, open learning, mobile learning, and developing effective complex problem solving techniques through multimodal approaches that conform to universal design.

Müberra Yüksel has completed her Ph.D. at the department of Political Science, Binghamton University (SUNY), USA, in 1989. She has experience in organizational theory, communication, conflict management, and policy analysis. During 1991–1995, she held positions as an Assistant Professor at Bilkent University in Ankara, Turkey. From 1998 to 2003, she was an adjunct lecturer at the Bilgi University's (Istanbul) MBA Executive Program. She has been the chair of Advertising Department of Kadir Has University in Istanbul between 2004 and 2010, where she is currently an Assistant Professor. Her research interests include human resource management, organizational behavior, and communication.

AUTHOR INDEX

SUBJECT INDEX